D0879661

The Mottled Screen

Mieke Bal **The Mottled Screen: Reading Proust Visually**

Translated by Anna-Louise Milne

Stanford University Press   Stanford, California

Translated from the French manuscript
Images proustiennes, ou comment lire visuellement.

Stanford University Press
Stanford, California
© 1997 by the Board of Trustees of the
Leland Stanford Junior University
Printed in the United States of America

CIP data are at the end of the book

Acknowledgments

I gratefully acknowledge support from the Rockefeller Foundation, Bellagio Center, and the University of Amsterdam. I thank the Université de Paris III Sorbonne Nouvelle, where it all started, and Columbia University, where I finished the book.

Philippe Hamon, Marina van Zuylen, and Ernst van Alphen were greatly helpful, critical, and inspiring. As always, the ASCA community provided intellectual stimulation.

M. B.

Contents

Figures

Double page references are given for all the quotations from Proust's novel *A la recherche du temps perdu*. The first reference is to the C. K. Scott-Moncrieff and Terence Kilmartin translation published in 1981, cited as "SK" by volume and page; the second reference, following the solidus, is to the four-volume Pléiade edition prepared by Jean-Yves Tadié and his team, published in 1987–89, cited as "P" by volume and page. In many cases the translation of Proust's text has been significantly modified, but the pages in the Scott-Moncrieff and Kilmartin translation are nevertheless given for ease of reference. The quotations from *Contre Sainte-Beuve* are translated here, but because no adequate published English translation exists, references are given only for the original edition. The quotations from *Contre Sainte-Beuve* are cited as *"CSB"* by page number. In all cases the emphasis in the quotations is Bal's own. The fragment "Solitary Pleasure" has been quoted from *Writing and Fantasy in Proust*, Carol and Paul Bove's 1986 translation of Serge Doubrovsky's *La place de la madeleine*, but where necessary that translation has been altered. Whenever available, English translations of secondary sources have been used, but page references are to the original French texts, to conform to Bal's other references to these works.

This study features many subtle puns and plays on words, some of which resist translation. Consequently the reader will find a certain number of translator's notes intended to clarify the sense of certain passages and allusions.

The Mottled Screen

Introduction

How can an image be written? And once written, how can it be read? This book is dedicated to this question of method, which it develops through a "visual" reading of Proust's *A la recherche du temps perdu* and selections from his *Contre Saint-Beuve*. The relations between text and image in Proust's work will be explored in all their complexity. In no passage of the novel are the paradoxical implications of the literary image made clearer than in the repeated mise en abyme in which the signature of a childhood friend of the hero of *A la recherche du temps perdu*, Gilberte, is described graphically.

Gilberte, herself the image of the taboo placed on the name in that she rejects and changes her own name, writes both badly, in other words illegibly, and well, since she creates a beautiful form. Emblematic of the difficulty of seeing, which only grows with desire as well as with closer inspection, the first description of her signature suggests an extreme illegibility caused by an excess of pen strokes. The effect of this signature is delayed: the joy that the narrator should have felt at receiving a note from her must wait until he has deciphered her scrawl. Much later, when the narrator is in Venice with his mother, the same signature leads him to think that Albertine, whom he knows to be dead, has been resurrected. All that saves this mise en abyme from incoherence is the question it raises of what is involved in image-writing, that is, in a "flat" writing.

The hero has just met Gilberte for the first time as an adult: he brushes against her, watches her, and then is introduced to her without recognizing her as his childhood friend. When he receives the telegram in Venice, he does not see the signature of his correspondent, as is the case with all telegrams. Nevertheless, and despite his earlier failure to recognize her face, he is able to describe her signature, which he saw once as a child, from memory and in such minute detail that all concerns for plausibility are suspended (SK 3.671 / P 4.235). The signature is, of course, the paradoxical sign that guarantees the authenticity and the originality of the *absent* subject. It is the most characteristic index, and yet it is also capable of being falsified, of being made into an icon. This is the very nature of the sign. Through Gilberte / Albertine's signature, the imaginary graphics and the image of *grammè* or "trace," the importance of the visual for Proustian poetics is sketched out and "signs itself."

The narrator of *La recherche* "explains" the philosophical implications of this poetic: "How often, when driving, do we not come upon a bright street beginning a few feet away from us, when what we have actually before our eyes is merely a patch of wall glaringly lit which has given us the mirage of depth!" (SK 2.435 / P 2.712).[1] If depth is a mirage, then the two-dimensional image is in one sense "flat," but in another sense has a depth of a very different kind. In what follows I explore the consequences of such a paradoxical vision for a possible reading of *A la recherche du temps perdu*. The significance of this vision to *La recherche* has yet to be studied in a comprehensive manner. I offer such a study and base it on the hypothesis that the references to visual images, the frequency and the importance of which for this novel have been pointed out many a time, are of fundamental value for the poetics of this work.

The motivation for this importance is not a simple aesthetic preference, nor does it follow from a simple exploration of a particularly rich domain of perception and sensation. I hope to show how the "flat" imagery of Proust integrates multiple stances, multiple needs of not only an affective order, but also a perceptual, epistemological, and poetic order. I shall attempt to analyze those well-known aspects of Proust's imagery—the obsessional voyeurism, the recurrent interest in visual art, the numerous and frequent metaphors borrowed from the domains of

2

optics and photography, the practice of narrative ambiguity in the descriptions, the visual fantasies, the fascination with flatness and the absence of volume—within a homogeneous framework.

I refer to this framework, this grid that structures my reading and forms the outline for a poetics, as *flatness*. I selected this term for its insistent and ambiguous quality. On the one hand, it implies the absence of depth and volume. Thus it emphasizes the disappointing and deceptive nature of fiction's *"mirage* of depth." The reader accepts a literal and concrete flatness as the price of admission to the diegetic universe of the novel and is rewarded by an almost total freedom of the imagination. On the other hand, far from being systematically associated with the exalted aesthetics of art, flatness also tends toward the banal,[2] such as is found in Charles Bovary's conversation, which is "flat like a sidewalk," and in the salons of Mme Verdurin and the Duchesse de Guermantes where the conversation is also flat in the metaphoric sense of the term. This particular flatness balances *La recherche*, which would otherwise suffer irrevocably from "elevated language." The principal thesis that this study develops is, then, that the tension *between* and the inharmonious resolution *of* the two meanings of the word "flatness" constitute a central impulse to Proust's literary project.

But literature is a verbal art. The visual domain can only be present within it by means of different subterfuges. The principal means of visualization is, of course, metaphor, which causes something "to be seen" in a way not revealed by the literal meaning, in a way only accessible through visualization. Furthermore, represented space is very often depicted with visual images. The narrator describes what he sees or what he saw when he was younger, and this gives a particular importance to the looking subject, whom I call the *focalizer*. But sometimes this gaze is "doubled," and what is described is often not a space or a vision but a visual representation: an image, a painting, an engraving, or a photograph. Or the visual nature of the image is "underlined," such as when the thing seen is described as if through a magnifying glass or a telescope, or as a projection from a magic lantern, or as a shot framed in the lens of a camera.

Taken in its entirety, *La recherche* has been likened to a cathedral, the overall composition of which has been described many a time. Thus it

3

can be considered as having been granted a visual form, that is to say, a form that is spatial as opposed to temporal and sequential. Georges Poulet, among others, has often remarked on the importance of Proust's preference for juxtaposing rather than superimposing images, which gives *La recherche* as a whole the appearance of an immense composition. The work is a collection of stained-glass windows or a retable made of predellas cleverly arranged: "The discontinuous multiplicity of episodes, identical until this moment to a series of isolated and juxtaposed pictures, is found to make room in the mind of him who embraces everything within it, for a coherent reality of images that relate to one another, mutually illuminate one another, and, so to speak, *compose themselves*" (*L'Espace proustien*, 132). Echoes of this type of formal aspect can also be found at a more detailed level, in the grain of the text. My particular concern is to analyze one specific aspect of this composition: the use of visual images, artistic or banal, explicit or implicit, around which the writing forms itself or deforms itself into what we can think of as properly visual writing. I call this generating aspect of the novel that stems from the visual, *figuration*.

It is a visualizing aspect of the text, but it remains an effect of language. Literature, after all, works within the medium of language. If we take into account this self-evident fact, then each visual image is first of all a verbal image and refers only indirectly, at the level of its meaning, to the visual images of other categories. Thus we could say that metaphors are verbal images of mental images, while descriptions are verbal images of perceptual images. Both the mental images and the perceptual images are capable in turn of referring to graphic images, which are visible, but only by means of a chain of mediations. The optic dimension is often interposed, less as an image than as the means for an image, in order to underline even more insistently the fact that these images are, after all, the products of language. In this way, this study of visuality in literature constitutes the counterpart to my own *Reading "Rembrandt,"* a study of the discursive aspects, that is, the narrative, rhetorical, and propositional aspects, of the image in Rembrandt. The question "how to read visually" complements the question "how to look discursively." The two studies suggest modes of understanding within a culture of exchange and interaction between the two "sister arts." They position themselves within the growing domain of the parallel study of text and image.

The choice of placing the set of visual domains at the center of this study stems principally, then, from my fascination with all narrative forms of visuality. Thinking back, my interest in the concept of focalization, the importance I have accorded to the subjectification of this concept, and the close attention I have paid in the past twenty years to narration as a mode of discourse, all derive from the same source. Put briefly, my work has grown out of the realization that subjectivity is formed by a perpetual adjustment of images passing before the subject, who makes them into a whole that is comprehensible because it is continuous. Having a certain continuity in one's thought depends, at a level that is more subliminal than conscious, on having a certain continuity in one's images.

But continuity is not the same thing as coherence. This distinction is another source of interest that informs this book. Having studied both historically and sociologically very diverse texts and images—the modern novel, the ancient and incomplete fragments that make up the Hebrew Bible, the paintings, engravings, and drawings of Rembrandt, all often very strange—I realized I was constantly coming up against that which eludes the coherence of these objects. My attention was systematically arrested by the detail that seems out of place, the contradiction that tears open the work, the monstrous element that reveals the flaws and the disparities and, because it provokes astonishment, offers a source of never-ending possibilities for the understanding of these images.[3]

Given the double impulse of my interest in the crossover between image and narrative discourse and of the heuristic possibilities offered by flaws in the text, I was quite naturally drawn to Proust. His work is solidly narrative, rich in imagery, and strongly focused on the process of apprenticeship, and yet troubling in its strangeness, in how it seems to flirt with incoherence, in how it delights in paradox and contradiction by means of both verbal and visual lies. I found it irresistible.

While I approach *La recherche* first and foremost as a visual novel, it is also a novel in which the subject is threatened with failure. The variability, the pluralization and the breaking-up of the subject leads, as Hubert Damisch would say, to a situation in which "the subject hangs only

5

by one thread" (*L'origin de la perspective*, 354). It is to this thread that the limbs of Proust's puppet-like characters are attached. The novel is written in the first person, but, as we know, *je est un autre*, "I is other." And by way of a rejoinder to this otherness, it quickly becomes clear that the other is "I." The narrator's identification with Swann, Saint-Loup, and Charlus is of the same order as the strange "flatness" of the character Albertine, who moves on the waves of the hero's desire without ever expressing the slightest will of her own. Like them, she is a projection of the narrator, and like them she remains nonetheless unknowable to him. For although the other is "I," I remains irreducibly other.

The subject is, then, constantly in danger of being absorbed into the other. This threat to the subject is *figured*, is given form, in the flat image that the narrator, as focalizer, can both contemplate fully and never know. Reduced to a flat surface, the image confronts the subject at the limits of vision. From a distance, the spectacle loses all life, colors disappear, and the movement of the sea is stilled. Close up, everything becomes muddled. When the hero leans to kiss the cheek he so desires, he is unable to feel any pleasure because he is too close to see it. As Gaston Bachelard has already said, in the visual domain, there is a rift between minute detail and clarity.[4]

The problem for the subject is that he wants to develop *himself* by brushing up against the other, represented in both the external world and human beings. But the other in Proust's work always flees, thus creating a conflict that possesses and defines the subject. In this study I explore this conflict from the angle of the image. The investigation will be carried out according to a restricted number of polarities that characterize the image: light and shade, as in chiaroscuro, clarity and indistinction, superimposition and juxtaposition, and narration and exhibition. The positions that Proust takes with regard to these polarities are invariably paradoxical. Sometimes shade is a better guarantor of visibility; sometimes volume cannot be grasped, while a flat, even banal, surface has more substance and thus offers a more solid support for the narrator's sensualist epistemology.[5] At both ends of the dialectical movement, which is itself fleeting, lies the two-dimensional image, the flatness of which appears as a permanent temptation to the subject who desires the total "possession" of his prisoner, a representation of the subject-desiring-knowledge.

The two-dimensional image is flat; it is also a platitude. I call this characteristic of the image its "flatness," but we must keep constantly in mind the conjunction between visuality and banality, which Proust reveals in all its sublimeness. As such, "flatness" is an image of writing. And it is, at the same time, a model for writing, not as an aesthetics of visual art, but as a literary aesthetics based on "flatness." It is also the major issue at stake in writing, its principal difficulty and an inextricable interweaving of affectivity and epistemology. The central desire in *La recherche*, which tells of a coming-to-writing, is to found the subject. The question is, then, how to resolve the insoluble conflict that makes "I" other while all the time rooting, as if in a transplantation, the other in the "I." Finally, "flatness" is also the metaphor for writing as a graphic art.

Each of the three following parts is given over to one particular aspect of Proustian flatness. They each begin with a metaphor central to the aspect in question, and the various chapters that make up each part follow the different dimensions of this metaphor. In Part I, I analyze the relations between Proust's writing and visual art, but only from the point of view of figuration. Art is not considered here as aesthetics in the way that the discipline of art history would understand it. Rather I take art to be more of an impulse toward emulation. It serves as a take-off point for an exploration of the possibilities for "putting down in writing" aspects of everyday life that give "flatness" an essential relevance. The analysis works around Jean-Baptiste Chardin's *The Skate*, a painting whose importance to *La recherche* is inversely proportional to the explicit mention it receives in the novel. This analysis suggests that the predilection for the image extends far beyond the level of epistemology. Indeed, it reveals an active involvement in the sensual domain, where disgust is perhaps more evident than pleasure. The initial metaphor that guides this exploration is that of the mottled screen, evoked in order to celebrate the activity of reading. The fact that reading needs the translucent effect, colors, and "flatness"—the word "screen" has Lacanian resonance—makes it the point at which literature and visual art converge.

7

Having established the intimate relation between the visual domain and Proust's writing in Part I, in Part II I explore this relation in greater detail. I do this with the help of the metaphor of the magnifying glass. The significance of this metaphor extends, however, far beyond the purely artistic. The magnifying glass introduces a poetics of the detail, for it is at this level that we find a conflict underpinning the whole of Proust's novel, that between perception at a distance and perception up close.

I then address the reflections on "flatness" according to the alternatives that the novel sets up and then rejects in favor of "flatness." The central metaphor in this case is the swelling hillsides, which are often evoked as an image of a woman's breasts. They represent a source of sensual pleasure that has "volume," but which is visible only from a distance. The reader will recall the description of Albertine naked, when her breasts are perceived as separate entities, detachable from her body. Between the hillsides, which remain out of reach, and the breasts, which lack "attachment," there are many ways to gain access to the breast's sensuality; yet it is the image of the breasts of two women pressed flat against one another that Proust gives us and which plunges the narrator into a jealous rage that lasts a thousand pages.

The masculine metaphor of the fountain, with all its vulgar sexuality, serves in its turn as a directing principle of the reading in Part II. Like the swelling hillsides, the fountain is invested with remarkable sexual significance, as can be seen in the small fragment known as "Solitary Pleasure," which Serge Doubrovsky made famous. It reappears often in *La recherche* both as a real object—Hubert Robert's fountain in the Prince de Guermantes's garden—and as a detail of itself, decomposed into those less glorious elements of masculinity otherwise known as "drips." This image of the dripping fountain contrasted with the first description of the father in the scene of "the bedtime drama" at Combray, where the father's weakness is imagined not as physical but as psychic. The pictorial character of this scene constitutes the essential mechanism that enables the son to identify with the father and to refuse this identification, a wavering that writing pictorially enables Proust both to say and not say at once. Broken up into fragments or details, the elements of masculine identity that suit the Proustian subject's needs ap-

8

pear like the pieces of a puzzle. He uses these to make forms that provide a "ground," in the sense once again of a flat surface, onto which the subject draws, paints, or projects the images that are necessary to him.

Finally, in Part III, I join the optical to the graphic. Motivated by the frequency of explicit references to photography in both the diegesis—Saint Loup's photograph of the grandmother—and the narrative, I venture to make photography the most revealing—and, of course, to reveal is the very essence of photography—mechanism by which to understand Proust's poetics. The snapshot, an image taken rapidly, is the metaphor for the writing of time in space. Taken in series, multiple snapshots become a sort of "contact sheet." This term is itself absent from the text of *La recherche*, but it describes well the type of writing that frustrates any attempt to write time in an image. Of all the characters of this novel who are loved, sought after, misunderstood, and desired, Robert de Saint-Loup is the one who represents Proust's visual poetic in the most "detail." His image resembles an engraving of a stylish dandy. His movements are serialized visually as a series of still images reminiscent of the work of the nineteenth-century scientific photographers. Robert's movements do not take place in time, only in space, and he transforms the Proustian universe into pure space.

All these forms of visual writing tighten the links between the affective, the epistemological, and the literary aspects of Proustian visuality. These aspects shed light on one another and they combine to make sense in a play of reciprocal composition. Thus, to give just one example, an example that is nonetheless particularly relevant, the description of Albertine naked and the voyeurism scene at the Guermantes' home both lead to a specific and essentially visual view of homosexuality as an experimental "science." Homosexuality is portrayed as an experience of knowing the other beyond the conflict between close-up vision and long-distant vision. The model of love for the same sex is that of a woman's love for a woman, not because of some sort of sexual jealousy, but because this loving relation is one of "pressing together," of two surfaces covering one another, and not one of penetration. Accordingly, jealousy is encountered in the course of the "ethnographic" voyage of discovery. The first episode of this voyage takes place when the hero sees Albertine's breasts pressed against those of Andrée in the casino at

9

Incarville. The last stage occurs a long time after the jealousy has disappeared; it is played out in Jupien's hotel when the hero watches Charlus lying flat on a bed, bound like Prometheus to a rock, seeking the satisfaction of his desire in blows inflicted upon him.

In its account of the vision of vision in Proust this study intends to be partial in both senses of the term. By focusing on detailed frames of the text, it aims to draw out an aspect of this work that gives it a great originality and a truly modern sensitivity. It is this originality and this sensitivity that enables us, I think, still to see something new in Proust.

part one

**The Mottled Screen:
Figurations of Visual Art**

When we have been smitten by one painter, then
by another, one may end by feeling for the whole
gallery an admiration that is not frigid, for it is
made up of successive loves, each one exclusive in
its day, which finally come to stand end to end,
reconciled in one whole.

—Proust, *A la recherche du temps perdu*
(SK 3.58 / P 3.572)

... I tried to find beauty there where I had never
imagined before that it could exist, in the most
ordinary things, in the profundities of "still life."

—Proust, *A la recherche du temps perdu*
(SK 1.929 / P 2.224)

chapter one

This Is Not a Painting

The mottled screen, which Proust uses to evoke the young Marcel's reading, is a metaphor that tells us how to read visually. When one says "Proust's images," one thinks of painting. To ignore the massive investment that Proust makes in this art form seems out of the question. He presents numerous works of art as both metaphors and narrative figures in *La recherche*, but in doing so, he does not use the magnifying glass of the connoisseur, the detailed perception of which would betray the author's hand metonymically. To give a rather peremptory summary of received opinion: one wouldn't go to Proust for advice when buying fine art.

It is remarkable that Proust's rejection of the detail in the matter of art is even explicit. Detailed perception, where painting is concerned, is a resounding failure. No "correction" is supplied to remedy the ridiculousness of Biche, who tries to look closely and, in so doing, fails to see anything:

> "I went up to one of them," he began, "just to see how it was done. I stuck my nose into it. Well let me tell you! Impossible to say whether it was done with glue, with soap, with sealing-wax, with sunshine, with leaven, with caca!" (SK 1.278 / P 1.250)

This is a blatant parody, even though it is directed not only at a member of the little clan who claims to be an amateur of the arts, the later El-

13

stir, but also at a prestigious and serious predecessor such as Rembrandt, about whom similar anecdotes abound. Furthermore, it might be tempting to deny anything other than the parodic force of this passage if it were not for the fact that it undeniably resembles the other moment of close-up perception when Marcel kisses Albertine. On this occasion the force of the passage is so striking that it would be impossible to ignore its implications, despite the irony which, once again, is not missing:

> Suddenly my eyes ceased to see, then my nose, crushed by the collision, no longer perceived any odour, and, without thereby gaining any clearer idea of the taste of the rose of my desire, I learned, from these obnoxious signs, that at last I was in the act of kissing Albertine's cheek. (SK 2.379 / P 2.660)

Close-up perception is reduced to nothing in the aporia of the detail, a theory which dates back to Gaston Bachelard. Looking at something close up splits the subject in two, making communication between minutiae and clarity impossible.[1]

The question raised in these two passages has nothing to do with art. Proust is neither a painter nor an art historian. In the discourse on painting there is no detailed elaboration of the visual image. Rather, as soon as the image is described, it comes to life, and the painting dissolves into "life." My concerns are not, then, with aesthetics, or with the meaning of the essayistic discourse in *La recherche*.[2] Proust was, after all, only an amateur. In fact, his remarks about painting are so eclectic that he could be accused of an inconsistency in taste.[3] There is no doubt about this. But it is almost as if one were to accuse him of being a cry baby or of lacking in will, of being selfish and insincere, snobbish and possessive, rather than considering him as a master writer for whom all of these attitudes are raw material.[4] His "taste for painting" is an important taste, and has more of an oral aspect than is immediately apparent. It is a taste that passes through painting; it is not, to put it according to Derrida, "taste in painting."[5] To accuse Proust of suspect taste is to read the whole of his novel as an essay; it is to subscribe to a naive realism, for which the author had nothing but contempt; it is, thus, to ignore his writing.

Of course, it is not possible either to reduce the nonetheless inter-

esting possibilities for an aesthetic reading of Proust to the rather caricatural search for "sources" or for models for the prolific and genuinely
museum-like work of the character Elstir. It is no more possible to restrict such a reading to the verification of works of art by well-known
artists evoked in *La recherche*. Beyond such a study of "sources" lies the
project of defining an "impressionist," a "realist," or a "cubist" aesthetics that can be identified in the poetic style of the work itself. The relation between text and painting in its "structural and technical aspect"
rarely manages to avoid the double constraints placed on it by the explicit elaboration in the novel of thematic and poetic statements.[6] Such
a project is also quite different from my concerns in these chapters. An
aesthetic reading of Proust is certainly interesting in a specific sense, and
it overlaps with my interests on various occasions in *La recherche*. There
remain, however, fundamental differences between the two approaches.[7]

There is another possible approach, which is also not mine, one that
is more "literary" in the sense that it takes into account the function of
the descriptions and the evocations of paintings in the novel as a fictional
text. This approach also shows more diversity. For example, Sophie
Bertho (in "Asservir l'image") assigns functions to these descriptions according to their place in the novel as a whole. On certain occasions the
image has a psychological function and characterizes the person who is
looking at it. In this manner Swann, who remembers Bloch because "he
looks so like the Bellini portrait of Mohamet II" (SK 1.105 / P 1.96;
Bertho 26), appears as an art expert and, to be precise I would add, as
an "orientalist." The very same Swann falls in love with Odette *because*
she looks like Botticelli's Zipporah, and thus he comes to embody the
rhetorical function because he allows himself to be influenced by what
he sees (SK 1.244 / P 1.220; Bertho 27). The two functions bear one another out, since Swann's love for Odette makes him appear as a lover
who "desires according to the other," that is to say, as a romantic, according to René Girard (in *Mensonge romantique et vérité romanesque*). Further, the structural function makes way for a reflexive function, which
Bertho describes as a mise en abyme.[8] She cites the similarity between
the kitchen maid and Giotto's image of Charity, a similarity which is
once again signaled by Swann. The common point between these two
would be the truth of the Platonic statement that "the idea of a thing is

15

never congruent with the thing" (Bertho 29). Only the ontological function escapes narrativity. It is assigned to the paintings that "stand still in a *description* that symbolizes the very meaning of the work" (32).[9]

This approach is relevant from a literary point of view, but in a symmetrical compensation for the "art history" approaches, it subordinates painting to writing and helps make the procedures involved in the writing more effective either by participating in their elaboration, as in the first three cases, or by transcending them and consequently by clarifying them, as in the last case. The interest of this type of approach for an analysis of Proust's novel is not in doubt; simply, in the more limited framework of my study of specific visual effects, it must be left to one side.

I approach painting in Proust by studying it as *figuration*, in other words, by projecting onto it an entirely literary poetics that is nonetheless articulated according to principles derived from the fundamental characteristics of painting, which are that it is an image and that it is "flat." I do this by means of a few identified paintings and a few *figures* of painters, who are, so to speak, chosen by Proust, but who are not characters in the novel. These figures are at once named historical figures, figures of paintings, and figures of writing. The art of these painters has been adopted by Proust for the process of *figuring*—of giving form and meaning—which he does by means of it and against it. The detailing of writing according to visual art takes place at this level.

It is Proust himself who chose these figures. In a short text "Marcel Proust par lui-même," which contains a list of preferences much in the manner of a child, he cites as his favorite painters Leonardo da Vinci and Rembrandt. He devotes another essay to the latter, "Rembrandt," which dwells longer on Ruskin and on the spectator than it does on painting. In "Chardin and Rembrandt" he does not discuss the Dutch painter until the few last pages. There are but a few remarks and allusions to da Vinci. On one side, then, I would place Rembrandt as a figure called up to serve in the figuration.

Chardin, who is not cited as a favorite painter, is nonetheless the favored subject of the essay just mentioned, "Chardin and Rembrandt." Throughout *La recherche* numerous references are made to him. Furthermore, he is placed in one respect opposite Rembrandt, who is classed among the "greats," and for Proust, he represents the alternative that must be taken into account. But if I have chosen Chardin as the second "figure of figuration," it is most of all because of the place accorded to one of his first paintings in the essay, and indirectly in *La recherche*. A very singular vision of art and of life emanates from the evocation of this painting, and this vision contributes significantly to the semantic content of the poetic notion of "flatness." Is it not surprising that Proust declares himself such an enthusiast for Chardin, given that this painter has nothing to do with impressionism, which has so dominated the discussions of Proust's aesthetics? This is but one more reason for analyzing his role.

But this does not mean that the text should be subordinated to art, even to the art of these great artists. Although Proust's hero may well be an apprentice, it must not be forgotten that this apprentice is one character among many, and that it is not he who is in control. On the contrary, the writing is without doubt that of an author who intends to be received as a master, and it is this writing that concerns us. If such a naive subordination is rejected, the specificity of the relations between text and image remains to be explored. I attempt such an exploration starting with a Proustian image. As a provisional indication of what is to follow, I start out with a metaphor that seems to me to be truly, if modestly, "of Proust": the mottled screen.

Proust uses the metaphor of "the mottled screen" for the first time in connection to reading. The sentence that it introduces is one of those which seem almost unbearably long, so long, indeed, that one hesitates to quote it and even more to shorten it. In its length it speaks of all the philosophical platitudes of the young and naive Marcel, who has yet to find, strictly speaking, his *place* with regard to reading or images. The mottled screen is one of two proper metaphors in the sentence.[10] Its status as a metaphor means that it is introduced and given a certain modality by the expression "the sort of," which belongs to a familiar and slightly casual tone of speech. This is a symptom of childhood, which is manifest again in the "gosh" expressed in response to a strikingly beautiful scene. So there is nothing extraordinary about this, nothing "artistic." Nothing very specifically visual either, beyond the actual metaphor. But a certain "flatness" is delicately established here.

Marcel, on the insistence of his grandmother, is in the garden. The

17

sentence, like the move to the garden, occurs just after the crucial passage in which Marcel is reading in the shade of his room, which follows in turn the unforgettable evocation of the kitchen maid as Giotto's Charity. This sequence is important. Here is the sentence:

> Upon the sort of screen mottled with different states and impressions which my consciousness would simultaneously unfold while I was reading, and which ranged from the most deeply hidden aspirations of my heart to the wholly external view of the horizon spread out before my eyes at the bottom of the garden, what was primary, my innermost impulse, the rudder whose incessant movements controlled everything else, was my belief in the philosophic richness and the beauty of the book I was reading, and my desire to appropriate them for myself, whatever the book might be. (SK 1.90 / P 1.83)

I will come back later to the sequence of the three passages. Let us leave aside also the irony directed at the young novice reader, which becomes rather heavy in the sentences that follow, and which works against a "serious" reading of the utterance. What interests me here, as a guiding principle to a "flat" reading of painting in Proust, is the fact that painting is called upon during the course of the novel to serve as a rival to this simple activity of *unfolding* or *displaying*. This rivalry should not be taken lightly, and Proust has already spoken of it to warn us indirectly against an "art history" reading of his evocations of paintings ("Painting cannot touch the one true reality of things and thus compare with literature except on the condition of not being literary" *CSB* 112).

In this passage, which describes both different states and their simultaneity as well as hidden depths that are flattened out before the eyes like a horizon (this horizon in the garden is necessarily seen fairly close up, which suggests a parody of the more grandiose horizon of the sea), we have a description of vision. The mottled screen, as a figure of the unfolding of simultaneous, different states, is a metaphor that inscribes variations and nuances of color on a flat image. Thus the metaphor functions as a concentrated figuration of variations of all sorts, among which are those governed by time, for which visuality serves as a ground, in the material sense of the term—in other words, as a screen. It is a quite different screen from the translucent and clear one that is so important in Zola's naturalist poetics. Let me start by comparing the evaluation that the narrator gives, perhaps a little defensively, of his "taste in painting":

> When one has been smitten by one painter, then by another, one may end by feeling for the whole gallery an admiration that is not frigid, for it is made up of successive loves, each one exclusive in its day, which finally come to stand end to end, reconciled in one whole. (SK 3.58 / P 3.572)

Marcel's reading in the garden is defined as "flat" in the manner of a projection screen. It is the result of an unfolding before the subject of that which is internal and hidden to him. A "flat" reading will be guided by the visual image that is presented as a painted work. But the definition of this reading according to the mottled screen must not be forgotten. It is to be distinguished from an aesthetic reading that takes the novel's references to painting as a starting point, as an utterance, rather than as a mode of enunciation.

Indeed, to read visually, it seems to me to be useless to ask whether "these leaning boats," or "these churches emerging from the waters," and "these hulls, vaporized by an effect of the sunlight and made to overlap one another by the perspective" really have anything to do with plastic art (Henry, "Quand une peinture," 210). In the case of the picture of the port at Carquethuit (SK 1.894–96 / P 2.192–94), all the evidence points to the impossibility of considering it as a case of referential plastic art. There is no more classic piece of ekphrastic virtuosity to be found in *La recherche*.[11] In it the vision of the picture appears like one of those states unfolded onto the mottled screen. Indeed, this is said quite explicitly: the description is "motivated" as an example of metaphor and is, thus, to be placed among the "essayistic" moments of the novel.[12]

Elstir's painting is the figuration of a problem linked to the mottled screen. "It multiplies the localities while preventing their localization" (Guillerm, "Le goût en peinture," 147). The very multiplication of pictorial details, personified as if they represented artist figures or characters, is inscribed as successive states coexisting simultaneously. This "reading" of the painting is a function of the narrator's vision, as is his reading of the studio, of which it is a "dis-figure."[13] The description of the picture, the most striking example of ekphrasis in the novel, becomes, as Jean-Pierre Guillerm has remarked, "a disordered 'scene,' a

19

sum of visibilities that thwart any separating-out and that reduce the modalities of vision, like a museum" ("Le goût en peinture," 147). The two key terms here are "disordered" and "scene," both figures of the separation that produces lack and reassuring re-re-assembly. This "disorder"—and it should be noted that the French word also carries the meaning of defeat—is a measure of the state of things in the rivalry between literature and art, as it is staged by our narrator.

In contrast to those studies which place the emphasis on painting as opposed to poetics, here it is a matter of shifting the emphasis from art to the image, from aesthetics to the visual, from the depth of judgment to the superficiality of flattening as a figure of appropriation. Indeed, the child narrator put it very clearly as he read in the garden: he wishes to appropriate the philosophic richness and beauty that he sees around him. Nonetheless, to isolate art as the form of Proustian "flatness" seems to contradict my attempt to shift the emphasis. The point is that, for Proust, art is, above all else, flat. Even the statues are two-dimensional, as is shown in the famous description of Françoise that doubly denies all "volume" to the servant (SK 1.57 / P 1.52). Art is also flat in the sense of being banal. The literary aesthetic prevails over the visual aesthetic, but the latter provides raw material for the former.[14]

But there is perhaps no more convincing example of the "flatness" of art than the juxtaposition of the passage in which Biche, the future Elstir, speaks in a way both admired in the diegesis and mocked by the narrator and the reader (SK 1.278 / P 1.250), with the passage in which Albertine is kissed (SK 2.379 / P 2.660), despite the pronounced irony clearly present in both cases. These two passages were, of course, already juxtaposed in terms of their relation to the problem of close-up perception. They "theorize" close-up perception by fragmenting it into "details," thus representing in a totally negative mode the approach toward the object of desire. In the case of the first passage the object in question is the work of art, "technically . . . even better than either Rembrandt or Hals." In the second, it is the woman with whom, a long time ago, Marcel decided to "have" his novel (SK 1.976 / P 2.268). Biche gets lost in the vagueness of snobbish talk, talking to say nothing ("It's all there—but really, I swear it!"). The narrator continues in his efforts. Too close to see properly, he pursues his quest by compensating for the crushing of his senses, as a result of his closeness, with a description of the invisible face that could not be more detailed while being nonetheless nonpictorial. This last resort is a parenthesis, a detail of the novel itself, which describes the infinitely small, adding a comparison with the artistic image of a genre much practiced by Rembrandt and Hals:

> (No doubt, compared with that earlier look, the voluptuous expression which her face assumed now at the approach of my lips differed only by an infinitesimal deviation of its lines but one in which may be contained all the disparity that there is between the gesture of "finishing off" a wounded man and that of giving him succour, between a sublime and a hideous portrait.) (SK 2.379 / P 2.661)

A gesture of "finishing off" or one of "giving succour": are these last two pairs of metaphors a parallelism or a chiasmus? The difference separating the two possible combinations of metaphors also separates life from death for the subject of this failed perception. Moral questions are buried deep in the poetic ambiguities.

This conflation recalls a passage that will be discussed in more detail later: "There are people whose faces assume an unaccustomed beauty and majesty the moment they cease to look out of their eyes" (SK 3.65 / P 3.579). Once again the description has "made the most" of a visual example borrowed from Elstir's stock. The eclecticism in the representation of Elstir's work gives this reserve of images a considerable evocative potential. For example, it would be quite wrong to refer to some real masterpiece as a source for the following description: "An isolated straight tress gave the same effect of perspective as those moonlit trees, lank and pale, which ones sees standing erect and stiff in the backgrounds of Elstir's Raphaelesque pictures" (SK 3.65 / P 3.579). However, thinking along the lines of the Japanese "manner" of this description, we could view it as a recycling of a "scene [that is] more picturesque than natural" (Uenishi, *Le style*, 27). It might even appear as a fairly nasty abuse:

> At one time it was an exhibition of Japanese colour-prints: beside the neat disc of the sun, red and round like the moon, a yellow cloud appeared like a lake against which black swords were outlined like the trees upon its shore. (SK 1.862 / P 2.162)

This description is sinister, especially if it is placed in relation to the description of Albertine's sleep, which I analyze in Part II and in which the tress of hair takes on proportions gigantic enough to blind vision. With its black swords, it reveals that the picturesque is able to serve masters other than great painters. Inserted into a reflection that begins "But as often as not they were, indeed, only pictures; I forgot that below their coloured expanse lay the sad desolation of the beach," this description only makes the narrator's case worse.

The image, seen in detail, loses its sensory characteristics, but it also represents another danger of "flattening," and that is the confusion of subject with object. By losing sight of the difference in scale, such an image runs the risk of suppressing this distinction. In the ekphrasis of the port at Carquethuit there is an effect of representation that oscillates between, let us say, impressionism and optical error, which is, however, an incompatibility in painting (Descombes, *Proust*, 282–84). Visibility requires distance, but distance, as we shall see, empties the sea of its colors.

It is here, caught in this dilemma, that Proust's distinction between his two favorite painters takes root and develops. In Chapter 2 I sketch out how Proust is to be distinguished from Rembrandt by his very "Rembrandtism." His taste for Rembrandt, his desire to appropriate this work in its poetics of figuration, is the site at which his eventual difference with the art of this artist develops. His investment in Chardin's work is greater, more intense. Here the stakes are of an order that massively overwhelms, that stretches well beyond the level that it is customary to assign to the domain of poetics. In both cases, the objective will not be to trace a literature "in the manner of," but rather to witness a loving interaction that is sometimes polemical, sometimes violent, and through which Proust's "mottled" poetic destiny is played out. Furthermore, it is not at a stylistic level, but rather at the level of the figuration that this interaction is to be found. The term "metaphor," made too vague by Proust himself, gives only an insufficient sense of the contours of this figuration.

chapter two

Rembrandt, Perhaps

Proust's predilection for Rembrandt is undeniable. But what are the properly poetic reasons for this predilection? It is not in the short descriptive notes such as "a Rembrandt style hat" (SK 1.263 / P 1.237) or "his whole manner exuded that gentle gravity which constitutes the broad and unctuous charm of certain portraits by Rembrandt" (SK 2.704 / P 3.78) that we will find them. Certainly these comparisons are quite "exact" in their comparative function: before reading the name, one *sees* the portrait of Jan Six in the last example, and this is due to the masterful stroke of literary emulation. They are but further examples of the interminable series that makes up the long tradition of "cultural" comparisons. To use art as a point of comparison is nothing new: Balzac and Stendhal had already done that.

Sometimes, however, what appears to be an example of such a strategy unexpectedly turns into its opposite: the comparison and the thing compared change places as if the relation between apprentice and master could be reversed in the same manner. This cannot avoid creating an ambivalence of sorts, as can be seen in a certain violence, such as is shown in the passage at Doncières when the hero experiences another of his lessons in looking:

> In a little curio shop a half-spent candle, projecting its warm glow over an engraving, reprinted it in sanguine colour, while, battling against the dark-

23

ness, the light of a big lamp bronzed a scrap of leather, inlaid a dagger
with glittering spangles, spread a film of precious gold like the patina of
time or the varnish of an old master on pictures which were only bad
copies, indeed, transformed the whole hovel, in which there was nothing
but rubbish and old crusts, into a marvellous composition by Rembrandt.
(SK 2.95 / P 2.395)

At first glance, the "marvellous composition by Rembrandt" is the point
of comparison, while the small shop is that which is compared. The
agent of this comparison—its motive, which is then turned into an agent
by the activity that it initiates—is the light. Indeed, the small candle is
very Rembrandtesque, even though its effect—the blood-like color—is
less so. This transformation operates, then, through the intervention of
the engraving, reminding the reader of the double intermediary of
Swann and the grandmother (SK 1.43 / P 1.39). And before Rembrandt
is able to intervene, a battle between light and shade has to take place,
giving rise, in turn, to the dagger.

As for the visual *tone* of the passage, the Rembrandtism of this description is only superficial, it consists only in the costumes, theatrical
props, and accessories mobilized to produce its semblance. The piece of
leather, the knife, the stump of a candle are also only details gathered
together to signify, "to make you see," a painting by Rembrandt. We do
indeed *see* it, and we also see the aspect of Rembrandt that is "staged"
or "played out" here. There remains, however, the spangles. Are they
not more "Elstirian" than Rembrandtesque? As for the poetical *tone*, the
words to note are those that figure battle, as well as the word "master,"
and, especially, the disappointing and temporary nature of the transformation. If we read the passage against the grain of the meaning it is
ultimately given, in other words against the image of the "marvellous
composition by Rembrandt," it all seems in the end to be nothing but
rubbish and old crusts.

Of course, it would be pushing things a bit far to read this passage
completely against the grain by making it into an ironic text in which
the Rembrandt-effect is revealed to be fake. But such a reading, be it only
marginal, even subliminal, is not totally impossible. My point is that the
relation to the master, to mastery in general, as well as to the most admired masters, always remains ambivalent. And it is the possibility of

such a presence that makes this description in turn something like a "mottled screen." The thing seen, thanks to the color effects produced by light and shade, the chiaroscuro, becomes first and foremost a flat image. As in the effect of the glittering of the spangles, we no longer see very well what there is in there.

For the Rembrandt-effect is presented here, above all else, as an effect of chiaroscuro. To remark on this effect is almost a banality in the traditional discourse on this painter. Transforming bad copies into art is the defining activity of all amateurs and imitators. This is the very description of a *trick*, or a basic type of artifice. It is rather like a recipe, as Swann, the masterful stockbroker who exchanges recipes for artistic subjects of conversation (SK 1.17 / P 1.16), understands so well. And the word "crusts," does it not indeed figure as a shifter between semantic fields by giving an idea of the edible and the surface or layer as both exchangeable and flat?

Nevertheless, chiaroscuro is not only a banality. Proustian "flatness" is always more complicated. In the banal conception of Rembrandt, which is concerned with the transformation of meager poverty into "patina," the important factor is the effect of the candle or the lamp. In a poetic appropriation of this effect, chiaroscuro becomes crucial in a different way. Light and shade are central to the celebrated passage on reading that is symmetrical to the passage on reading in the garden in which the "mottled screen" makes its appearance. Indeed, the former passage is the shade to the light of the latter. The little figure of the yellow butterfly, which precedes this passage, overdetermines its importance:

> I would be lying stretched out on my bed with a book in my hand. My room quivered with the effort to defend its frail, transparent coolness against the afternoon sun behind its almost closed shutters through which, however, a gleam of daylight had contrived to insinuate its yellow wings, remaining motionless in a corner between glass and woodwork, like a butterfly poised upon a flower. (SK 1.89 / P 1.82)

Nothing Rembrandtesque about this. This passage differs from the Doncières passage in every possible way, like night to day, to put it rather aptly, and the delicacy and the quivering of the yellow butterfly's wings are at the heart of this contrast.

It is important that this description, while being the opposite of the description of the shop in Doncières, constitutes the "shade" to the "light" of the reading in the garden. This uncertain position, relative in all respects, is contained within the quivering of the wings. And though the Rembrandt-effect at Doncières may seem both vulgar and dim compared with this passage, we must not be tempted too quickly to read a facile contempt for Rembrandt into it. The quivering in question could well be the poetic counterpart to that which, in an *image*, would be the more subtle aspect that emerges when Rembrandt throws light onto some anodyne element of the picture, thereby placing the face in shadow *in order that it be better seen*.

Now, if we suppose that Proust simply borrows an aesthetics from visual art, we fail to perceive the conditions necessary for the transposition of this chiaroscuro into literature. It must be taken not as a mode of representation or as an artistic ideal, but as a way of pursuing the aesthetic effect that belongs to the specific enterprise embodied within the image or the text. In other words, it must be understood as the destiny of the enterprise. Proust describes it when he writes: "The configuration of a thing is not only the image of its nature; it is also the word of its destiny and the trail of its history" (*CSB* 112). It is in this sense that Rembrandt's chiaroscuro underpins the text. This paradoxical, subtle but essential lighting illuminates, by means of a contrast with light, that which is in shade. The importance of this lighting in *La recherche* is well known, and in this sense, we could indeed say that the work is situated "on Rembrandt's way." The figuration of Proust's Rembrandtism is located, then, within this domain.

Furthermore, it is also in this domain that Proust departs from Rembrandt, since there is a real rivalry justifying the choice of literature as art. When Proust says, in the remark already quoted, that "painting cannot touch the one true reality of things and thus compare with literature except on the condition of not being literary" (*CSB* 112), it is advisable to take this utterance to be reversible. If painting should not be literary, literature should no more be pictorial for fear of failing to realize its own possibilities. The following passage offers the proof of this assertion:

> This dim coolness of my room was to the broad daylight of the street
> what the shadow is to the sunbeam, that is to say equally luminous, and
> presented to my imagination the entire spectacle of summer, which my
> senses, if I had been out walking, could have tasted and enjoyed only piece-
> meal; and so it was quite in harmony with my state of repose which . . .
> sustained, like a hand reposing motionless in a stream of running water,
> the shock and animation of a torrent of activity. (SK 1.90 / P 1.82)

This passage has been discussed so much that it is difficult to add anything new.[1] Its content is that of a plea for metaphor, which, in a Rembrandtesque manner, is capable of bringing out the qualities of the
other side of the chiaroscuro. But this plea is expressed by means of
metonymies, or rather, by means of a to-ing and fro-ing (Genette,
"Métonymie chez Proust") between these two figures, which we could
call a *shimmering*. The totalizing effect, the interest of which for the "impressionist" Marcel is well known, is not at all Rembrandtesque. It is part
of the very search (*recherche*) in which Marcel is engaged: the attempt to
capture time simultaneously calls upon comparison with visual art in
general.

The last image is the one that strikes us most ("a hand . . . torrent of
activity"). Indeed, it makes its impact felt, and I have cause to come back
to it in a later chapter. Here, the important thing to note is that the relation between light and shade, the chiaroscuro, seems to be at the heart
of the reading experience, even though the metaphor of water pushes
it from its central place. The pause in the simultaneity of "pieces," which
would have fragmented the experience if it had taken place in narrative,
in time, corresponds to the effect we see in Rembrandt's historical painting. But this pause requires another dimension in literature. The dim
coolness, a figuration of Rembrandtism in poetics, begins as the object
to be compared, for which the comparison is elaborated, but it ends up
being relegated to the position of serving as a *ground* for something else.
The image of running water containing a motionless hand is an image
of activity associated with the shimmering fountain, which is absolutely   **27**
central to the hero's preoccupations analyzed later. It goes beyond and
overflows the frame created by specifically Rembrandtist pictorial figuration.

In Rembrandt's work, as is well known, it is in the shady corners that the essential is to be seen. In a self-portrait, for example, the large rim of a hat places the eye in shadow. And, because we are forced to look harder, we see the eye all the better. It is a clear case of displacement. We can say, therefore, that, contrary to what happens in Rembrandt's work, Proustian figuration of the position of the painter's mastery is imbued with ambivalence. The figuration of chiaroscuro is not a means of dividing the visual field in order to displace the accents, but rather a fundamental effect of mobilism: in literature, light and shade are perfectly interchangeable. The appropriation and the surpassing of the earlier master's work are, after all, both quite normal practices from one artist to another, from one form of art to another, or from one medium to another.[2]

Thus, the short essay "Rembrandt," contained in the *Literary Beginnings* (*CSB* 659–64), reveals nothing of great interest for the Proustian Rembrandt. It is rather an occasion to celebrate, not the painter, but the thinker Ruskin—another model and cause for emulation—and also to marvel at the shimmering effect ("pearls that shine dimly" *CSB* 659). In "Chardin and Rembrandt," only one page, which comes at the end of the essay and seems almost out of place, extols Rembrandt's art. But this is done in terms that provoke fear, all the while emphasizing a mobilism that is much more Proustian than it is Rembrandtesque: "We will see that the objects are nothing by themselves, empty orbits whose light is the changing expression" (*CSB* 380). We also find: "all the torments of death," "bolts of fire," "glittering, enameled, glowing windows" (*CSB* 381). The last sentence of this incomplete text is itself incomplete, ending on "the anger for . . . " I regret slightly that I cannot speculate on the meaning of this end and the continuation that it both suggests and represses.

The essay "Chardin and Rembrandt" does not make much of Proustian Rembrandtism. It presents itself as a stroll in the Louvre. The pedagogical aim of this stroll is to review common attitudes to everyday life among young people by means of these two painters' art. One of the paintings, which is only briefly discussed, is *The Slaughtered Ox* (Fig. 1). This is, in fact, of all the Rembrandts in the Louvre, the one that comes closest to the still lifes that are the central concern of the essay.[3] And,

Fig. 1. Rembrandt van Rijn, *The Slaughtered Ox*, 1655. Paris, Musée du Louvre (copyright Photo R.M.N.).

rather than the dead beast, Proust mentions only the woman to the right of the painting, whom he describes as "turning round" (660), thus turning away from her a little fast. Nevertheless, this painting offers a good counterpart to Chardin's *The Skate*, which he has previously discussed in detail. This turning away strikes me as an important gesture in that it suggests a good deal about the figuration that Proust bases on visual art. Not only is his literary Rembrandtism nowhere to be found in the explicit evocations of the master, the same can be said of the other figuration of visual art, his Chardinism.

chapter three **Chardin Reads Proust**

The relation between the arts is seen best if one respects the specificity of each as well as the dialogue between them. Can we, then, in an anachronistic reversal of perspective, speak of Chardin reading Proust? In other words, does Proust's text shed a different light on the Chardin we think we know? With *The Skate* (Fig. 2) we discover an art at once disgusting, disturbing, and fascinating. The painting provokes the utmost repulsion, thereby appearing as the ultimate redemption of abjection through art. The few words I say about this painting here do not claim to offer an exhaustive analysis. I limit myself to giving a reading of the painting that is informed by Proust as we have come to see him.

The Skate occupies an exceptional place in the painter's work, and, in presenting it for the occasion of his nomination to the Academy in 1728, Chardin intended to surprise. The painting could not have failed to make its mark, and ever since it has been the object of much critical analysis.[1] Here, I attempt to define, according to this painting, the idea of a "mottled screen," which is to function as a guide to our reading of the text. First, the painting is, in its form, literally a screen: the central figure of the skate appears as two triangles spread out to form a diamond.

This diamond is also like a crossroads: in it meet the different angles of vision located in the four corners of the painting, like the faces in the four corners of ancient maps. At the top, staring out of the ghostlike

Fig. 2. Jean-Baptiste Chardin, *The Skate*, 1738. Paris, Musée du Louvre (copyright Photo R.M.N.).

face, are the "eyes" of the fish, eyes which are no more than signs of the eye, *trompe l'oeil*, because what they in fact represent are the gills. These blind eyes dominate the scene. In the left-hand corner are the living eyes of the cat, which seem almost to look directly into the spectator's eyes. In the right-hand corner is the round opening of the cauldron, where the handle is joined to the pot. This opening takes on the form of an eye once the spectator is alerted to the representation of vision in the painting. Finally, the eye of the dead fish lying at the base of the painting is so well trained on the spectator that it becomes difficult to avoid it. The fish is also the focus of the cat's stare, a stare which suggests perhaps lust, but seems, above all else, threatening.

The significance of this form is inevitable: the diamond shape, the representation of the body splayed open as if martyred, and the disposition of the corners all bring to mind the Crucifixion. But here the traditional form of the Crucifixion has been reversed in several different ways. First, it is the external surface of Christ's body that appears on the cross. This externality is underlined by the wounds in his side and in his hands and feet. In contrast, it is the inside of the skate that is exposed; the body is opened out before us. Second, the body of Christ itself forms the shape of the cross, with the torso and legs as the vertical support and the arms forming the horizontal line. Thus the arms and the legs are themselves the extremities that point away from the body. With the skate, however, the body is a unified surface, and its outer limits encompass the whole of the body, which is spread out within them.

And finally, the body of Christ has real volume. Indeed, this volume is essential to its nature as incarnation. The theological concept of incarnation has had a profound impact on the possibilities for pictorial representation of Christ, as Leo Steinberg has shown (see his *Sexuality of Christ*). The body's volume is represented, in particular, in the weight of the dead body by showing how the chest slumps forward, as can be seen in many frontal images. The skate, however, seems hardly to have any volume. Or rather, an extreme effort has been made to minimize this volume. This contrast is all the more striking in that the skate is also shown to be most definitely "hung," nailed like Christ on a hook that is clearly represented. The two flanks of the dead fish have remained surprisingly stiff, which serves to emphasize their breadth. The comparison with the much smaller skate painted by Chardin a few years later makes the breadth of the earlier skate all the more striking.[2]

If we superimpose these three departures from traditional images of the Crucifixion, we can describe the "flatness" of this image as encompassing or containing the whole body, which has been opened out. Thus the body figures the unfolding as a representation, in other words, as a display. Taking into consideration the ideology surrounding the death of Christ, we are even more struck by this difference. While it is theologically crucial that he be incarnated, it is equally important that the idea of the spirit taking leave of his body should dominate his death. Indeed, when the women go to visit his tomb, they find it empty. For our skate, which is, after all, just a vulgar animal, things happen rather differently. Its tomb is the kitchen, and its resurrection is to be none other than the combined result of the foods lying around it. Of course, Christ will also be eaten, and he is often symbolically represented by the figure of the fish, but the consumption of Christ only occurs through the mediation of a form that is supposed to be his body, and that, in fact, bears little resemblance to it. Ultimately, the symbol is quite reassuring.

Against the background of the flat body exposed here, our eye is drawn to particular elements, or perhaps details, of the canvas. The cat catches our attention first. Should we not consider it almost a second principal character: a figuration of the gaze that faces the flatness? The cat's position and posture also remind us of the cat in Manet's *L'Olympia*, which looks aggressively at the indiscreet spectator. We might expect the cat to look hungrily, but this seems to be a very aggressive and destructive hunger. In this respect, it is not unlike the account that Serge Doubrovsky gives of Marcel's lust as he eats the small cake called a madeleine (see *La place de la madeleine*). The cat's attitude reveals an urge to attack, or at least to defend itself from attack. This attack could not possibly come from the fish, which is only too dead and no doubt the victim itself of an attack. The cat seems, then, to be offered up as a counterpoint, "in the name" of the skate: an eye for an eye. And the skate, in turn, seems simply to look up as if to say it can do nothing to resolve this hostile confrontation.

We shall return to the cat shortly, because, as we shall see, Proust took a particular interest in it. We shall talk about its paws, which tread gently on the oysters in their shells. And we shall find that the liquid surrounding these oysters seems to take on a strangely elastic consistency, like in those second-rate paintings of Venus by artists like Bouguereau in the Orsay museum in Paris, in which Venus, who is supposed to emerge from the water, in fact seems to walk upon the waves as if they were the paving stones of a road; or like Cabanel's Venus, who seems to lie upon the water as if it were a hard cushion. The communication, or the transition, between Venus and the water in these paintings is unconvincing. How, then, does the cat treading magically over the liquid in the oysters in Chardin avoid being second-rate? What makes this all the more striking is the fact that the liquid surrounding the oysters is, without doubt, watery. Indeed, the water is even sufficiently transparent to prompt an allusion to the episode of the glass jars in the Vivonne. In his essay, Proust makes a real drama out of the cat and the oysters. But this aspect of flatness, too limited to one meaning to have great weight, hides another dimension of flatness, about which Proust doesn't speak, but which he uses in his practice.

We have to look closer at the other details of the canvas, all of which are "instrumental." First, the knife: instrument of penetration, of course, but which appears in the painting to have lost its point.[3] Like the other objects that seem to lie along a certain line, the knife is deflected. It is aimed at the center of the body, which it has no doubt just finished opening up, but its final point is hidden by the tablecloth, which Proust describes as *rounded* or *swollen*. It is—and we must run the risk implied in this word—as if the knife were visually castrated before it can castrate. The other oblong objects, the handles of the skimmer, the saucepan and the jug, as well as the neck of the bottle, are all carefully deflected from the line that would lead them to the inside of the body.

This is most striking in the case of the saucepan handle. We have already encountered the image of a handle in the second metaphor of the passage introducing the mottled screen. There the handle appeared as a rudder, introducing an element of marine vocabulary that fits well with the "sea monster" of this scene. Moreover, the term "rudder" establishes a contrast in the figuration of flatness. A rudder is hard, phallic-shaped, and especially "always in movement" in order to control the tendency to stray from a path. Attached to the body of the pan and provided with a small eye, the pan handle seems to reply to the cat's stare. But even more clearly, it seems to aim precisely at the point to which our eyes are led if we stare into the body of the fish. As in Charles S. Peirce's notion of an index, the continuation of the pot handle strikes the spectator's vision and cuts it off. The act of penetrating the inside of a body, even if it is only with a penetrating look, is far from simple.

Clearly, this painting lacks penetrable depth.[4] It is in this respect, in particular, that it can be distinguished from Rembrandt's *Slaughtered Ox*.[5] The very device of depth in painting, of perspective, is used here to confound a sense of depth. The wall, which holds up the fragile exteriority, seems to turn around a corner just behind the flank of the skate on our left. This corner is necessary in order for the cat to be at the same depth in the field of vision as the skate, allowing its gaze to participate in the figuration of the diamond-shaped screen on a flat surface. But the sink on which the objects are lying does not fit with this corner, almost as if

35

it were intended to reveal the artifice of this perspective. It functions as a sign that indicates, without actually signifying, an impossibility. In this way, the cat appears to stand both "behind" the skate and "on" the screen. It is both outside in a kitchen scene, and inside in a body, which is exposed, open, flat, and impenetrable.

But it is not only the inside that we see here. This picture is so effective, particularly as a figuration of Proust's poetics, precisely because the outside and the inside are represented at the same time, together with that most complex problematic that their simultaneous representation creates. We see the skin of the fish, but also what is covered by that skin. The guts have been removed, but we can still see the fragments of these internal organs.

If we look closely, we're struck by the extent of the opening of the body. This wound, as François Lecercle says (in "Le regard dédoublé," 121), invades the painting, like a detail that blinds and yet both informs and gives form. Under the grotesque face, turned slightly to the left, are what could be two hands reaching out from the body, or wounds hollowed out of the surface. The hook, a reminder of the power to kill, is taken from the inside of the body. Like the nails that pierced the hands and the feet of Christ, there are traces of blood on its surface. But it is also shiny, and the whiteness that represents this shine is repeated on the inside of the fish's body.[6] We even have the impression of ribs a little to the right, which leaves us wondering whether the body is not, in fact, transparent.

There is a definite lack of clear distinctions here. Indeed, this is the very nature of the "mottled" effect: the body seems to have a transparent lightness, and its inside and outside appear at one and the same time in an infinitely nuanced range of color, which is also light. The colors in question are those of mother-of-pearl, of a rainbow, with particular nuances to be found in the white. This white manages to dominate the redness of the body by appearing through it. It all seems rather disordered, and, of course, order depends on the possibility of making distinctions. Chardin is said to have avoided ostentation by using this sort of disordered and careless display.[7] But the scene we have before us in no way suggests spontaneity. No kitchen ever looked like this.

So what does it look like exactly? What is the purpose of the objects such as the folded cloth that is hanging over the saucepan, or the knife from which the blood must have been wiped, perhaps on that very cloth? Why the studied emphasis on the soiled and the disordered? All these oblong objects—weapons?—cross over one another, creating a breathtaking tension. It is definitely a scene, but the scene has nothing to do with a kitchen. It seems more like a battlefield. So there is a scene being staged, but it is not articulated. All the objects disappear into one another, either under or over the others. On a rather prosaic level, without the skate—without the flatness-screen—all we see are small objects scattered around. There is a lack of articulation and depth. We see only a hostile confrontation between the oblong objects and the lines of vision. In this respect, the painting is already significantly Proustian. It brings to mind the unlikely details in the painting of the port at Carquethuit by Elstir, who is himself a compendium of the history of art. The narrator describes this painting in a manner that explores the possibilities of representation, while seeming to talk only of metaphorization.

The Skate is, without doubt, the *pièce de résistance* of Proust's essay "Chardin and Rembrandt," which appears in *Contre Sainte-Beuve*. It clearly far outdoes Rembrandt's *Slaughtered Ox* inasmuch as once the author has described Chardin's painting, he has nothing left to add. The *Ox* also represents the inside and the outside at one time, which is the source of its elemental force. But this ambiguity, so profoundly important for Proust, is represented by Rembrandt in a three-dimensional image. A sense of perspective is so well deployed in this painting, by both the representation of space and the chiaroscuro, that the spectator almost has the impression of being invited to penetrate into the body. That Proust devotes so much of his essay to one of these painters, and so little to the other, must not be understood as a judgment of aesthetic value, but rather as an indication of Proust's own poetic practice. The emphasis he places in this essay is completely a function of his own needs. **37**

So is Chardin, then, an ideal of flatness, in the two senses of the word? Before we consider this painting in the light of Proust's writing, in the light, that is, of his writing on this painting, let us first look quickly at the other painting that Proust addresses in this essay: Chardin's *The*

Buffet (Fig. 3). In this painting there is nothing comparable to the troubling, ghostlike atmosphere of *The Skate*. This canvas seems almost to be the reassuring counterpart to the other, although there are some undeniable echoes that give a certain cause for anxiety. There is no cat, but there is a gun dog, whose muzzle and eyes are directed longingly toward the food on the dresser. We can detect certain references to the mottled screen in the overall lack of distinction between inside and outside: the oysters, like those tread upon by the cat, are about to fall; the knife is half buried, while being clearly directed toward the visually empty center. The empty center, in fact, allows us to see the support holding up the dish. The rather strange position of the tablecloth, attached, one supposes behind the upright dish, seems to be too far forward and, consequently, forms a flat surface with the dish. The small still life on the right-hand side of the canvas, composed of very Proustian glasses and jugs, reveals the same uncertain, discrete light that we saw on the pan, the skimmer, and the knife handle in the other painting. By way of an emblematic sign for the mottled screen, there is the half-peeled lemon, a traditional display of virtuosity that is, consequently, rather flat, in the other sense of the word. This lemon reveals both the inside and the outside, the yellow and the white, the skin and the flesh, both simultaneously flayed open.

This painting would be qualified without any hesitation as a still life, as would *The Skate*, although the latter is recognized as exceptional. But this is no reason to consider it a model for Proust of "acute observation of both the physical and the moral nature of an object," or to see it as proof of a "love for the real," as Taeko Uenishi was tempted to do in her aesthetic reading of painting in Proust (see her book *Le style de Proust et la peinture*, 29). Leaving aside the relation between the physical and the moral, this approach understands the whole genre of still life, defined according to thematic principles, to be homogeneous, unified, and always identical to itself. To pursue this approach requires us to consider that Proust accepted this commonplace. To talk of acute observation where Chardin is concerned, however, seems far from appropriate. His still lifes are very different from those of Lubin Baugin, where our eye is forced into an almost fanatical fixedness, as with the wafers in *Dessert with Wafers* in the Louvre museum (Fig. 4). This fixedness is provoked

Fig. 3. Jean-Baptiste Chardin, *The Buffet*, 1738. Paris, Musée du Louvre (copyright Photo R.M.N.).

by the formalist hyperrealism, which is offset, but only just, by the plate that is tilted toward the spectator.

The thematic of still life is one that calls attention to the relation between the subject and the objects of everyday life, between the spectator and his or her bodily needs. It can be distinguished in this sense from history painting, which tends to entertain the spectator with more grandiose subject matter. It is also to be distinguished from painting in which space is represented in a linear perspective, which reduces the body of the spectator to an eye, and the eye to a disembodied point.[8] But the attention implied in still life to the relation between the body and the subject, an attention that spans the whole of the history of art, does not always resolve the anguish of corporeal being with simple recourse to observation. Chardin's place in this tradition is quite particular. And Proust's interest in him, specifically through these two paintings, shows that he was aware of this particularity. This awareness makes itself felt in his text.

According to the analysis I have developed so far, the quality of the mottled screen in Chardin's paintings is achieved by means I would term stylistic. By this I do not intend to refer to the idea of a significant feature or development in the history of art that would normally define a "school." Rather, I mean the figuration of the mechanism of flatness that is at work here, a figuration by means of which the inside and the outside are simultaneously present, without ceasing to play against each other through nuances of "states" and colors. This figuration is constituted by the composition, not only of the scene, but also of its representation—the lack of depth as a sign—and the arrangement of the lines of vision and the objects. But its importance is most clearly underscored by the extremely subtle game played between clarity and indistinction that underlines its nuanced and oscillating nature. Some points are much sharper, more focused, than others, and this clarity has nothing to do with the depth, or with the distance between the foreground and the background, as it would in the case of a photo taken on a large aperture, for example. The impression is not one of objects observed vigilantly. Rather, it is as if the painter's eye was slightly inattentive to the objects, preferring to roam aimlessly, but intimately, over them (Bryson, *Looking at the Overlooked*, 92).

Fig. 4. Lubin Baugin, *Dessert with Wafers*, mid-seventeenth century. Paris, Musée du Louvre (copyright Photo R.M.N.).

The lack of clarity in form and the uncertain contours and planes in Chardin's painting have often been noted. And various commentaries have been offered suggesting that this was an attempt to experiment with the new optical theories of his time.[9] According to this interpretation, which is no doubt valid, the painting would be an attempt to record faithfully the real movement of the eye skimming over the painted surface, since this was how vision was then understood. According to this interpretation, it is not a simple matter of an excess of realism. The "thinking" of the painting is more active than would be the case with a straightforward application of the realist conceptions of the period. The painter adopts a certain mode of thinking in order to be guided by it in the process of painting, which is an act situated in a particular culture. Painters, like writers, have to work within the conceptual structures of the culture in which they operate. As Michael Baxandall says, "Painters can't be social idiots" (*Patterns of Intention,*

41

75). Ideas are active, and "active ideas do not float, they are brought to bear" (75).

Of course, it is no doubt in a vulgarized form that an idea is adopted by a painter, since painters are not philosophers (no more than writers are necessarily connoisseurs of art). The impact of Locke's ideas on perception is revealed by means of the particularly Chardinian figuration of a distinction in vision that is dominated by two optical facts. On the one hand, there is the eye's capacity to adapt in order to see clearly objects that are situated at varied distances. In other words, the eye can accommodate variety in depth. On the other hand, there is the question of "sharpness." This term refers to the different degrees of distinction across a field of vision, which is a question of variability on a surface.

According to this interpretation, Chardin is showing a fiction. And the fiction is the idea that the eye can travel adventurously across an image, stopping on the points of clarity like a migrating bird on branches it comes across during its journey. The fictive aspect of all this is obviously the chance nature of the stop-off points. The journey that lets the eye drift, is, in reality, highly organized, and this organization is in turn figured, or staged, by the rudder/handle. This interpretation certainly has the advantage of emphasizing, in terms of the mode of painting, the "flat" character of the image. It suggests that because of the unequal division of clarity, the elusive sharpness causes us to travel across the surface, more than in the depth, of the space represented.

Chardin's forms tend toward a fluidity that gives them their tactile and temporal quality. Bryson comments: "as though he were trying to paint peripheral rather than central vision, . . . to suggest a familiarity with the objects . . . , and that nothing anymore needs to be vigilantly watched" (*Looking at the Overlooked*, 92). It is as if these were portraits of time, but not of a narrativized time following diegetic lines. If there is diegesis, it consists in the adventures of the vision that simultaneously presents those states which, as Proust said, "ranged from the most deeply hidden aspirations of my heart to the wholly external view of the horizon." The mottling—multicolored mother-of-pearl, infinitely detailed white, reddish pink, flesh and blood—results from this multiple simultaneity. It is a very Proustian effect.

This particular quality of Chardin's art, even though it is invoked in order to intensify the flatness of the mottled screen, does not need the thematization of the latter. It can also be seen at work in canvases that share neither the same bloody and threatening thematic nor the same emphatically flat arrangement that we saw in *The Skate*. These canvases lack even the mitigated allusions to these features that we found in *The Buffet*. Let us take what is perhaps an extreme example of the absence of this thematic and this arrangement. Nothing in the simple *Silver Goblet* leads us to think that there is an attempt here to enter into polemics with history or perspectival painting; nothing evokes a battlefield torn apart by a fight to the death (Fig. 5). Everything is in a minor modality: the objects are laid out in an ordered manner, but without insistence. The goblet is indeed silver—in order that it "sparkle" more than tin?— but it looks nothing like those luxury objects found in the ostentatious Dutch still lifes. In fact, it only just enables the traditional game of reflection, and even then, there is no excess.

Three aspects remind us of the earlier canvases, although they are like weak symptoms, subliminal, and they are only visible in an intertextual reading. First, there is the spoon handle, which is placed on the diagonal, thus recalling the half-hidden knife. There is a light patch on its side, and the foreshortening suggests a lack of depth. Second, there is the reflection of the fruit in the goblet, which extends the series of images, the second of which, made up no doubt of a combination of "real" fruit (but this is beside the point), is gigantic compared to its original. Right inside this single reflection there seems to be a stripe that divides the surface into two cheeks. This reflection, which presents a stepping back from the fruit, represents a sort of visual penetration. Finally, the rather cramped perspective of the table makes it seem excessively narrow. This perspective runs counter to depth.

But if this canvas also contributes, no less indeed than the others, to the figuration of the mottled screen, albeit more modestly, it is because both sharpness and indistinction run across it freely. The gaze of the **43** spectator is in difficulty: either it assumes a mimetic stance and remains vague or inattentive itself, or, by accepting the fiction, it travels from one point to another. It is turned away or narrativized; it imitates or it plays

Fig. 5. Jean-Baptiste Chardin, *The Silver Goblet*, 1767–68. Paris, Musée du Louvre (copyright Photo R.M.N.).

the game. And if the gaze is narrativized in this way, it is absorbed by the same token. The distinction between inside and outside, between subject and object is no longer reliable. Moreover, the tactile quality that results from this blurred effect suggests that touch offers an alternative to the frustrating, perhaps even disturbing split necessarily implied in vision, and all the more so in close-up vision. The point is that this form of perception requires a relation of direct contiguity between subject and object.

The intimacy of Chardin's still lifes invites the spectator to enter without inhibitions into the space that offers such an attractive tactile proposition. But it also and at the same time stages the difficulty of such an entrance. I suggest that this particular Chardin, the Chardin of *The Skate* to begin with, but also the Chardin of the seemingly less disturbing *Buffet* and the other still lifes, is, so to speak, a reader of Proust. Like our author, he is sensitive to the insoluble tensions that accompany perception as the mode in which a nondisembodied, participating subject apprehends the world. Chardin sought to figure simultaneously these difficulties and, in the visual mode that he made his own, to propose certain solutions, however provisional they may be. He sought these solutions by way of a diegetic, dispositional, and modal flatness. In this sense he "follows" Proust; he echoes the literary problems posed by our writer.

The Skate is, then, a very Proustian painting. But there is also a Chardinism in Proust, beyond the author's taste for this master's actual paintings. By Proustian Chardinism I mean a figuration that interacts with these paintings in order to adopt from them the principles that govern the figuring process. These are principles that enable Proust to say in his writing that which is unsayable without this detour, that which is incomprehensible without this intertext. Proust uses three Chardinian principles, each embedded within the next. First, he stages, then "flattens" the most vulgar aspects of everyday life. This action occurs at what we could call two thematic levels or two levels of utterance. Next, he examines the capacity to "contain" offered by the flat image in terms of its potential to encompass and to cover, which includes the indispensable range of colors in mottling. Chardin's paintings make use of the screen for the juxtaposition and the unfolding of different layers or images, which fill the imagination. This happens at the figurative but nonthematic level, which is situated at the level of the enunciation rather than that of the utterance. Finally, he renders the focus uncertain by distributing unequally and in a seemingly arbitrary manner that clarity and indistinction which is situated prior to the division between utterance and enunciation at the level of the discursive mechanism that makes the very enterprise of Proustian writing possible.

Let us first consider the staging of flatness. The most direct reference to *The Skate* appears in the passage in which the narrator of *La recherche* says he owes his discovery of the beauty of everyday life to Elstir (SK 1.929 / P 2.224). It must be remembered that Marcel had previously been disgusted by the scene of the end of a meal:

> At the most we would occasionally linger, after finishing our lunch, to chat to her, *at that sordid moment when the knives are left littering the table-cloth among crumpled napkins.* (SK 1.746 / P 2.54)

Here we have a case that is structurally homologous to the sliding of the metaphor into metonymy that Genette highlights (in "Métonymie chez Proust"). The link between the moment and the disgust is metonymic: it is the moment, the temporal dimension of the spectacle, that removes all pleasure from the meal. The narrator adds that he had to look at the sea in the distance in order to overcome this disgust:

> I compelled myself to look farther afield, to notice only the sea, to seek in it the effects described by Baudelaire and to let my gaze fall upon our table only on days when there was set on it *some gigantic fish, some marine monster,* which contrary to the knives and forks, was contemporary with the primitive epochs in which the Ocean first began to team with life, at the time of the Cimmerians, a fish whose body with its countless vertebrae, its blue and pink veins, had been constructed by nature, but according to an architectural plan, like a polychrome cathedral of the deep. (SK 1.746–47 / P 2.54–55)

Although the theme may reinforce the relation, it is not first and foremost the thematic declarations of this passage that bring to mind *The Skate*. Rather it is the figuration. Let us not be mislead by the architectural plan: it is, above all, a *plan* of a *polychrome* cathedral. And the object that helps overcome the disgust, that cures the problem of a close-up view of the flatness of everyday life, is most definitely a *monster*, a *marine* monster, whose characteristics required to exercise its therapeutic function are precisely those which characterize the figuration of *The Skate*. The dimension is described not only as *vast*, in other words by the term that characterizes flatness most perfectly, but also by the subtle coloring and transparency of the body. Here, the second principle of Proustian Chardinism, *encompassing,* begins to be woven into the first, the staging of everyday life. One might also read a trace of the battle in the "contrary to" that opposes the monster to the knives and in the napkins, which are crumpled or "defeated" according to the double meaning of the French word *défaites.*

The narrator explicitly refers back to this passage in order to correct his attitude to the scene, behaving in this respect like the young apprentice who has wisely learnt his lesson from the great master. Here we see Elstir as "good for anything"; but in this case appearances are deceptive:

> I would now happily remain at table while it was being cleared . . . , it was no longer solely towards the sea that I would turn my eyes. Since I had seen such things depicted in water-colours by Elstir, I sought to find again in reality, I cherished as though for their poetic beauty the broken gestures of the knives still lying across one another, the swollen convexity of a discarded napkin into which the sun introduced a patch of yellow velvet, the half-empty glass which thus showed to a greater advantage the noble sweep of its curved sides and, in the heart of its translucent crystal, clear as frozen daylight, some dregs of wine, dark but glittering with reflected light, the displacement of volumes, the transmutation of liquids by the effect of light and shade . . . , and where in the hollows of the oyster-shells a few drops of lustral water had remained as in tiny holy water stoups of stone; I tried to find beauty there where I had never imagined before that it could exist, in the most ordinary things, in the profundities of "still life." (SK 1.929 / P 2.224)

There are two levels of meaning here that are both situated outside the space in which I am developing the aesthetics of Chardinian flatness. First of all, there are the numerous terms that refer to convexity as opposed to flatness: "glass," "the noble sweep of its curved sides," "in the heart," "volumes," the "tiny holy water stoups." But we should not allow ourselves to be misled by these references. This passage does not lend itself to being read as a metaphoric but realistic description of what the focalizer sees in his mental vision while the hero daydreams. In other words, this is not an implicit comparison in which the painting is the point of comparison and the table the thing compared. These terms convey the description, which is realistic, of the *effect* of the painting in

48

question. And this effect is due to the inscription of an illusion on a flat canvas. The canvas intervenes, thus displacing the table and changing the very development of the story. At the end of the paragraph, the table has become the point of comparison, which is examined because of its capacity to bring painting to mind.

A further potential point of tension for my analysis of Chardinian flatness lies in the numerous elements in this passage that "speak to" the impressionist Elstir, especially where the visual metaphor (see Henry, "Quand une peinture") is concerned, as in the random presentation of optical errors and the explosion of points of transition in a shimmering effect. This particular aspect seems to work as a middle term, establishing a contact between the ordinary and the pictorial by means of the impression, which is indeed "impressionist," that the sun creates on the sea. In fact, the passage is composed of an overlapping of different aesthetics and semiotics. I would like, however, to emphasize those words and expressions that have been less systematically noted than others.

The yellow velvet, which is introduced into the discarded napkin, is Proustian above all else. On the one hand, it is linked to the network of references to yellow circulating between the quivering butterfly and the fatal yellow patch that kills Bergotte. On the other, it participates in the poetics of the detail that cannot be detached from its surroundings. It is, of course, impossible to miss the allusion to *The Skate* in the "broken gestures of the knives still lying across one another," which in this description, however, play a minor role rather than constitute a full thematic repetition. Then there is also the aspect of the "battlefield" and the dis-articulation of the "scene." The "swollen convexity of a discarded napkin" underlines the intertextual reference.

Doubrovsky has thoroughly examined the obsessional character of the spherical roundness of the little madeleine. Here we see this roundness brought into play in a distinctly Proustian project by means of the "swelling" in the napkin. Certainly, we can at least say that Proust seems to be sensitive to this form. In the previous passage, prior to his learning experience (SK 1.746 / P 2.54), the napkin was only crumpled. The term "swollen" seems nonetheless to be appropriate in its visual sense. In Chardin's painting, the tablecloth is swollen around the lower edge in the middle, and the effect created by this swelling is astonishing, since this three-dimensional form appears here to serve the cause of . . . flatness. This is the case because this tablecloth takes on its swollen form in order to neutralize the inevitable perspective of the representation of the battle of knives, that is, to mask the depth that is indispensable to this representation.

The swelling around the right-hand edge of the crumpled tablecloth is also a line of demarcation that delineates a drawing. With its fine, snake-like folds, which look rather like arteries, the tablecloth forms a sort of repetition of the body of the skate. The quarter circle that it fills, thus, neutralizes the edge of the counter, which is a symptom of depth. This form repeats symmetrically the slightly curved line of the upper part of the skate. The folds of the tablecloth fall not in front of the edge of the counter but rather onto it. The knife seems now to be nailed down, trapped, while the handle of the saucepan comes out of this second body as if for a counter-attack. Indeed, it was this handle that broke the line of vision of the spectator who wished to penetrate the body of the skate.

What we see at play in this well-behaved episode of the apprentice who learns his lesson, under the cover of a noble simplicity, which is slightly too clearly proclaimed, is, in fact, the battle between the knife and "flatness," a fight to the death to determine whether the body is to be penetrated or not. The issue is one of visual penetration, but for Proust, this dimension is difficult to separate from the tactile. The penetration contested here is based upon flat exposure rather than on a narrow entry-way. After all, the road in Elstir's painting was only the effect of an optical illusion. Although this violent struggle may well result in a greater appreciation of still life, the novel, through its figuration, shows all the more the cost of this lesson. Still life is the battlefield of nature.[1] The close-up perception in question here, the contemplation through the magnifying glass that Chardin's painting represents, does indeed produce monsters.

The essay "Chardin and Rembrandt" should be read from now on as a "novel": reading in the grain of the text, it seems more like a narrative or a poem than the elaboration of an argument. Beginning with "Take this young man" and presenting the latter as disgusted by the remains of his meal, just like Marcel in the passage cited (SK 1.929 / P 1.224), the essay proposes an aesthetic of the everyday in the same way as the passage we have just read.[2] This aesthetic is, however, grounded in disgust and bears the traces of this provenance. Indeed, the author does not let up about this disgust, evoking the feelings of "disquiet," "ennui," "nausea," and "spleen" in a passage of almost a page in length. A "knife lying on the half-cleared tablecloth" and "the remains of a bloody and insipid-looking lamb-chop" are the objects described (*CSB* 372). A context is added, like a stage set: the young man's mother is unwinding her red wool. There is even a cat to complete the scene.

That the mother must be included in this spectacle of disgust, even though it is a mother quite unlike Marcel's Mamma, brings to mind that other passage in which disgust appears, disguised this time in imaginary delights:

> That forbidden and unfriendly dining-room, where but a moment ago the ice-cream—with burned nuts in it—and the finger bowls seemed to me to be concealing pleasures that were baleful and of a mortal sadness because Mamma was tasting of them while I was far away, had opened its doors to me and, *like a ripe fruit which bursts through its skin, was going to gush out into my intoxicated heart* the sweetness of Mamma's attention while she was reading what I had written. (SK 1.32 / P 1.30)

I am quite prepared to acknowledge that this is a description of desire and of love, but there is no doubt that the fruit is definitely beginning to rot. The imagined gushing-out threatens also to soil. And, after all, it is not up to Marcel's mother to give his love the form of a gushing or spurting outward. This breaks her, bursts open her skin, which the child needs so desperately in order to sustain himself with kisses.

The young man sick with disgust who is featured at the beginning of "Chardin and Rembrandt" does, then, resemble Marcel closely, and—given that "I is other"—he enables the mother to be represented with a more marked ambivalence. Proust the doctor sends him off to the museum to be cured by paintings, to see some Chardins and some Rembrandts. The young man comes back much revived. What was the secret of his cure? Above all else *The Skate*. Having enumerated several Chardins, citing the titles with only a few introductory words, the description continues: "the interior of a kitchen in which a live cat walks

51

on some oysters, while a dead skate hangs from the wall" (*CSB* 373). But here the title is omitted. "Chardin and Rembrandt" then continues to evoke different paintings with their titles. A little later *The Skate* reappears, this time with its title.

There is something unsettling in this description of a therapeutic expedition to the museum. It is all a bit uncanny, and the first symptom of this is the delay in revealing the title. The painting that dominates the whole of the text is named only when death and nausea are evoked ("scenes that disgust you, dead fish"). To name or not to name: this is a serious decision for this author who names two of his novels after this very notion and who, moreover, fetishizes names even as he refuses, to all extents and purposes, to let his readers know the name of his hero. What problem is there with naming? We should take a look at what is said about the effect of Gilberte's name, which is invested with all the charges associated with naming. The reader should recall the transformation of Gilberte's signature into a dis-figure of writing. In the following example, this function of the name is quite clearly brought to mind:

> The name of Gilberte passed close by me, evoking all the more forcefully the girl whom it labelled in that it did not merely refer to her, as one speaks of someone in his absence, but was directly addressed to her; it passed thus close by me, in action so to speak, with a force that increased with the curve of its trajectory and the proximity of its target. (SK 1.428 / P 1.387)

In the first part of this passage the description of the name resembles a pragmatic theory of the sign in general; then "in action" the name becomes a projectile, a weapon, the relevant characteristic of which is its curved flight, reminding us of a "sketched" version of the swelling hillsides and the fountain.

Now, a projectile presupposes a distance, "a depth." The object projected comes from the inside out, propelled with force. Because Gilberte's name stems from the inside, this dimension of the name places in peril the whole delicate enterprise in which the novel is involved. To name is also to fix, to make a *painting* of the spectacle of disgust, which was until now an event. It is to place it there, outside oneself. By throwing the subject toward the outside, all the painful but indispensable gain made with the help of the marine monster in its capacity as mottled screen is placed in danger. Hence the subliminal hesitation to name this painting in particular. It is nothing more than a momentary stammer, or rather, a displacing of focus. The delay in naming signals the passage from a thematic of flatness to a "flat" enunciation.

Immediately after this presentation of the spectacle of sublimated disgust, the narrator takes the education of the young man in hand again, offering such platitudes as "If all this now seems beautiful to look at, it's because Chardin found it beautiful to paint. And he found it beautiful to paint because he found it beautiful to look at" (*CSB* 373). Clearly the role of diligent apprentice to the great master of looking does not go together with either depth in thought or subtlety in expression. This continues for a good page. Then Chardin intervenes, disguised first as Marcel, then as Rembrandt, the painter of chiaroscuro. *The Buffet* is introduced as a transition, and it is described in detail by means of a comparison: like a "Princess woken, everyone is brought back to life, takes back their colors, begins talking to you, living, lasting" (*CSB* 374).

The first particularity of *The Buffet* mentioned is "the half folded-up tablecloth next to the knife placed to one side, with its whole blade showing." These battlefield effects are attributed to the servants' haste and to the guests' greediness. This is a diegetic motivation that betrays the force of these effects perfectly. The tiered fruit dish, filled with fruit, is figured as an object of desire: "peaches chubby-cheeked and pink like cherubs, inaccessible and smiling like immortals." The dog, which cannot reach them, "makes them all the more desirable for being truly desired." All this seems quite peaceful. Is that to lull us into a sense of security? Indeed, the dog immediately becomes less innocent. This change takes place because the dog knows how to look: "His eye tastes them and, in the dampish down of their skin, he chances upon the sweetness of their flavour" (*CSB* 375).

This seems to be a reaction to the tactile interpellation so typical in Chardin. But this reaction is attributed to a character who, because he is inside the diegetic space, can proceed at any moment from looking to acting. The following passage announces the young hero's astonish-

53

ment before the spectacle of glass in water, of glass jugs in the Vivonne: "As transparent as the day and as desirable as fresh-water streams, the glasses with a few mouthfuls of smooth wine basking in them as they would in the back of the throat, are standing next to glasses that are already nearly empty, as emblems of scorching thirst would stand next to emblems of satisfied thirst." The description of the glasses is repeated almost word for word in the well-behaved episode in *La recherche*. It ends with the oysters "fresh like the sea-water they offer us." The inside and the outside are in harmony here.

But this harmony won't last. Between this ekphrastic passage and the following description of *The Skate*, an element intervenes that not only disturbs this idyll in order to take the essay toward its first climax but also inserts a criminal element. This intervention takes up a separate paragraph, as if to indicate more clearly its transitional character. A mottled screen in itself, this passage is so marked by a change in tone that it displaces the whole enquiry to another level.

> Fresh water lies in a bucket on the ground, still disturbed by the foot that gave it a vigorous shove. A knife, hidden in a vigorous gesture, indicating the great haste of pleasure, lifts up the golden discs of lemons, which seem placed there by an impulse of delectation, completing the trappings of voluptuous delight. (*CSB* 375)

Why does this dim corner of the painting provoke this change in tone? Let us suppose that it serves more as a pretext, that it was necessary to figure what the rest of this painting still has to offer, which does not fit well with the idyllic description. A break was necessary, and it took the form of a discursive rupture. The repetition of the word "vigorous" clearly suggests the urgency of the matter, the "great haste." Knives and pleasure: here lie, it seems, "the trappings of voluptuous delight."

This delight had already been brought into the foreground. The chubby-cheeked peaches were the object of the gun dog's lust, and the reader should recall here Marcel's fantasies in which he imagines being bitten into by Gilberte (SK 1.437 / P 1.396) and also the extreme importance he gives to the approach of Albertine's cheeks. It makes no difference if he eats or is eaten, since the voluptuous incorporation is neutralized, and also crushed, on the image's surface.

The essay speaks of a pictorial language, an "imperative and brilliant language," "the significance of its form, which is so brilliant before the eye and so dim before the mind" (*CSB* 374), in a language that itself recalls Rembrandtesque chiaroscuro and Elstirian shimmering. But the subtext, the "novel," inscribes a completely different discourse in which violence and voluptuous delight combine forces in a collusion, the index of which is the repetition of "vigorous." This transitional paragraph raises the tone in preparation for a second climax, which introduces a different sort of pleasure and anxiety.

"But now come into the kitchen": thus begins the passage in which *The Skate* is described in detail. The kitchen is "fiercely guarded by a tribe of different-sized vases," and this personification inserts an imaginary element that makes the description into a proper ekphrasis. But more precisely, this beginning prepares the discursive terrain for the atmosphere of a battlefield and for the violence, which is not only a precondition-condition of the voluptuous pleasure, but also constitutes the mechanism for its realization. "On the table, the active knives, which go straight for their target, are lying threateningly and inoffensively idle" (*CSB* 375). This sentence defines effectively the dead aspects of still life, even as it transforms the knives into military instruments, in other words, into weapons and at the same time into a race of warriors. Threatening and inoffensive at the same time, their idleness depends on the battle being a defensive war formalized in mime—the pure sign.

The sea monster, which had such a calming effect on the Marcel who was unable to stand the filth of everyday life, is introduced here as a "strange monster, still fresh from the sea in which it undulated." To describe the fish as fresh seems excessive: it has already been gutted and abandoned, hence it is not just out of the water. This freshness creates an association between the marine characteristic and two other notions that are necessary in order that the beast reconcile the close-up vision of the table with the distant and colorless vision of the sea. First, it evokes the feeling of life, which is quite aptly called "strange." The blind eyes of the fish, its bizarre hands/holes, and its grotesque mouth all indicate that it is indeed a living creature presiding over this scene.

Furthermore, the freshness makes the evocation of desire possible, even though this is slightly paradoxical, given that it stems from a mon-

55

ster. The essay says of this strange monster that "the sight of it mixed greedy desire with the curious charm of calm or stormy seas, of which it was the incredible witness" (*CSB* 375). Words such as "curious charm" are effectively displaced when one wonders to what extent this sanguine ghost, which seems falsely alive, could provoke greed. The point is that we have already left behind the actual descriptive discourse. The flat image is called upon to ensure the capture of time, which is presented much more emphatically as problematic in the passage cited earlier in which the sea monster also introduced a prehistoric existence (SK 1.746 / P 2.54). Far from being an imitation or a respectful and admiring emulation, Proust's Chardinian writing serves as a foundation for the complex edifice of the work. Rather than being aesthetic, this Chardinism is made to serve eroticism and its paradoxical secret representation.

This brings us to a third principle of Proustian Chardinism, which is, in short, the mechanism indispensable to the enterprise of writing. As Doubrovsky has demonstrated, the memory matrix that generates the search (*la recherche*) is essentially of an oral order. However, at the level of actual experience there is a certain rivalry between the senses—between "shape and solidity" versus "smells and flavors." Here only one element of this whole intervenes, and it is that which establishes the unequal distribution of clarity and indistinction that characterizes Chardin over and above the thematic and referential aspects of his paintings. This distribution is also characteristic of the screen-memory.

In fact, many of the words in this passage about *The Skate* reappear in the evocation of the sea monster. In order that the latter be sufficiently voluptuous to satisfy the close-up view of it, its freshness must be emphasized. For there remains one more operation to be carried out, and that is to pass from the "saltiness" of the sea to "filth," which must be distinguished from the filth of the table that caused Marcel's disgust.[3] As Proust says, it is important that "you can admire the beauty of its vast and delicate architecture, colored with red blood." The young man, who is grammatically assimilated to the addressee of the text, in other words, to the reader, is the double of the author who suffered from disgust, and this disgust is such that the admiration of beauty seems barely to be its proper antonym. But this assimilation helps to introduce into the whole the essential element, which is color. In "delicate" we recognize the formal frailty of the butterfly; "vast" is the very word to describe the formal and spatial dimension of the fish as a whole. However, "colored" means it is painted, but without there being any distinction in detail: that which is colored is painted as a whole.

The cure for disgust is freshness, which only the color of the totalizing paint can guarantee. There has to be fresh blood in order that the cannibalistic young man be cured. As a means of combating filth, blood is spread all over the painted surface / colored skate. The point is that "it is open." The plan of the polychrome cathedral is sketched out because the body is opened up. Indeed, this building comes out of this opening, like Combray out of the cup of tea: "blue nerve-ends and white muscles, like the nave of a polychrome cathedral" (*CSB* 376). What we see here, more explicitly than in the passage from *La recherche*, is that the transition between the close-up view and the distant view is made possible by means of the opening-up and the flattening-out of the body.

Opened up, the body functions like a magnifying glass. This opening, however, must be carried out by means, not of penetration, but of a spreading-out, an exposing. And this exposure, this exhibition in the style of Chardin, can be sustained because the strange distribution between clarity and indistinction enables the gaze both to be absorbed or incorporated into the image and to travel across its surface, stopping where it wishes, or rather, where it can (bear it).

This image invites a certain greediness; indeed, it invites more than a simple gustatory greediness. The opening-up, a cruel act in itself, is also, by means of its magic ability to produce the mottled screen, a condition of or a mechanism for violence. And this constitutes the second musical pause in the pleasure of this passage. This time the climax is of a feline nature. The author says things about the cat that—according to a realist reading—are so wrong from a visual point of view that they become very revealing for a poetic reading. A most glaring misrepresentation is that the cat is said to fix "the glint in its eye . . . on the skate." While this is wrong from a realist point of view, it is very true from the point of view of the libidinal investment in the spread-open body. Moreover, this cat is taken as an emblem of the unconscious, or, at least, if we prefer not to employ psychoanalytic vocabulary unnecessarily, of that which is added to the level of the conscious composition ("super-imposing on this aquarium the obscure life of its more knowledgeable and conscious forms" *CSB* 376). The cat "maneuvres the velvet of its paws with a slow haste over the raised-up oysters." The sentence quoted earlier, which staged a live cat on dead oysters, seems here to be re-versed: a (dead?) cat on live oysters. Under the cover of a prudence that is said to counterbalance the greed and the daring, what follows justi-fies a sadistic reading of the slow haste that makes the (live?) oysters rise up (in pain?).

Indeed, the pleasure is described, or rather, is fabricated with words that evoke sadism, thereby transforming the domestic drama into a cli-mactic lyricism:

> And one can already hear, at the moment when the precarious pile of fragile mother-of-pearl will tumble under the weight of the cat, the small cry of their crack and the thunder of their fall. (*CSB* 376)

"The small cry of their crack" makes for a sadistic gasp. A foretaste of the orgasm represented by the thunder, the small cry is the "product" of the walking on water that creates such a bad effect in paintings like those by Bouguereau. The subtlety of Chardin's painting is "reaped" here by that of Proust. The author expands this subtlety with an erotic charge, which is for him a very typical response. This is the Chardinian Proust rewriting the Proustian Chardin.

The evocation gets to the point of being almost lewd. We understand, then, the crucial importance of the transition from "saltiness" to "filth," eliminating on the way the first meaning of "filth." In order to work as a cattleya would for Swann's ecstasy, the skate must be fresh, more fresh, or let us say, more emphatically fresh because the painting requires it. Flat in the extreme, the painting offers "flavor and smell" rather than "shape and solidity." It is the other side of the little madeleine.

In *Sodome et Gomorrhe I*, the collocation of "saltiness" and "filth" (in French, *salé* and *saleté*) reappears in a context that is clearly erotic and, moreover, recalls the disgust of the first stay at Balbec. In order to fill the erotic frame fully, the association is attributed to Charlus. Two evo-cations occur, no more than one page apart, right in the middle of the diagnosis of sexual inversion, which is often qualified as stereotypical and sentimental. This diagnosis follows, of course, the very "flattening" description of the meeting between Charlus and Jupien seen by our narrator, who thus completes the necessary triangle:

> [The solitary man] loiters upon the beach, a strange Andromeda whom no Argonaut will come to free, a sterile jellyfish that must perish upon the sand. (SK 2.649 / P 3.27)

And, in a exorbitant lyricism, which reveals wild enthusiasm, the narrator identifies himself with these inverts, whose "inversions" the discourse of the essay is analyzing, in other words, is detailing and classifying, as in this example:

> Jellyfish! Orchid! When I followed my instinct only, the jellyfish used to revolt me at Balbec; but if I had eyes to look at it . . . I saw an exquisite blue girandole. Are they not, with the transparent velvet of their petals, like mauve orchids of the sea? (SK 2.650 / P 3.28)

The reader is well aware of the extent to which botanical metaphors dominate this scene. They constitute the semantic center of the almost Linnaean classification of homosexual "types," all the while making this classification epistemologically confusing. Our narrator, novice though he may be, nonetheless does not choose to be seriously identified with the faithful of the Verdurins' little clan, who see Charlus as "this painted, paunchy, tight-buttoned personage, reminiscent of a box of exotic and dubious origin exhaling a curious odour of fruits the mere tasting of which would turn the stomach" (SK 2.1075 / P 2.1044). It is significant that the French expression "vous soulèverait le coeur," translated here as "would turn the stomach," has been translated elsewhere as "stirs the heart."[4] Torn between disgust and emotion, sentimentality rages, and the epistemology is sacrificed to linguistic appropriation.[5] Instead of allowing the language, with all the difficulty implied in maximizing the precision of translation, to direct the translator who wants to understand toward the point indicated by a serious approach to flatness or banality, the choice was made to erase the disgust, thereby obliterating the sublime that it generates. It is perhaps not necessary to add that it is homosexuality that falls through the cracks between the French expression of disgust and the English expression of sentimentality.

We might almost forget how little the diagnosis applied to him by the essay is actually merited by our young man, who is sick with disgust because he is perhaps not sufficiently "other" than "I." In opposition to the Duchess of Guermantes's comment about Zola, "His is the epic dungheap! He is the Homer of the sewers!" (SK 2.518 / P 2.789), it is the lyrical dungheap that belongs to the narrator of *La recherche*, and this dungheap, because it is contiguous with the saltiness of the sea, ceases to be a dungheap.

He is very thorough in this cleaning-up process, and often the metaphor employed to this end precedes the thing to be compared, thus making the latter literal. Hence the great importance of the freshness of the skate, and, indeed, the fantasy provoked by Chardin's cat responds almost point by point to that other sadistic climax, on which the narrator sadistically spies. Here we have an incomplete but metaphorically touched-up image of an orgasm, the ambivalent visuality of which is translated into "noise":

> It is true that these sounds were so violent that, if they had not always been taken an octave higher by a parallel plaint, I might have thought that one person was slitting another's throat within a few feet of me, and that subsequently the murderer and the resuscitated victim were taking a bath to wash away the traces of the crime. I concluded from this later on that there is another thing as vociferous as pain, namely pleasure, especially when there is added to it . . . an immediate concern for cleanliness. (SK 2.631 / P 3.11)

We have no problem in understanding where the crime comes from here, but what about this bath? What excessive freshness!

And this is the end of our exploration of Chardinian figuration. Having come to the end of the novel of *The Skate*, the essay quickly takes the upper hand. But this can happen because Proustian Chardinism has been well and truly established in this noisy end to this long paragraph. So, what is actually comprised in this Proustian Chardinism? The answer is given in the same sentence, a little earlier than the climax and as the "theory" of this ensuing pleasure:

> The eye that likes to play with the other senses and to reconstitute with the help of a few colors, more than just a whole past, a whole future, can

already smell the freshness of the oysters that will wet the cat's paws. (CSB 376)

The cat as a personification of the eye, which plays mercilessly, is already becoming wet, like in female masturbation, with the help of a few colors. . . . The mottled screen is charged with much more than "philosophic richness," as was stated by the metaphor presiding over its creation.

It is also possible to confer a female sensuality on Rembrandt's *Slaughtered Ox*. If the stakes involved in Chardinism were only this sensuality, then Rembrandt would have done just as well. But the point is that we cannot consider this aspect in an isolated way. The "thunder" is only possible "with the help of a few colors." It is only because the image insists so much on its own flatness that the open body can serve as a screen for the voluptuous feline activity. And it is by means of this spreading-out, this exhibiting, of the body as screen that the flat form of the skate can encompass, in the sense both of sheltering and discreetly exposing, the "torrent of activity" taking place before it.

After this second climax, in which violence constitutes pleasure, the essayistic writing comes to dominate, making the piece at once insipid, phenomenological, and imbued with the most classic type of oedipalism. It loses all novelistic interest, except to the extent that it marks the limits of the ability of the young man sick with disgust to regain enough strength, by means of this exercise in bodily hygiene, to throw off the father. The essay continues to glorify Chardin, but it does so in reference to him as a portrait-painter, which he was hardly at all. The self-portrait has caused people to dismiss the personage of Chardin as effeminate. But in his condescending generosity toward old people, the author of the essay moves from still lifes, where he had found "his" place so well, to the self-portrait where the "I" is more than ever "other." Chardin, the master-homeopathic doctor, described as an "old woman" (CSB 377) becomes himself a flat image (Fig. 6).

But beneath this condescension can be seen a trace, not of the pushing to one side of the master who has done his job, but perhaps of the "history" of the story, of the lost time, and of the young man's apprenticeship. Here we see, projected onto the self-portrait, an appropriation of Chardin's femininity, which he assumes as his own, although this is

Fig. 6. Jean-Baptiste Chardin, *Self-Portrait* (also called *Portrait of Chardin Wearing Spectacles*), 1771. Paris, Musée du Louvre (copyright Photo R.M.N.).

the result of a scruple of unconscious justice. As Doubrovsky put it so well, "To be a writer is, above all else, to have being, but being is to have others' being in me" (*La place de la madeleine*, 92). Chardin, by flattening himself, "gave" him the power to unite with the flat image, to be in it, or even, to be it. But once the deed is done, the author must not stand still. Proustian writing is a reading, and all readings are readings of the

Fig. 7. Henri Matisse, *Luxury I*, 1907. Paris, Musée National d'Art Moderne, Centre Georges Pompidou.

Fig. 8. Francis Bacon, *Triptych May–June* 1973. Private collection, Switzerland (courtesy of Marlborough Fine Art, London).

self (SK 3.911 / P 4.490). The subject of the novel, a fragile young man who is fortified, has to be the only subject-reader-of-the-self. Is this the reason for the importance, in this fight to the death with the flat image, of capturing not only the past but also the future?

If we must turn all of this into "aesthetics," that is to say, not into an aesthetics of visual art, but into visualizing tendencies contained in Proust's writing, then not only is Proust's Chardinism to take the upper hand, surpassing Rembrandt's importance in the figuring process, but also Elstir must be considered as a screen that serves as a cover—a "cover-screen" perhaps.[6] Rather than try to categorize Proust as a symbolist or a cubist, I look elsewhere to discover his pictorial descent.

Prior to Proust, there is, then, the Chardin of *The Skate*. Later, there are those painters who in turn explore the limits reached in a refusal to recognize and to accept that the body as a penetrable solid is the only source of voluptuous pleasure. Already in painting contemporary to Proust we find Matisse's images, which are so flat that they offer the spectator a simple juxtaposition of a plurality of "shots." It is as if Chardin's points of sharpness have each become a complete image (Fig. 7). Later and more emphatically, it is on "Francis Bacon's way" that we

64

have to look.[7] On the one hand, Francis Bacon's painting provokes disgust even as it demonstrates an affective and pictorial power that keeps the spectator from turning away. On the other hand, his work is an exploration of the possibilities of representation that ignores the limits between inside and outside. In *Triptych May–June 1973* (Fig. 8), the body, whose limits are systematically transgressed, is also in the act of vomiting.[8] It is a case of *dégoût oblige*: the disgust requires it. After all, the jellyfish is far from sterile.

Between the two passages on reading, the one in the bedroom with the yellow butterfly, and the one in the garden with the mottled screen, there appears the little kitchen maid who, according to Swann, looks like Giotto's Charity. The reason for this likeness is her belly, which is large like a basket and seems, thus, to be a detachable piece: "She was beginning to have difficulty in bearing before her the mysterious basket, fuller and larger every day" (SK 1.87 / P 1.80). If we consider the fresco in question, we see that this comparison is stretched significantly: the figure of Charity does carry a basket, which seems quite full although extremely light if we judge by the effort it seems to demand of the woman's arm as she holds it in one hand; but she carries the said basket quite clearly to one side of her body.[9] In Proust, then, this belly brings to mind a fragment rather than a detail, an indexical sign rather than a thing. Once this belly has been detached, we are left with only a flat girl. With her belly, looking like a fresco, she is just as flat.

part two **Voyages of Discovery**

It will be necessary, for example, to interrupt (disfigure) the luminous projection of subject desire with the comic relief of features.

—Samuel Beckett, *Proust*

One couldn't live under a microscope or in slow motion. It would make you go mad.

—Nathalie Sarraute, in Simone Benmussa's *Qui êtes-vous? Nathalie Sarraute*

What a difference there is between possessing a woman to whom one applies one's body alone, because she is no more than a piece of flesh, and possessing a girl whom one used to see on the beach with her friends on certain days.... Life had obligingly revealed to you in its whole extent the novel of this little girl's life, had lent you, for the study of her, first one optical instrument, then another, and had added to carnal desire the accompaniment, which multiplies and diversifies it, of those other desires, more spiritual and less easily assuaged, which do not emerge from torpor.

—Proust, *A la recherche du temps perdu*
(SK 2.375 / P 2.657)

chapter five **Optical Instruments**

Toward the end of *Le Temps retrouvé* Proust complains that his literary enterprise has been misunderstood. He is offended by how his critics have used the metaphor of the microscope to say that his writing gets lost in detail:

> Even those who commended my perception of the truths which I wanted eventually to engrave within the temple, congratulated me on having discovered them "with a microscope," when on the contrary it was a telescope that I had used to observe things which were indeed very small to the naked eye, but only because they were situated at a great distance, and which were each one of them in itself a world. (SK 3.1098 / P 4.618)

The opposition that he establishes in his response could mislead us here. The narrator does not contradict the "detailing" that characterizes his work; rather, by changing the optical instrument in the metaphor, he indicates the specific nature of the relation between the subject and the object of vision, a relation that we know to be highly variable. This relation is determined above all by distance.

Microscope or telescope, the optical instrument that enlarges is an indispensable metaphor of a poetic order. In the following section I take as my starting point the idea that such an instrument gives form to an important literary question. At the end of the sentence the narrator states his conception of the status of details within his text. While each tiny thing that he has gathered in order to engrave it in his temple—an image of longed-for permanence, if ever there was one—is a world in itself, they all also belong to the whole that is composed so carefully, as if it were a work of architecture. Here we have, then, the subject of this chapter—the Proustian detail and the "optical" focus that is required to make it function as a poetics. We move on from art to the optics that underpin it. Let me make clear right from the start that there is a continuity between the technique of enlargement and the visuality provoked by such an instrument. The optical prosthesis provides the technology that enables one to *see* better by seeing larger.

Proust invokes all sorts of visual prostheses to refer to "detailed" perception. But the instrument does not always have the effect of helping close-up vision. The following is an example of almost the contrary effect: the optical instrument is invoked twice, a few sentences apart, in order to "displace" or to "forget" the details and substitute something else in their place. Moreover, the first instrument does not enlarge; rather it adds relief. Substitution is opposed to flattening: it is a means of resisting "flatness."

> I had just slid them [the conversations at Mme de Guermantes's dinner-table] into the internal stereoscope through the lens of which, as soon as . . . we wish to receive our life only from other people, we give depth and relief to what they have said and done. (SK 2.569 / P 2.836)

> Through the magnifying lenses, even those pronouncements by Mme de Guermantes that had struck me as being stupid (as for example the one about Hals pictures which one ought to see from the top of a tram-car), took an extraordinary life and depth. (SK 2.569 / P 2.837)

The optical instrument in *La recherche* is a recurrent structuring metaphor. It provides the articulations necessary in the often problematic joints between the great truths that the author hopes to engrave in his temple and the minute things that he also intends to reveal as being each a world in itself. The latter intention is not simply a matter of dimensions or of modes of perception. It also brings the focalizing subject into question.

The frequent occurrence of the magnifying-glass metaphor has been commented upon by others, who do not fail to point out its very diverse functions. In his classic essay *Proustian Space*, Georges Poulet describes with remarkable accuracy a typical case of such a metaphor. Citing a reference to this instrument in the description of the church at Balbec, a reference that also demonstrates perfectly the metonymic motivation theorized by Genette (in "Métonymie chez Proust"), Poulet writes:

> "In the name of Balbec," he writes, "as in the magnifying-glass of one of those penholders one buys at seaside resorts, I perceived waves rolling around a church of Persian style." If the gaze is aided by a sort of magnifying-glass, it is not to enlarge the objects, but rather to isolate them, to put them into relief, and thus to reveal much more sharply the surprising nature of their conjugated presence. (*L'Espace proustien*, 119–20)

If we follow Poulet here, the magnifying glass functions in this case as a stereoscope in that it "puts into relief." It is not, then, the precise technology that counts, but rather "the technological" in a larger sense, of which the instrument is an index. However, the technological represented by various optical instruments, even when they are stereoscopic, is used mainly to add relief in a strictly figurative sense. In fact, the metaphor is used either to frame and to delineate, or to focus a field of vision, in the photographic sense of the term. On other occasions it is used to enlarge, not the object, but the difference or the visual distinction between the object and what surrounds it. Elsewhere it helps characterize the subject who is doing the looking, whether that subject is having difficulty in seeing, or is seeing too well, or rather not enough. All these functions of the whole metaphoric network created with the optical prosthesis are put to use in the elaboration of a subtle and complex poetics of detailing. If this particular metaphor seems especially apt in the elaboration of this problematic, it is because the detail in *La recherche* is presented first and foremost as being visual.

The detail in Proust does not lend itself to other general characterizations. All of the uses and the meanings of the detail in the epistemology of the period occur in this work, but their functions and their effects are varied:[1]

> The clinical detail, that symptom of the subject's state which "indicates" another reality, such as the grandmother's voice, which betrays the old lady's imminent death;

71

The "earlobe" detail, upon which Giovanni Morelli based the branch of art known as "connoisseurship," and which survives today despite the loss of belief in its feasibility. The fact is that this metonymic sign of the *master's hand*, which is also somewhat surreptitiously indexical of the *master-connoisseur*, offers the reassurance that art, at least, resists valiantly and romantically the flattening of the postmodern subject.[2] Proust has a good laugh over this with his character Swann;

The detective detail, which is an "index" in the classic sense of this genre: metonymic of both the criminal and the crafty detective, it structures jealousy in *La recherche*, both that of Swann and that of Marcel;

And finally, the realistic detail, which refers to the whole from which it has been cut. Synecdoche of a world, infinitely contained within the signifying madness, this detail is made problematic by the many metaphors is generates. Yet it remains a "realistic detail" in Proust's poetics.[3] This sort of detail is perverted in that it comes to signify nothing other than realism itself, as Barthes analyzed it in his conception of "the reality effect."

All these details are synecdoches, and they become quite extraordinary in the context of *La recherche*, which breaks the bounds of even the most fantastical fable. But epistemology is one thing; poetics is another, even though they are both based upon a semiotics or a logic of the production of meaning.[4] Moreover, this distinction overlaps with another distinction, which I explain by borrowing Vincent Descombes's terms (*Proust: philosophie du roman*, 23–30). He distinguishes between the essay and the novel, or between theory, epistemological or aesthetic, and practice in the form of novelistic writing. It is the implicit and marginal poetics that interest me here. And this poetics, which is generated by the practice, reveals, as we shall see, a predilection for the visual detail.

72

While there may be a poetics of the detail in Proust, the text first rejects all its "erroneous" versions. Thus we see the failure of Aunt Flora, to whom had been communicated "some most interesting details about the cooperative movement in Scandinavia" (SK 1.26 / P 1.24). Aunt Flora fails in her signifying mission by drowning the details in vagueness, in noise, as information theory calls it.

But the sense of the detail does not depend solely upon the subject. Aunt Flora could not stop the detail from signifying in any case, and what it signifies is precisely the insignificance of the aunt. There is no escaping so lightly from synecdoche. Here her insignificance stems precisely from her inability to give any details. In the same way the Curé of Combray, unable to reconcile the pictorial with the temporal—"even if he cared nothing for the arts, he knew a great many etymologies" (SK 1.111 / P 1.101)—flounders in nonsignifying arbitrariness.[5] The Curé's sin, if we can say such a thing, is an excess of temporality.

Things work a little better where the victims of jealousy are concerned. After all, jealousy, the primary epistemology of the novel, like police detective work, is a science of the detail. The desperate battle for truth between Swann and Odette, who persist in their game of hide-and-seek, is played out by means of the detail. But this detective-type detail is not easily appropriated. Odette is the first to use the detail as a weapon, but she soon finds herself held prisoner by it:

> Yet she must say something, and there lay within her reach precisely the fact which she wished to conceal and which, being the truth, was the one thing that had remained. She broke off from it a tiny fragment, of no importance in itself, assuring herself that, after all, it was the best thing to do, since it was a verifiable detail and less dangerous, therefore, than a fictitious one. (SK 1.303 / P 1.273)

The narrator states quite clearly why, from the point of view of a "jealousy-based" epistemology, Odette is wrong to expose the truth by means of a detail. But first it is important to say that she is also wrong from the point of view of a semiotics of the detail: Odette's "fragment" is a synecdoche, not of the text—the lie—but of the referent—the truth; not, that is, of the surface, but of the depth; and, even more incriminating, not of the present in which Odette is trying to reassure Swann, but of an inadmissible past that she wants so much to hide.[6]

This passage already seems, then, to belong to the poetics of the detail as the narrator understands it. Indeed, this is stated with utmost clarity immediately afterward in one of those passages which distinguish

73

the essay from the novel, all the more strikingly so in this case because Odette would never have been able to understand it, had she "heard" it:

> This fragmentary detail of the truth had sharp edges that could not be made to fit in, except with those contiguous fragments of the truth from which she had arbitrarily detached it, and these edges, whatever the fictitious details in which she might embed it, would continue to show, by the surplus matter and by the gaps she had forgotten to fill in, that its proper place was elsewhere. (SK 1.303 / P 1.274)

Whenever something is detached, it creates edges, and here lies the great danger and violence resulting from this gesture. Surplus matter and unfilled gaps are the central elements of Proustian poetics, elements that render vain the violence in the act of detaching.[7] The diegetic detail at play here is not in itself visual—or, to be more precise, its register of meaning is not specified. But the (meta-) language that explains how it functions semiotically "colors" it with visuality.[8] The violence of the detaching is, incidentally, all the more terrible in that the science of the jealous man consists in a fragile equilibrium between knowledge and ignorance, an equilibrium that is always about to collapse:

> It is better not to know, to think as little as possible, not to feed one's jealousy with the slightest concrete detail. (SK 3.17 / P 3.534)

The visual prosthesis has a vital function in this delicate epistemology of jealousy.

No scene reveals this better than the one in which the character who holds the knowledge that generates the jealousy is also and crucially the person with bad eyesight. I am referring to the scene of the "dance breast to breast" at the little casino in Incarville (SK 2.823 / P 3.190). The narrator insists upon the fact the "ill that these words spoken of Albertine and Andrée had inflicted upon him" would work gradually like a slow poison, or like the sort of writing that is found in the character and the text of Esther. It is in this way that the detail, far from being asystemic, takes on a strictly narrative function.

In the introduction I mentioned Gilberte's signature as a mise en abyme of the poetics of flatness. This emblem is "inflated with meaning" through the mediation of a detail that circulates throughout the whole work, and the detail in question is an allusion to the biblical text, recycled by Racine's play about Esther. The presence of the Book of Esther in *La recherche* is almost obsessional, and with good reason. It can be explained principally by the emphasis placed on writing in it. As we know from the Bible, Esther manages to prevent the catastrophe that threatens her people by first concealing her identity, then by revealing it at the right moment, and finally by making the most of the delay implied by writing in order to "countersign" the death sentence with a decree that nullifies the effectiveness of the time bomb that was Aman's first decree.[9]

In her first appearance in Proust's novel, Esther is the figure of yellow, which is the color of her dress in the stained glass in the church at Combray ("the yellow of her dress was spread so unctuously, so thickly"; SK 1.63 / P 1.60). She is also the figure who keeps secret the fact of belonging to a particular group, and Proust develops this in his notion of "being of them," which serves as a principle of selection for the elite of the "accursed race," be it of Jews, artists, or homosexuals. Esther is the figure in the closet that signifies a combination of secrecy and choice.[10] The third dimension of "Esther," text and character, but also character-text, is the less well known but equally relevant dimension introduced by her being the incarnation of the signature as speech act that "does things with words."[11] Writing in this case has the power to initiate action, but the action is delayed. The signature is the word of a specific person "put down in writing."

It is because of this aspect of Esther that Proust is able to use this character-author-text in order to integrate aspects of his own literary enterprise with the visual mechanism that underpins it. The poetics of his work must be understood and appreciated in the effects produced by the integration of epistemology with affectivity, sexuality with aesthetics, sensuality with poetics. In the "dance breast to breast" episode, the poison, the delayed action of which is related specifically to writing in the Book of Esther, is generated by a problematic of vision that is embodied in failing eyesight.

The almost artificially drawn-out slowness requires that the medical knowledge of the focalizer, from whom the narrator is to learn—the doctor Cottard, both an expert and stupid—also be nearsighted, in all

75

senses of the term. Having forgotten his pince-nez, and being less of an expert on feminine beauty than Marcel, he asks "Are they pretty, at least? I can't make out their features." He is, however, the professional of medical clichés that enable him to *know*, rather than see, that "they are *certainly* at the climax of their pleasure." He underlines that his conclusion is based upon prior knowledge and not upon perception when he adds: "It is not sufficiently known that women derive most excitement from their breasts." In the gap between perception, for which the necessary optical instrument is missing, and knowledge, which allows a certain deduction, lies the hesitancy upon which the epistemology of jealousy depends, like a parasite. The details of Odette's account of her activities also play within this gap.

Swann, who does not believe himself to be duped by the poison administered by his mistress, also fails to see the semiotic implications of Odette's speech. Neither true nor false—and is that not the essential characteristic of aesthetic discourse?—Swann accepts it nonetheless in his heart of hearts, and hence becomes more and more worried, uttering the vague statement "that doesn't fit with the fact that she didn't let me in." But this acceptance fails to acknowledge the force of the "surplus matter and the unfilled gaps," words that echo back in poetic terms to the glass jars in the Vivonne when the surplus itself filled in the gaps (SK 1.183 / P 1.166). These glass jars are very clearly presented as poetic: they are a mise en abyme of the poetics of to-ing and fro-ing associated with what I termed earlier the poetics of "mottling." They oscillate between being the container/signifier/point-of-comparison and being the content/signified/thing-compared, which already reveals the distinctions between epistemology, semiotics, and poetics, all of which are implied in the scene with the glass jars, as they are in that with Swann and Odette. The text only mentions the first aspect *explicitly*—the aspect of container/content—and alludes to the third aspect with the use of the word "image."[12] But the poetic aspect of the glass jars is definitely the one that projects its trace in what follows. As the novel continues, the subject, like Rousseau in the *Reveries*, is substituted for the glass jars. He puts to the test the poetic potential of drifting: "How often have I watched and longed to imitate . . . a rower who had shipped his oars and lay flat on his back in the bottom of his boat, letting it drift with the current, seeing nothing but the sky gliding slowly by above him, his face aglow with a foretaste of happiness and peace" (SK 1.186 / P 1.168).

This is the poetic potential of the detail that neither Odette nor Swann see. Having neither the choice nor the imagination to do otherwise, the latter can only play the same game as his mistress, pitting the same weapons against her:

> And making opportune use of some detail—insignificant but true—which he had accidentally learned, as though it were the sole fragment which he had involuntarily let slip of a complete reconstruction of her daily life which he carried secretly in his mind, he led her to suppose that he was perfectly informed upon matters which in reality he neither knew nor suspected. (SK 1.391 / P 1.353)

"Accidentally learned" is equivalent here to the unfilled gaps elsewhere. Swann thinks he can do battle with Odette's surplus matter using the complete life that she supposes him to know. Brilliantly playing out their interchangeable and disconcerting roles of author and reader, Swann and Odette reveal the impossibility of finding a resolution by means of details.

The semiotic battle between Swann and Odette later provides a model for Marcel's jealousy concerning Albertine. The difference is, however, that the latter is a much less substantial character than Odette. From the beginning, long before her escape and her death, this "fleeting being" is truly in flight. Consequently, the search for details becomes a real caricature of Swann's actions. Marcel, who, because he hardly ever leaves his house, depends upon others' help, embarks upon an interminable to-ing and fro-ing between a suspected detail and a confirmed certitude, only to lose that certitude, and thus have to set off on a further expedition. The source of the Nile remains always beyond reach.

And that is all for the good. For, as Doubrovsky puts it, this is how the narrator writes: the writing does not "reflect" nor does it "wed" jealousy's movements; it is jealous (*La place de la madeleine*, 90). It follows, then, that in order to understand the poetics of the detail in this novel, it is necessary to see which detail determines this jealous quest, this voyage of discovery in search of female pleasure that is always hidden and resistant. We discover that the gap that must be filled in this quest is, in fact, that gaping hole, those "huge blanks" (SK 3.93 / P 3.605) which leave a truth without any leftover fragments, without any kernels hidden deep down, from which the narrator could reconstruct something. The huge blanks are like those on a map that designate uncharted land. Archaeology is not a helpful model: the fragment cannot come to the rescue of the detail.

chapter six **The Magnifying Glass and the Journey to Spain**

Let us use the following passage to situate the Proustian detail as a figuration of vision. Coming in the middle of the narration, this passage has an important epistemological bearing on the poetics of the novel. Once again it is a question of knowledge. A fairly anodyne epistemological problem is posed, in which the subject of the knowledge is once more a doubting subject. Here, it is Mme de Villeparisis who, just like Odette, betrays herself by knowing too many details about the journey to Spain that the narrator's father is making with M. de Norpois at the very moment of the narrative:[1]

> And I wondered by what strange accident, in the impartial telescope through which Mme de Villeparisis considered, from a safe distance, the minuscule, perfunctory, vague agitation of the host of people whom she knew, there had come to be inserted at the spot through which she observed my father a fragment of glass of prodigious magnifying power which made her see in such high relief and in the fullest detail everything that was pleasant about him, and the contingencies that obliged him to return home, his difficulties with the customs, his admiration for El Greco, and, altering the scale of her vision, showed her this one man, so large among all the rest so small, like that Jupiter to whom Gustave Moreau, when he portrayed him by the side of a weak mortal, gave a superhuman stature. (SK 1.754 / P 2.61)

What makes this detail exemplary for my enquiry is that this passage juxtaposes very explicitly "a close-up shot" with "detailed" awareness, just as an unavoidable visuality is placed at the very heart of the "detective" question. The close-up shot is of the "host of people," represented as a whole body, and described as "minuscule, perfunctory, and vague." The rest of the passage corresponds word for word to this description as its contrary. "Perfunctory" is opposed precisely to high relief and fullest detail; "minuscule" is contrary to the effect of the magnifying glass. But, given the distance between the person supposedly doing the looking and the travelers who are the objects of her gaze, this glass is more like a sort of *telescope*. Finally, vagueness is opposed to the precision of the information. All of the information is presented as a view seen through some sort of eyeglass.

This description contains fragments of others, to which it replies: the "accidental" nature of the battle between Swann and Odette, the "glass" in the glass jars. This textual expansion, like a swelling or puffiness within the text, is generated by an informative remark made by Mme de Villeparisis. It assumes the metaphoric form of an eyeglass or visual prosthesis, and as such, it suggests the importance of visuality in the poetic practice of the detail in Proust. So, from the point of view of the subject of the vision, there is an ordinary eyeglass into which a piece of magnifying glass has been inserted. From that of the image, there is a juxtaposition of the large and the small. Strikingly, in this juxtaposition, the detail is large precisely because it has been enlarged. The detail here is the father, deified for the occasion. Marcel sees him enlarged, flattened, and at the same time, made godlike by association with a work of art.

Of course, according to the poetics of the detective-type detail, this particular detail of Mme de Villeparisis's clear-sightedness only betrays her epistemologically because the secret involves love. But the narrator, like James's Maisie, is too young to realize this.[2] However, the nature of the poetics of the detail in Proust is revealed rather in the fact that a magnifying glass is necessary in order to measure the enormity of the detail and to grasp its miraculous effect. For Proust, what counts in this passage is indeed the detail, which is contained within it like a mise en abyme. The magnifying glass is not to be found within the "essay," which deals here with the detective detail; nor does it belong within the diegetic epistemology based on questions such as "how does she know that, and what does she reveal in knowing it?" On the contrary, this magnifying glass and the necessity proven by its appearance here belong to Proust's poetic practice. The twists and turns of this text follow unfailingly the development of an anxiety, a jealousy quite different from that inspired by love. This anxiety inhabits the question of the postrealist modernity of the work, and it is generated by the desire to escape from binary logic by means of the visual detail.

Let us leave aside the names of the painters and the pictorial effects introduced in the passage. They are not a matter of simple aesthetics, as they are normally considered to be. Indeed, they are not the aim of the passage, but rather an effect of the development of the detail. They are the result of the magnifying glass with its two functions. On the one hand, the eyeglass is supposed to be applied to *"life"* by the diegetic character, Mme de Villeparisis. On the other hand, it is applied by the character-focalizer, the young Marcel, to the *vision* that his interlocutor helps to display, without knowing it. In other words, once one starts looking into the detail, the painters and the pictures appear out of the narrator's pen, just like the houses of Combray appeared out of his cup of tea.

The important aspect to notice in the reflexive relation between the character and the focalizer, and then in the relation between these two agents and the text that follows, is not in this case the overlapping of the subjects, such as we saw in the scene between Swann and Odette. This type of overlapping is the cause of the true detail's failure. Rather, the enlargement process, which functions indifferently in both a microscopic and a telescopic sense, is important here as a poetic truth. The "prodigiousness" of the poetics in question is after all the fact of having "prodigious *magnifying power.*" The detail in the passage *presents itself* as a detail: a fragment of glass inserted into—not detached from—Madame's eyeglass, in which appears a gigantic image of Monsieur. There is an important nuance here: the instrument of the enlarging is inserted into another optical instrument, the ordinary eyeglass, which produces a flat but vague image. We should hold onto this example as **81** a provisional definition of the detail according to Proustian poetics.

Odette's detail, far from being an archaeological reconstruction of the (false) truth she wants to communicate by means of the "edges" that Swann reads so well, becomes a simultaneous interpretation of the (true) lie that surrounds it. At first sight the image produced by the magnifying glass does not imply a change in meaning; it is not, therefore, a metaphor.[3] The detail of the glass juxtaposes, in a manner that is both diegetically and textually simultaneous, the close-up shot—"minuscule, perfunctory, vague," the importance of which cannot be overemphasized—and the godlike detail.

This does not mean to say that there is no displacement, or even substitution, that is well and truly tropological, but this is at another level. For Mme de Villeparisis knows what she knows, not because she applies her self-betraying amorous interest to Marcel's father, but because she displaces this interest, passing from M. de Norpois, the unspoken object, to the object-father, who is only made godlike by the dumbfounded son looking obliquely through the magnifying glass that is actually trained on the person next to the father. Thus one single magnifying glass is pointed at two different people, both wrapped up in one another, according to whoever is holding the eyeglass.

This piece of glass is an exemplary self-reflexive detail. It is both detail and fragment, trope and non-trope, metonymy and synecdoche, flat and bulbous, visual and imaginary, and this at various levels. What it signifies above all is the danger in conceptualizing the detail by opposing it to its neighbors. This "theoretical" lesson to be learnt from Proustian practice is relevant to Georges Didi-Huberman's attempt to define a neighboring concept by means of its difference from the detail. He elaborates this concept in reference to that most famous Proustian detail, the little patch of yellow wall attributed to Bergotte, who attributes it (no doubt wrongly) to Vermeer's *View of Delft*. This little patch of wall causes Bergotte's death (SK 3.185 / P 3.692).[4] Didi-Huberman names this concept the *patch*, in honor of Proust and in reference to his use of the term. He takes the concept from this famous passage in Proust and presents it as being useful in the analysis of painting "in the act."

According to Didi-Huberman, the patch in painting can be defined as a sovereign accident, an unstable index and an intrusion of the very act of painting into the representation, which, rather than being structured by this patch, is torn open by it ("Appendice," 313–14).[5] The author continues his definition by focusing on the ambiguity of the color of the little patch of yellow wall. This ambiguity stems from the possible alternatives of applying the yellow in question to the wall or to the patch, according to the different aesthetic attitudes of the readers. Is it a yellow patch of wall or a patch of yellow wall? For the reader who attributes the yellow to the wall, it is a detail; for the other who attributes it to the floating term "patch," it is related not to the referent, but to the act of painting. When applied to the painting, the yellow is a patch, a patch of color, of paint in all its materiality. What we should retain from this patch is the fact that Bergotte was jealous of the yellow that kills him. The important aspect about it is less its supposed luminous effect than its ontological composition, so to speak. And this links it all the more directly to Proust's writing: "I ought to have gone over them with a *few layers* of colour." Thus it is superimposition that provides for a reconciliation between the flatness of the image and the textual swelling that produces it.[6] Bergotte's comment also indicates the function of color, and of yellow in particular, as that which conveys the "precious" character of the patch.

Didi-Huberman continues by tracing the features of these patches in Vermeer's work. He is particularly drawn to the color red, beginning with the red splash at the elbow of the woman in *The Lacemaker*. At first glance this red splash represents a mess of red thread, a mess that conflicts glaringly with the peaceful atmosphere of the painting as a whole. But it is already a patch in that it provokes a "second" vision. In a referential sense it is disproportionately large and totally incongruous against the background of the cushion. It does have a form, but that form is meaningless. As opposed to the detail, which is always there, the patch "appears," it "stands out." It is more aggressively present than it seems, so much so, in fact, that we might say it is staring the viewer in the face, thus blinding her.

Mme de Villeparisis's detail was after all quite obvious in its method: Marcel, who is made to appear younger for the purpose of the demonstration, does not perceive the substitution of the biological father for the social father and, therefore, he is able in a rather childlike way to see **83** his father enlarged. The vision through the magnifying glass is possible because of both distance—de Norpois made invisible—and proximity, which results in an enlargement that blinds Marcel. Thus blinding is an integral part of the self-reflexive sense of this detail.

Didi-Huberman's insistence upon color primarily focuses on precisely that color which is nonreferential: Proust's yellow, which is nowhere to be seen in Vermeer's painting. If the little patch of yellow wall is capable of killing Bergotte, it is not because this yellow as described exists in Vermeer's painting, but because it "exists" in Proust's novel. It is because it is an active or performative signifier, rather than a referent "put down in writing." This yellow brings to mind echoes of the passage in which Marcel is reading in the "dim coolness" of his room at Combray (SK 1.90 / P 1.82). This Proustian color has the same form as the butterfly flitting before the child. Here is the yellow that kills Bergotte:

> His dizziness increased; he fixed his gaze, like a child upon a yellow butterfly that it wants to catch, on the precious little patch of wall. (SK 3.185 / P 3.692)

The yellow here is literally displaced, right in front of our eyes. From the patch of wall, to which it still remained attached in the previous sentence of the account of Bergotte's death ("and finally, the precious substance of the tiny patch of yellow wall"), it passes to the butterfly. Patch of wall, patch of yellow, yellow butterfly: the series, which is unified by the *detail* of the butterfly, signifying fascination and mobility of both light and reading in these two passages, definitely suggests that the color is important, but also that the color takes on a certain form. This form is mobile, so much so, indeed, that it is dizzying; it is light and fine—like an ideal detail.

It is perhaps because this little patch of wall and this yellow are textual that the concept of a patch is useful. Yet its use lies not in opposing it to the detail, but rather in viewing it as a subcategory of modes of detailing, that is, in understanding it as an insertion, and not as a detached piece or a fragment.

Perhaps the "patch" is not a simple detail, not because it fails to signify, but because it signifies too much. Part of the definition of the patch, as we now understand it, is to lead to errors of perception on the part of the person who is almost too attentive to it. It questions the possibility of visual attention, which turns out to be fatal for Bergotte. And Proust does clearly suggest that this attention is hindered by the violence applied to the delimitation of the patch. In other words, it is important to look more closely at the difference between "detaching" (a fragment) and "inserting" (a detail).

There are many passages in which Proust uses the very word "patch," or its equivalents,[7] and most often the amazement produced by the effect of light borders on an anxiety, which takes the form of a threat of violence. Here is an example:

> And so it was that, for a long time afterwards, when I lay awake at night and revived old memories of Combray, I saw no more than this sort of luminous patch [*pan*], sharply cut out against a vague and shadowy background, like the panels [*pans*] that the sudden explosion into flame of a Bengal light or a searchlight beam will cut out and illuminate in a building, the other parts of which remained plunged in darkness. (SK 1.46 / P 1.43)

This passage proposes a poetics of the patch by means of its practice. The word "patch" is followed by one designating fracture, and this sharp "cutting-out" in turn establishes a distinction between light and shadow. Contained within this opposition, a latent violence is already present, and it explodes—hence, necessarily, the metaphoric fire. The metaphor insists upon its status as artifice with the idea of a "Bengal light," which is a firework and thereby implies an artificially created display.[8] But its necessary role in the poetic creation of the patch or panel of light stems nonetheless from the violence with which it explodes into flame. This violence is made more acceptable by the addition of another metaphor, the searchlight. With the violence of the "sharp cutting-out" Proust is playing on two levels, that of the creation of the patch of light, and that of the poetic detailing introduced by the metaphor.

As for the creation of the patch, the rest of the passage foretells the anxiety it produces. We come quickly to "the opening of the dark path from which M. Swann, the unwitting author of my sufferings, would emerge, the hall through which I would journey to the first step of that staircase, so painful to climb." Next, the evocation of the patch of light turns back on itself but in a way that leaves all luminosity behind it, recovering only the idea of sharp cutting-out and darkness: "isolated from all its possible surroundings, detached and solitary against the dark background, the bare minimum of scenery necessary . . . to the drama of my undressing."

As for the second matter in question here, the functioning of the metaphor in all of this, I shall mention only briefly that master of metaphors, Elstir.[9] While this character and his studio-museum may be unsatisfactory as a "ground" for Proustian aesthetics (Henry, "Quand une peinture métaphysique"), his art or rather his images are the embodiment of the challenge presented by metaphor. Faced with the paintings by Elstir in the Guermantes' gallery, the difficulty of this metaphoric challenge is made quite explicit. I am referring here to a descriptive passage that recalls the one I just quoted, not only because of the theme of the patch, but also and especially because of the network of meaning it creates that links blindness—the optical error—sharp or violent cutting-out, and the effect of "flatness," which in *Combray* keeps the threatening father figure at bay, although still without success:

> How often, when driving, do we not come upon a bright street beginning a few feet away from us, when what we have actually before our eyes is merely a patch of wall glaringly lit which has given us the mirage of depth! (SK 2.435 / P 2.712)

Here, Marcel has made progress in his enquiry, but the magic lantern of his childhood is still standing firm a few lines earlier, and the father figure comes and interrupts his contemplation a few lines later. The violence of the light is also the violence of cutting-out, which detaches, blinds, and flattens.

To begin with, it flattens meaning. And sometimes, this is a good thing:

> I had been led by some effect of sunlight to mistake what was only a darker stretch of sea for a distant coastline, or to gaze delightedly at a belt of liquid azure without knowing whether it belonged to sea or to sky. (SK 1.894 / P 2.192)

But we must not forget the conditions of this delight. They include the abolishing of the referential color and the substitution of the imaginary color. As Descombes put it so well: "To choose a view is to cut out a picture from the spectacle of the world" (*Proust*, 273), and if Elstir is so expert in the practice of cutting-out—"this little square panel of beauty which Elstir had cut out of a marvellous afternoon" (SK 2.436 / P

2.713)—it is also because he manages to put the color-patch, which is self-reflexive, in the place of the fleeting color, which is referential.

It is perhaps not a coincidence that the violence necessary for the creation of the patch—creation by cutting-out and flattening—takes a particularly aggressive form, indeed a fatal form, when faced with the vision of Albertine asleep. This vision is broken up into pieces:

> Her hair, falling along her pink cheek, was spread out beside her on the bed, and here and there an isolated straight tress gave the same effect of perspective as those moonlit trees, lank and pale, which one sees standing erect and stiff in the backgrounds of Elstir's Raphaelesque pictures. If Albertine's lips were closed, her eyelids, on the other hand, seen from where I was placed, seemed so loosely joined that I might almost have questioned whether she really was asleep. At the same time those lids gave her face that perfect continuity which is unbroken by the obtrusion of eyes. There are people whose faces assume an unaccustomed beauty and majesty the moment they cease to look out of their eyes. (SK 3.65 / P 3.580)

This here is the cutting-out effect that constitutes the detail as a patch.

First of all each element is detached: the hair is "put beside" the color, if it is not actually "put to one side," and then it is cut up even more. The tress separated from the hair undergoes a process of differentiation that establishes it as most definitely fragmentary. First, it is described as "straight," which distinguishes it from the wavy nature of the hair. Second, it is enlarged, as if by a magnifying glass, to become a tree. But, almost as if to insist upon the fact that this enlargement is an effect of the image, that is to say, of "flatness" with all its implications, the tress is "ironed out" by the deceptive device of perspective. Both artificial and shadowy, these trees evoke a sinister atmosphere. They are moonlit and therefore nocturnal, sickly as if already condemned—"lank and pale." Thus they grow straight out of the metaphorizing palette of Elstir.

Marcel, who is involved in an exploration of visual violence, is quite happy about this cutting-up. Albertine's way of talking is too "contemporary," but here she is silent, with her lips closed, almost as if she had breathed her last breath—she dies soon anyway. This effect is, of course, produced by vision and controlled by the focalizing subject. But the clo-

87

sure of the body is to be taken to much greater lengths.[10] The most striking thing, as far as I am concerned, is how this vision of Albertine violently closes her eyes. The narrator says that the eyes seemed to be half-open. This puts his visual enterprise of producing a patch into danger: if the woman is not asleep, she cannot be peacefully and totally cut into pieces.

But, by worrying about the narrator's chances of success, we are only underestimating his ambition. Since this doubt is simply, like all the rest, a visual effect or a particular way of focusing on the object, it only serves to magnify the visual performance. The fact that these very eyes can also be completely removed from the face reveals the effect of flattening that the eye can apply. It is clear that the issue at stake here is enormous. Beauty "offers itself" only if it is blind, because, in order for it to be accessible, in order for it to exist, the subject who sees it must not be seen. Doubrovsky has already made the same point: "It is the invisible man who watches Albertine sleep" (*La place de la madeleine*, 116). Here lies the whole history of the nude, which has tended to be female.

Like Oedipus taking his revenge, the price of viewing the body—exploded into fragments, broken into different patches, even broken-down—is that the blindness is projected onto the object. "Beat it, son, that's my place": this discourse, which has parental resonances to which I shall return, is appropriated here in a visual manner by means of dead trees. Despite all his synthetic efforts, it is by means of a parasitic opposition that Marcel manages to *see*. This is no small matter.

Let me come back to the glass of prodigious magnifying power. It is in this way that we should understand the patch in visual literature. It is a detail that proclaims its own status as detail and prescribes how it is to be read. In other words, it is a detail, with all that implies of ambiguity and difficulty in interpretation, but it is a particular type of detail: it is a detail that *details itself*, and as such it passes from being referential to being self-reflexive. Accordingly, a patch, in its capacity as detail, produces an enlargement effect signified within the novel itself. In this sense the red splash in *The Lacemaker* is indeed a model patch. The possibility of the emergence of the patch is better understood if we reread the passage about the magnifying glass. Both here and there, the "message" of this effect is that, being linked to the enormous structures of sexual difference, it must contaminate the text that is given over to analyzing it. Perhaps it can be understood as the effect of the subjectivity that spurts out from the text, as Didi-Huberman has so well suggested.[11] We could quite easily replace this terminology with that of the decoy—"miroir d'alouettes"—elaborated by Naomi Schor, who uses a vocabulary of flatness, of illusion, since blindness has no gender bias. In our paradigmatic example, the mistake that results from this detailed visuality is precisely one of enlargement. The gaze that is foregrounded in the text is that of Mme de Villeparisis, and yet in her eyes the father is neither enlarged, made godlike, nor flattened.

Mme de Villeparisis's magnifying glass deceives Marcel, who is blinded by it and thus sees a godlike father appearing out of it.[12] Juxtaposed to a weak mortal, who is given the feminine grammatical form for no apparent reason except to be flattened[13] and substituted for another, this father is also quite monstrous, badly integrated and subject to a change in the "scale of vision." Far from being formless, his form is actually detailed in this enlargement and as such it is deformed. The concept of the patch, which suggests a visuality without form, visual "noise," perhaps does not, in fact, account for all the relevant aspects of this category of details.

Let us take as a pictorial example, in the original meaning of the term, that infamous representation of Bathshebah's leg in Rembrandt's painting *The Toilet of Bathshebah*. The top part of the leg is turned toward the viewer, the knee, which is crossed, is hidden by the letter she is holding, and the lower part of the leg is turned incongruously toward the attendant (Fig. 9). I read a conflict of two genres in this leg, both of which require specific modes of reading. For the genre of the nude, the body must be properly visible and, therefore, turned toward the viewer. For the genre of history painting, the event taking place, which already contains the next event, must be plausible. In order that the attendant can beautify the woman, so that David will take her and leave her pregnant, which sets off a whole succession of violent events, her leg must be turned toward the attendant.

The artist could have accomplished this double allegiance to two different genres without attracting such attention to it. He could quite sim-

Fig. 9. Rembrandt van Rijn, *The Toilet of Bathshebah*, 1654. Paris, Musée du Louvre (copyright Photo R.M.N.).

ply have crossed the knees in the other direction, the left one over the right. The distortion, or deformation, is, therefore, necessary—perhaps not desired by the painter, but necessary for the painting as double discourse in conflict with itself. By disfiguring a figure so perfectly formed,[14] the disfiguration in the detail of the leg figures in a negative rhetoric of "neither one nor the other." However, although this detail is not referential, it is not by that account deprived of all form. On the contrary, it is because of its double form, its excess of form, that it disfigures the referentially recognizable woman. She is disfigured in order to allow a certain self-reflexiveness to express the conflict in the pictorial practice of this work between genres—the nude and history painting—and internal and external needs.[15]

Neither the concept of the patch according to Didi-Huberman, nor that of the detail in the common sense of the term, helps us describe this leg. The excess of form in this deformed leg recalls the excess of information that the magnifying glass was able to provide. But it also recalls the butterfly, which, small but so yellow, gave a flickering, mobile, and overdetermined form to the patch of wall that was "yellowed" by Proust's text.

I propose to call this type of overdetermined detail quite simply a dis-figure. It is disfiguring as a result of an excess of form, and as such it is related to denial that is absolutely not necessary and is, therefore, excessive: effective negative surplus, the effect of which is proven by the theorist's insistence upon nonsense. A dis-figure is the visual equivalent of a Freudian denial. This enables us to examine the cost implied in the Proustian poetics of the detail, although we may find ourselves forced to reserve the term "patch" for more restrictive use on the occasions when self-reflexivity effectively takes on a formless form, as opposed to an excess form. Both of these possibilities are deforming, both are no doubt self-reflexive, but the hypothesis creeping in here is that Proust's novel, which is after all an irreducibly literary text, even though it is charged with visuality, needs dis-figures more than it needs patches. Moreover, these needs are overdetermined in visual terms.

Now is the moment to reconsider the notion of "literary visuality." Figuration is clearly distinguished from figurativeness, which is the usage of tropes and which has been so well analyzed by others.[16] Here I am attempting, quite differently, to ignore as much as possible the distinction between "literal" and "figurative." Sometimes it is in metaphors or comparisons that figuration begins, and this is the case when a visual image is invested with the figuring function or the power to give form, that is, visual form, to that which follows. But it is not because it is a trope that a word, an evocation or the representation of a thing, serves as a blueprint for the writing. So where is the visual situated in a literary text? How can we read "visually"?

I am considering Proust's text in this respect under the sign of the Wittgensteinian idea of "language games."[17] The concept of image—which implies generally, but not always, an idea of likeness, of resemblance, or of similitude—has in the past been analyzed according to its use in five domains. The graphic domain is that of painting, which we have already considered, and photography, which we will look at later. The optical domain is that of mirrors, projections, lenses, and glasses, the recurrence of which in Proust has raised the questions I am currently examining. A third domain is that of sense data or appearances, which are related to perception. Then there are mental images that are encountered in dreams, memories, ideas, and fantasies. Finally, at the other end of the spectrum, is the verbal domain, related to which is the domain of metaphors and descriptions. These domains could be broken down even further. It is a "family" of concepts. They all refer to images, but these images are of widely divergent semiotic and aesthetic status.[18]

These five domains are not only strongly represented in Proust, they are also thematized in this work, both as part of the theoretical reflection, the essayistic dimension of the novel, and in the collection of fictional representations that constitute the novelistic dimension of *La recherche*, to which this particular study is devoted. Their presence is at once strong, constant, and confused. The graphic domain alone "fills" the work: it causes it to "swell up" with all the descriptions, evocations, references, and allusions related to visual art. But this domain is not only relevant in terms of this semantic or thematic network. Its importance is transformed from being semantic to being syntactic, so to speak, when the images, which are visual objects in this domain, figure the text, informing and forming it by imposing upon it certain developments that, without this link to the visual, would lose a lot, if not all, of their meaning and their richness. These are the images on which the dis-figure superimposes a self-reflexive dimension.

The optical domain, traditionally represented by the mirror, is figured here much more often by methods of projection—the magic lantern—and by visual prostheses, on which I am hoping to shed some light: magnifying glasses, Brichot's huge glasses, pince-nez. In the case of Saint-Loup, the visual prosthesis is mobile; in that of Cottard, it is not there when he needs it.[19]

Perception is no doubt the best-studied domain in Proustian studies. Indeed, Proust makes frequent comments about it, and his whole work can be considered as an apprenticeship in perception. Making one mistake after another, the hero gradually evolves from naïveté, which causes him to believe what he sees, to knowledgeable worldliness, which enables him to superimpose the different levels of mistaken perception that the eye causes the subject to infer, until he eventually sees the "truth." I refrain here from commenting on the psychology and the philosophy of perception, analyzed convincingly by others.[20] During the nineteenth century, and Proust is decidedly a child of the nineteenth century, the optical instrument had a marked but diverse cultural presence.

For my purpose, visual perception is relevant only as a narrative mechanism, a mechanism that, according to how it is used by the subjective position of the "focalizer," establishes a motivation for the "appearances." This limitation is reinforced by another such limitation. The focalizing subject is most often considered to be a voyeur: a subject who sees without being seen, and whose gaze is charged with eroticism.[21] Later on, the well-known voyeurism of *La recherche* will be understood as an attempt to know the other, and this knowledge will both be recognized as the fundamental object of desire and admitted to be inaccessible. The nature of this voyeurism is above all else "ethnographic," a term which I hope reveals the epistemological stakes in play here. It is a question of how to study the other, that is, those other people whom one wants to know, having realized the radical otherness that separates them from the "I."

The domain of the mental image, as it is distinguished in the theory sketched out here, poses the immediate problem of categorization. Are we dealing with properly visual images? This domain is also extremely rich in Proust. I only concern myself with fantasies, dreams, and memories to the extent that they function as a ground for images whose referent is of a visual nature. I apply the same restriction to descriptions and metaphors.[22] Once again, the problem of different categories is posed here. First, it is obvious that figures and descriptions are not visual by definition, although, inversely, the evocation of the visual takes these as its preferred rhetorical forms. Again, I insist on respecting this restriction. On the other hand, metaphors and descriptions are only two specific forms of a more general verbal "imaging," which is more easily grasped by means of the concept of focalization, understood as a narrative mechanism that spreads before the "mental eye" of the reader a vision of the narrative content. It is quite clear how, in the case of Flaubert, expressions such as "one observed . . . ," "one saw . . . " invite the reader to stand behind the focalizer, who is anonymous in this case. The same can be said of the use of the "I" in Proust. This generalized "I" is invested with absolute focalizing power and identifies a position that the reader can occupy. While it is more subjectivist and more personalized, this "I" is nonetheless so volatile and so often endowed with perceptual implausibilities that its meaning is far from being individualist. In terms of the construction of images, this "I" is once more a mechanism that turns each notation of the visual into a describable image that is centered, although, in relation to this image, it is not clear whether or not the perceptual and perspectival center is occupied.

In this framework, we see that the detail for Proust must reconcile the fundamental requirements of his enterprise, which is to recuperate the past in the present by means of the latter. In this enterprise, Proust, like the Neoptolemaic cartographers of the late Middle Ages, comes up against the fixed image.[23] But far from being a discouragement, this fixedness constitutes both the challenge and the means of his poetics. He finds various solutions to this problem, and perhaps the best-known solution—the multiplication of points of view—bears a certain likeness to the strategies of cartographers:

> The multiplication of points of view in the form of faces and gazes that reveal the surface of the earth from partial and complementary angles.
> (Jacob, *L'empire des cartes*, 152)

We are familiar with those puffed-up faces that represent the winds strategically placed in the four corners of maps. We tend to feel a certain affection for them, for they seem sweetly childlike. But in so doing, we forget the semantic effect of the puffiness that creates an imaginary voluminousness in an image the flatness of which constitutes precisely both the problem and the advantage. And while this association is overdetermined by Marcel's obsession with Albertine's cheeks—the tendency is to associate this characterization with the famous kiss preceded

94

by a breathtaking number of preparatory shots ("in the short journey of my lips to her cheek, I saw ten Albertines"; SK 2.378 / P 2.660)—we should note that the text functions in an inverse manner to the maps. The multiplication of points of view, when it is the result of Proust's pen and Marcel's lips, becomes a multiplication of objects of vision. But it is rather the notion of a delegated gaze that I associate here with the detail-disfigure of the magnifying glass borrowed from Mme de Villeparisis.

For the kiss becomes the crucial example of the impossibility of seeing—the paradigm of the patch: "Suddenly my eyes ceased to see, then my nose, crushed by the collision, no longer perceived any odour, and, without thereby gaining any clearer idea of the taste of the rose of my desire, I learned, from these obnoxious signs, that at last I was in the act of kissing Albertine's cheek."[24] This impossibility, which seems here to be absolute, is the final result of a whole development, of an entire "study" of the sensorial imperfection of the body, and in particular, of the lips as an epistemological instrument. The difficulties that intervene are of various different orders: the perception is displaced, the object is transformed, the skin as a surface breaks up into "coarse grain":

> At first, as my mouth began gradually to approach the cheeks which my eyes had recommended it to kiss, my eyes, in changing position, saw a different pair of cheeks; the neck, observed at closer range and as though through a magnifying glass, showed in its coarser grain a robustness which modified the character of the face. (SK 2.378 / P 2.660)

The magnifying glass does not improve close-up vision; it modifies it. The object seen is a different one, and this displacement continues until the perception is reduced to nothing. The lens attributed to Mme de Villeparisis, however, allowed too much to be seen: an over-large father, whom the borrowed gaze (that of Mme de Villeparisis) totally failed to see. But this operation nonetheless functioned by splitting the vision into multiple elements.

In order, then, to use these relevant concepts, the distinction must be made between the patch, a detail that self-reflexively campaigns against form, and the dis-figure, a detail of a quite different category in which the self-reflexiveness overdetermines the form to such an extent that the

95

conflict between forms loses its first "banal" meaning and gains a poet-ically useful meaning that describes the desperate battle in which the maker of signifying flat forms is both caught up and confused. And the contradictory effect of the magnifying glass is precisely that the dis-fig-ure, which I am proposing as a detail so typical that it becomes a mise en abyme of the poetic process that it foregrounds, inflates the text, causing a swelling in the surface of the narrative.

chapter seven **Swelling Hillsides**

Suddenly I had the feeling that all events existed
simultaneously around me. Time became horizontal and circular; it was space and time at the same
time, and I tried to draw it. . . . But I was attached
to the horizontal, I didn't want to lose it, and I saw
the disk become an object.
—Alberto Giacometti, *Ecrits*

Beneath any carnal attraction that goes at all deep,
there is the permanent possibility of danger.
—Proust, *A la recherche du temps perdu* (SK 3.76 /
    P 3.589)

It seems clear, then, that the Proustian subject uses the flat image
to invent the nonexistent, to identify the impossible, and to spare himself
choices that are either too difficult or too unattractive. Dripping with
blood, nullifying any depth, encompassing a whole visibility, and exposing the opening of a body with no inside, the Chardinesque skate
comes, perhaps, close to his ideal. It is obvious that this ideal is not exclusively of an artistic and epistemological order. As we saw, it also possesses an aspect that links poetics to sensuality. But even the skate is not
sufficient to produce this link. There is a simple reason for this: Proust's
art is literary. Such an art is difficult to "flatten."

One of the characteristics of Proust's art is the production of long
sections of text from a small generating scene, a swelling that produces
spread-out or "flattened" meaning, remaining all the while a bulbous
presence. Hence the importance of the detailing, which is the paradoxical development whereby the infinitely small is enlarged into a textual
tumor and a torn-open flat image. Although the magnifying glass produces flatness, we should remember that it is itself rounded. The first
swelling or inflating of this type in the work establishes the rules for the   **97**
process.

In the scene of the maternal kiss, a central episode in the bedtime
drama with which *La recherche* begins, we find the first description in
which visual art is allied with literary art in order to produce an image

in the proper sense of the term. Let us recall how this drama ends: in a totally unexpected fashion, Mamma spends the night at the young boy's bedside. She would not have done so of her own accord, but the father sent her to gratify the child's longing. The mother, who seems herself to be intimidated by the father's absolute power, is, however, the one who actually decrees the supposedly paternal law: "We mustn't let the child get into the habit . . . " And the father, traditionally the embodiment of the arbitrariness of power, takes his lead from what he sees when he says: "You can see quite well that the child is unhappy, he looks distressed" (SK 1.39 / P 1.36). And the unexpected good fortune, the lucky order, leaves its beneficiary perplexed by this paternal generosity, unable to speak or to move: "I stood there, not daring to move." The only bodily function that the child continues to master in this delicate situation, in this fragile happiness, is the ability to see.

And what he sees merits our close attention:

> He was still in front of us, a tall figure in his white nightshirt, crowned with the pink and violet cashmere scarf which he used to wrap around his head since he had begun to suffer from neuralgia, standing like Abraham in the engraving after Benozzo Gozzoli, which M. Swann had given me, telling Sarah that she must turn away towards Isaac. (SK 1.39 / P 1.36)

How striking it is that this image of the father at this moment of supreme power, which is experienced by the overwrought child as a real power of life or death, is articulated indirectly, by a reference to a work of art, as if the power itself can only be made manifest indirectly. Furthermore, as a result of an accumulation of superimpositions, the artistic image is effectively "turned away." There is no such work that corresponds to this description.

If it seems impossible, if not quite insane, to distinguish in Proust's manifest interest in visual art a particular priority for one visual or pictorial "aesthetic," or an exclusive preference for one "period" in art history, for one school or for one tendency, this is because his interest is of a quite different order, at least in its libidinal aspect. This interest is libidinal to the extent that it directs and moves the text by exciting the subject, who needs this excitation while being perhaps unconscious of his need. These visual images, as artistic images, are of *fundamental* importance to Proust's writing, and this again must be understood in the literal sense of the term: they provide the foundations and support for the artistic value of this work, which intends to be monumental—once again, in both senses of the term. They are the ground for the work, as a canvas is a ground for a painting: they are the necessary but modest ground, indispensable but radically insufficient. However, between the visual art that is invoked and the literary art produced with its help, there is a necessary gap. This gap is much more than a simple difference in medium; it is also a difference in forms and means, in depth, background, and objective.

It is difficult, if not impossible, to imagine what sense an apparent pictorial aesthetic can have for a literary artist without realizing that between the two there is an ontological gap. This gap is the site of anxiety and voluptuous pleasure, two motives for the aesthetics. It is a question of ways of being, of possibilities for existing, of means of constructing a fully subjective and totally accessible existence: what does "I" signify? Who exactly has gone to bed early for a long time? And what is the relevance of the fact that this habit is broken at the moment when "I" looks at a nonexistent engraving?

If Proustian hesitancy sometimes takes the form of an uncertainty in taste, of a lack of coherence in the preferences expressed, even perhaps of a misunderstanding of the great movements of art, it is better not to take this in the negative sense of a lack of knowledge or of an incapacity or refusal to choose, but in the positive or constructive sense of a will to reserve simultaneously for oneself possibilities that are incompatible in pictorial terms. It is a will to place oneself simultaneously in different situations, in alternative modes of being and positions. Neither a disciple of Rembrandt, supposedly his favorite painter, nor of Chardin, the center of his early essay, Proust is only a follower of himself as an artist of writing. Simple vanity or ambition are not at issue here. Rather, what we see is the necessity of experimentation, generated within someone who is incapable of splitting himself in two, and **99** who, thus, has only the choice between all or nothing.

It is all a matter of possible positions and imaginations, of roles to be played and images that can be evoked. Even Doubrovsky, who was hardly hesitant in his desacralization of this writing, failed to grasp the full extent of Proust's ambivalence.[1] This ambivalence does not depend on the various maternal and paternal identifications, which Proust uses freely and variously, thereby creating an extraordinary richness and density. Nor does it depend on a lack of food or love, since this work is too egocentric, constructed from and around one subject, to begin an evaluation of the difference between the self and the other. This writing, that of the novel rather than the essay, is moved or pushed by a search or an enquiry (*recherche*) that is aesthetic in its means as opposed to its end. The "end," the inaccessible *telos*, is situated more in the direction of voluptuous pleasure, from where the writing emerges triumphant. The search carried out in this work is in one sense, perhaps a perverse sense, a search for a pleasure that lacks nothing, that monopolizes everything, and that is situated nowhere. The visual image provides a base and a screen, which are necessary but also necessarily provisional, for this pleasure.

I propose to follow some of the directions taken by the subject who tries to place himself within reach of a voluptuous pleasure that no known principle and no recognized sexual position can guarantee, and which, far from taking the visual image as an ideal example to follow, uses it and exploits it in order to reach an otherwise unimaginable climax. The image of the body's sensuality is imagined first of all in its female form through the specific aspect of roundness. This first exploration opens up the terrain for a more complex view of the traps that are specifically equipped to catch the Proustian subject.

These traps also take on a double aspect, that of positions and that of objects. As object-traps, located within the province of the feminine, they include the madeleine, of course, but also the boiling milk, cheeks, and peaches, all of which lead to the figuration of the breast, a site of sensuality that is presented immediately as perverse, and also a site that the Proustian subject resists—or that he cannot reach. The trap is staged and takes form in scenes that generate the narrative. The scenes I am referring to here are not so much those of the famous revelation of involuntary memory, which has been taken a little bit too literally. They are rather the scenes that have an opposite effect, an effect that I willingly, if a little metaphorically, qualify as traumatizing. They are intensely visual scenes, which stage, again intensely, the necessity of blindness. They are scenes in which the vision is so hurtful that the subject is unable to see it. Perception in these scenes has only just begun when it fails, and in this manner it initiates the ensuing narrative. They are scenes with *holes* in them. On the one hand, there is the "dance breast to breast" (SK 2.823–25 / P 3.190–92), and on the other, its sodomitical equivalent, the first scene of voyeurism in which the hero spies on Charlus and Jupien (SK 2.635–56 / P 3.3–16). The latter scene is, of course, the one of the "big bum." In both scenes the narrator's voyeurist position determines both the genesis of the story and the trauma that makes it inaccessible. It is a simultaneous conflict between sight and blindness.

These two scenes are scenes of visual initiation, in which the rounded or swollen form is the issue and the image, which is necessarily flattened in one way (literally, in the dance of the breasts) or another (figuratively, in the scene of sodomy). Following these analyses, I read the description of Albertine as nude as a successful end to this apprenticeship: successful to the extent that it manages the writing of an inhabitable position for the subject.

We have seen that the essay "Chardin and Rembrandt," from *Contre Sainte-Beuve*, can be taken as generating certain visual fantasies in *La recherche*; the same can be done with the piece known as "Solitary Pleasure," which disappeared from the Pléiade edition of *Contre Sainte-Beuve* but was brought back into circulation by Doubrovsky. Only a few fragments of "Solitary Pleasure" appear in the novel. One little sentence in it merits all of our attention: "Beat it, son, that's my place."[2]

In psychoanalytically oriented criticism it is more important than ever to remain close to the grain of the text, to remain as attentive to the literal as possible. This little sentence signifies quite clearly and directly the suppression of the father-sun, since this literalizing psychoanalytic figuration means that to take the place of the father is concretely to sit in his seat. But it is particularly by means of the indirect object, the thing to be seen, that this dividing-up of positions is imposed. Far from being suppressed, the thing seen, which is clearly maternal, is constituted as a frustrating but necessary image. It is this image that means that the subject, who is not satisfied with taking the father's seat by addressing him as the father to the child, must *also* close the curtain to cover, if only partially successfully, the thing seen.

The little sentence follows an evocation of the landscape, and the place or seat in question enables the contemplation of this landscape. We should focus, then, more closely on the terms of this evocation. The pleasure begins with a feeling of power that gives the young boy the sense of mastery over "infinity and eternity," that is, over both spatial and temporal totality (*CSB* / G 68). It is worth insisting that this feeling of power is at the base of the voluptuous pleasure provoked by involuntary memory. The moment of this power is punctuated by a sensation described in the following manner:

> At that moment, as far as the clouds might *puff up* over the forest, I felt that my mind went a little further, was not quite filled by it, that there was always *a small gap*. I felt the lovely *swelling hillsides* that were rising *like breasts* on either side of the river supported, like *mere insubstantial reflections*, on the powerful gaze of my pupils. All this *was resting* on me, I was more than all of it, I could never die. (*CSB* / G 68–69; emphasis added)

The italicized words constitute the outline or the skeleton of the visual fantasy on which the feeling of power *rests*, this last word being one we should take in the concrete sense of the ground evoked earlier. It is important not to underestimate the precariousness of the situation, underlined in the French text by the Flaubert-like conflict between the momentariness of the situation and the verbs in the imperfect tense of duration.

Even more important, it seems to me, is the *form* taken by the feeling of power. The landscape, with its swelling forms of clouds and hills, is presented as lying beyond the subject-ground. Indeed, this landscape presents problems of visibility. It is impossible to fix or immobilize the elements that compose it. And this is the first problem with the visual that calls for the literary by absolute necessity. The two elements appear narratively in successive stages, each one marked by a failure of the focalizing subject to integrate himself in the thing seen. The problem with kissing Albertine is thus announced. Clearly it is a problem with distant perception as well.

This attempt at integration, at absorption, is at least as important as the swelling form that is explicitly likened to breasts. Genette (in "Métonymie chez Proust"), of course, taught us once and for all to interpret the likeness as "necessary" because of its basis in contiguity. And this contiguity can only be situated at the phantasmic level, which is explicit in this frank description of masturbation. The puffed-up clouds, ephemeral forms, the value of which as a mottled screen should not be underestimated, do not quite manage to absorb the mind that asks only to lose itself in them. They fail to give enough support. In the first stage, then, the small gap cancels the integration.

The more substantial swelling hillsides are also narrativized by the pronominal verb of action "to rise," which already announces a certain competitiveness. This narrativization places them, then, in a second phase, in a second stage or attempt. But the integration once again fails, and this time it is because of the "flatness." Mere insubstantial reflections: they are only an image, even though this image is created by a gaze that claims itself to be powerful. The subject knows where to *place* this failure: "All this *rested* on me." This consistency of the subject, his strength as a ground, turns against him, since the words "I was more than all of it, I could never die," while they announce the ecstasy of the subject, also reveal the overflow, the dangerous spilling-out of the self. "All of it" is very heavy to carry. In the guise of denial, it is more than possible that death will intervene, but this death would not be a stop in time, which has effectively been averted, but rather a dissolution in space. Such a dissolution threatens the unstable clouds. Incidentally, according to a strictly paradigmatic reading of Proust's text, this denial is also inscribed like a syncopated beat relative to the possibility of dying, to Bergotte's inevitable death in front of the *patch*, the unformed form of flatness.

Implied by the difficulty in carrying these lovely swelling hillsides, which are endowed with an independent dynamism and are capable of "rising up" alone, is the failure of the gaze itself. This failure can be read 103 not only as a philosophy of the visual, but also as a consciousness of the human being's limits and as an unconsciousness of the difficulties implied in sexuality. The visuality that is questioned here is that of long-distant perception. And, it is immediately after this failure, that the little sentence appears, substituting the subject for the (paternal) sun. Textually speaking, it is after this usurpation of place that the subject closes the curtains. Thus he breaks with the long-distant view, but this break is only half successful: "The branch of the lilac prevented him from closing it." A little earlier, what is now represented as a branch had quite a different form: "making way for a young lilac, which . . . had passed its perfumed head through the half-open window." Nonetheless, it remains the taking of the father's place that enables the ejaculation, in turn, to "rise up." But the reader has to wait a little longer for this climax, since this "rising up" marks the abrupt transition between the inaccessibility of the mother's body and the impossibility of identifying with the father.

Proust's fundamental hesitation, which means that he never unambiguously subscribes to one particular visual aesthetic, stems from his will to suspend the temptation to decide between the different identifications open to him. The figurations such as the fountain, the spurting outwards, and, as a whole, the "masturbatory" writing, are clearly, in a primary way, figurations of male identification. But this writing, which takes the fragile form of a snail's trail, needs a ground. It rests initially, like the "torrent of activity" that rested upon the hand in the water, on the swelling hillsides and on the rounded napkin, thus drawing in the direction of a female identification. But the hills are too far away, and the clouds are too ephemeral. The first are only a reflection, a flat trompe-l'oeil, while the others leave a small gap.

This necessary ground, which is almost material, can have no better figuration than that of the leaf, the canvas, or the paper used in writing, painting, and photography. Once this extreme sensitivity to the need for a ground has been noted, it is clearer why objects are so often presented from the back or the wrong side. Even the madeleine, the little scallopshell of pastry "so richly sensual under its severe, religious folds" (SK 1.51 / P 1.46), is first described as "those squat, plump little cakes," which, with their sensual form, readily provoke an association with the maternal breast. But the other side intervenes immediately: "the fluted valve of a scallop shell" (SK 1.48 / P 1.44). I am reluctant to apply a female charge blindly to the scallop shell (*valve*), which some might have been tempted to do first because of the identity in consonants between "valve" and "vulva," and second because of the rounded form. The scallop shell here functions above all else as a ground, a space in which the plump form lies. It is, therefore, a back or a wrong side. It is flat and even slightly paternal, as opposed to welcoming and maternal. Between "plump" and "scallop shell," there is "religious," a descriptive metaphor that is metonymically motivated and which anticipates the extent to which the "plump" sensuality "is folded" over to meet the stipulations of the way-things-are-done, of the form.

Later we see the reason for the importance of the ground, which often takes the form of a significantly liquid materiality. But let us look first at its rival, in other words, at the rounded form with its power to attract and its inability to satisfy. This form is attributed in the first place to breasts. Concretely and literally, or, inversely, it throws the shadow of the breast onto other external objects. Here, for example, are some solidly real breasts. Swann, lover of female flesh, who establishes the norm, the normality, against which the narrator must fight his battle, is on the brink of death, but that does not stop him from looking deeply and longingly into the corsage of the woman who is talking to him:

> As soon as Swann, on taking the Marquise's hand, had seen her bosom at close range and from above, he plunged an attentive, serious, absorbed, almost anxious gaze into the depths of her corsage, and his nostrils, drugged by her perfume, quivered like the wings of a butterfly about to alight upon a half-glimpsed flower. (SK 2.733 / P 3.106)

We recognize the motifs that inscribe ambiguity in this "in-depth" image, such as the butterfly, emblem at once of the detail, the patch, and the mottling. But it is especially important to realize the extent of the insistent irony with which Swann's gaze is described. This irony is as serious as it is critical. It refers exactly to what it says: the depth of the gaze. We must take this seriousness at its word in order to see how this gaze is criticized later by the intermediary of the metaphorization of the sea. In this context, it seems justifiable to associate the word "sea" (*mer*) with its homonym in French, "mother" (*mère*).

In fact, we know that the sea has been placed from the very beginning within the maternal figuration, since this is the primary meaning of the exchange of characteristics between the sea and the mountain that Genette pointed out (in "Proust palimpsestes," 47–48). Seen through the "portholes," which commemorate the magnifying glass— that "rounded" detail which produces the enlarged flat image—the sea is said to be "naked," a "vast, dazzling, mountainous amphitheatre," with the "snowy crests of its emerald waves, here and there polished and translucent." And the roundness is presented in the form that we know from the fragment in *Contre Sainte-Beuve*: "Hills of the sea which, before they come dancing back to us, are apt to withdraw so far that often it was only at the end of a long, sandy plain that I would distinguish, far off, their first undulations" (SK 1.723 / P 2.33). From this the painting that serves as a point of comparison follows on quite naturally.

The hills, which associate the sea with a mountain and which Marcel has learned to appreciate from the master Elstir, are in the first place personified as female. Moreover, the relevant aspect of this vision is the distance, the teasing withdrawal that slows up the dance "back to us." But this withdrawal is also indispensable. Without it, how can the undulations be seen in all their subtlety of form and, significantly, of time, that is to say, of narrative movement? This does not alter the fact that long-distant vision is irremediably separated from close-up vision, of which Swann has granted himself the privilege. This epistemological divorce returns to declare the impossibility of depth at precisely the moment when the narrator is overcome with dizziness in front of the sea:

> After the toll-house, where the carriage had stopped for a moment at such a height above the sea that, as from a mountain-top, the sight of the blue *gulf* beneath almost made one dizzy, I opened the window. . . . Was it not like an index of *measurement* which, upsetting all our ordinary impressions, shows us that *vertical* distances may be compared with horizontal ones. (SK 2.927 / P 3.290; emphasis added)

The impossible battle to fill in the gulf between distant vision and close-up vision seems, then, to be closely linked to the difficulty in making the hills-breasts of "Solitary Pleasure" into something other than a flat and inaccessible reflection. The association between sea/mother/mountain is overdetermined by the problem of detailed vision and the penetration that the latter requires.

This association between sea/mother/mountain is so systematic and is so inevitably accompanied by sensual frustration, that it governs the representation of the failed kiss at Balbec (SK 1.995 / P 2.285). Marcel visits Albertine, at her request, while she is ill and thus spending the night at the Grand Hôtel. Anticipating the pleasure that he believes she has promised him by inviting him to her bedside, the first visual sensation provoked by Albertine in bed is that of a change in the proportions of her face. The experience of this attempt at a kiss is to be played out around the pivotal point between close-up and distant vision, and it ends with Albertine ringing the bell in alarm. Between the close-up vision of Albertine's face and the alarm-bell, there is a long description of the sea/mother seen from a distance. This description literally reworks several of the key terms of the fragment on solitary pleasure:

> The sight of Albertine's bare throat, of those flushed cheeks, had so intoxicated me . . . that it had destroyed the equilibrium between the immense and indestructible life which circulated in my being and the life of the universe, so puny in comparison. The sea, which I could see alongside the valley through the window, the swelling breasts of the first of the Maineville cliffs . . . all this seemed less than a featherweight on my eyeballs, which between their lids I could feel dilated, resistant, ready to bear far greater burdens, all the mountains of the world, upon their fragile surface. (SK 1.995 / P 2.285)

But the frustration, which the subject had known how to remedy provisionally in *Contre Sainte-Beuve* by partially closing the curtains and dislodging the father/sun, intervenes here in a more definitive manner when the end of the phantasmic description signals the alarm bells.

The last example of this intricate visual complex of psychoanalytical positioning is the hill seen from the window at Doncières:

> This comfortable room, which seemed like a sort of optical centre from which to look out at the hill—the idea of doing anything else but gaze at it, the idea of actually climbing it, being rendered impossible by this same mist. *Soaking up the shape of the hill*, associated with the taste of hot chocolate and with the whole web of my fancies at that particular time, this mist . . . came to *infuse* all my thoughts of that moment. . . . The hill might expose its gray rump to the sun's rays.[3] (SK 2.79 / P 2.380; emphasis added)

107

The mist, as is hoped, arrives just at the right moment (to put it as Mme Verdurin might), allowing, by means of synesthesia, the (close-up) incorporation of the distant view of the hill. The form of this hill, which is obviously rounded, is personified this time by reference to another part of the body, a part that serves in the playing out of transsexualization through the intermediary of Charlus. The mist brings the hill closer and makes it inaccessible at the same time. But this inaccessibility is required in order that the personification in the female form be possible.

The swelling clouds of *Contre Sainte-Beuve* are helpful in the incorporation of the "madeleine," but their help is metaphoric in this instance. The magic potion, the hot chocolate, only intervenes by association. But we know how vital the metaphor is for Proust. Thus it enables the narrator to "soak up" the hill, including its form. We are more than justified by this passage to use the term "figuration" for the result of the vision, at once distant and, metaphorically close-up, of the hill-breast that becomes a rump or a bum.

Here we are as close as one gets to success. Thus we are a long way away from simple appropriation by penetration, such as that which seems to satisfy Bergotte. Incidentally, the latter's mode of appropriation is also slightly contaminated by the Proustian rejection of penetration and is, therefore, lightened somewhat: "Pleasure that is but a little buried in the flesh is useful to literary work" (SK 3.181 / P 3.688). Far from penetrating the flesh, the focalizing subject is himself penetrated, but not by a hard object, rather by a potion, mist, or smell.

The rounded form, as soon as it is associated with the breasts, the belly, and the buttocks of the maternal body, is prohibited from any type of penetration, as was indicated in the scene of solitary pleasure. Let us recall the poor kitchen maid at Combray whose belly had at all cost—at the cost of an artistic intermediary—to be detached from her body prematurely. The fact that the word "basket" signifies the woman's rear in French slang is but one more reason to cut the connection linking this rounded form to the girl's body that is carrying it. This detachable basket, which motivates the association with the image of Charity that is otherwise so unclear, this doubly flattened belly, in a fresco and as a fresco, thus has no logical continuation. Once the pregnancy is at term, Tante Léonie dismisses its importance, and no more is said of either the girl or her inevitable child. In fact, nothing more is said of pregnancy, except metaphorically, or "in the hollow" of the text, in reference to Charlus.

The description is significant and functions here almost as a declaration of principle. This is not only the case because homosexuality in *Sodome et Gomorrhe I* is discussed in terms of a philosophy of fertility. Charlus is later presented as a mother who is hollow, that is, capable of incorporating all that matters in a question of taste: "and everything between painting and cooking" (SK 3.220 / P 3.713). This hollow gives a masculine value to the valve on the scallop-shell that made the "richly sensual" madeleine religious. This masculine value is to be extended to the small shells (*valves*) of color in Hubert Robert's fountain. Charlus as hollowed-out mother, whose fertility is to be a serious worry for the narrator, is revealed in his essence by means of the metaphor of pregnancy.

The "rounded" figuration is the object of a tenacious problematic of penetration as physical integration. At no point does it intervene without one version or another of its contrary: the hollow, on the one hand, or the detached piece, on the other. To put this more simply, it is never without the flat form, which represents the counterparts to "roundness" in the various figures of the *valve*, the ground, the incorporable liquid, the ray, the trace, the line, and the black trees. These figures are represented as fleetingly indistinct or destructively solid. The breast and the image compete around the figure of "roundness," and between them the focalizer insinuates himself, or finds himself trapped, thus becoming himself a problem. It remains for us to see the extent of this problem.

Marcel's suspicions about Albertine, which generate the jealousy that consumes him, thereby also generating the novel, do not begin at the moment of the famous scene at the little casino in Incarville. Marcel himself prefaces the narration of this scene with this metanarrative remark that motivates the short proleptic narration: "It was not on that evening, however, that my cruel mistrust began to take solid form. No, to reveal it here and now, although the incident did not occur until some weeks later, it arose out of a remark made by Cottard" (SK 2.823 / P 3.190). Why is it necessary that the narrator be accompanied and assisted in his quest by another man in this crucial scene that introduces the principal focus of the Albertine novel; and further, why is it necessary that this man be both a doctor and nearsighted?

But this remark, like so many others of its nature, is disappointing and deceptive. On the one hand, all the earlier narrative of the tyranny exercised over Albertine is motivated uniquely by a jealousy that is already in germination. The metanarrative remark about the order of the narration, that is, about the following description's status as prolepsis, is purely rhetorical, designed to underline the importance of this short narration of the "dance breast to breast" as a generative scene. A similar anachrony foregrounds its counterpart, the likewise voyeuristic scene in which Marcel spies on the encounter between Charlus and Jupien. On the other hand, insofar as this scene has a generative effect, it is not solely from Doctor Cottard's remark that Marcel's "narratogenous" jealousy develops. In fact, the jealousy is slow to form, and this slowness is figured by the strange blindness the narrator exhibits when he asks the very woman with whom Albertine "betrays" herself at the casino to guard over his prisoner. Blindness is inherent to discovery, which, by definition, is partial and uncertain.

Here we have, then, the development of a poetics of indirect perception, which is fundamentally important for Proustian visuality. Marcel, having declined the invitation to the casino from the little band of young girls, finds himself nonetheless obliged to go there accompanied by Doctor Cottard, whom he encounters by chance following the breakdown of the tramway. Such is, then, the implausible staging of the scene, which is constructed according to the model of picaresque adventures and resonates with that genre.

The young apprentice and the wise doctor settle themselves comfortably as spectators. The scene does not concern them except as a visual spectacle. The status of spectator is, therefore, a defining principal of the scene, like an initial division of narrative labor between the sexes. After the men have settled down as spectators, the genesis of the novel to come—*La prisonnière*—is established in three successive stages: the sound of laughter, the spectacle of the dance, then the sound of laughter once again. Marcel's earlier plan, to go to the Verdurins' home, at first alone and then with Cottard, is abandoned the moment he hears Albertine laugh. Hearing her laughter inspires in him "an irresistible desire" to stay with her (SK 2.823 / P 3.191).

The fact is that Albertine's laughter is a powerful operator, full of crucial elements:

> And this laughter at once evoked the flesh-pink, fragrant surfaces against
> which it seemed to have just brushed and of which it seemed to carry
> with it, pungent, sensual and revealing as the scent of geraniums, a few al-
> most tangible, irritating and secret particles. (SK 2.823 / P 3.191)

III

An example of the "necessity" of Proustian metaphors, this passage exposes better its multiple meanings if, rather than taking it to be a Baudelaire-like reworking of synesthetic correspondences, of which there certainly remains an echo, it is read in the contrary manner, that is, as literally as possible. My point is that the Proustian metaphor is necessary because it is always and above all else literal.

The "surfaces," which introduce colors the vital function of which is obvious, not only imprison, they are also instruments of flattening. "Brushing against" the surfaces has the same olfactory result as the breaking of the branches in the solitary pleasure: pungent, *therefore* sensual. "Revealing" is to be taken more literally than any of the other words, since it indicates that the laughter is a detective-type detail and is "photographic." Belonging to the semantic domain of visuality, this word introduces into the evocation of hearing the properly visual vision—the mental image—that is its result. The scent, on the other hand, is an essence capable of carrying over from the long-distant perception to the close-up vision that which sight alone, incapable of surmounting this epistemological gulf, is unable to capture. It loses its essentially immaterial character immediately to become the "bearer," thus the material ground, for the particles-details that together constitute the substance of jealousy. Tangible, they carry weight; irritating, they have an effect; and secret, they introduce the lack of knowledge, the epistemological deficiency, that is as essential to jealousy as its counterpart, knowledge.

The "detailing" of the laughter does not only inscribe the latter in the narration of the discovery that is soon to be made. It also already provides the details of the elements of this discovery, thereby reinforcing the Proustian suspense, which is always anticipated by the characteristic method of unraveling it. The narrator, having heard this laughter, is still happy, but to his misfortune, he wishes to inform Cottard of this happiness. The latter is not interested in happiness. He is interested only in his "professional point of view as a doctor" and all that this point of view enables him to reveal of his own person's synecdochic knowledge and value. The medicine of the period, with its clichés about sexuality and particularly about homosexuality, which it to all extents and purposes invented, makes itself heard through his mouth and seen through his eyes.[1]

But on this particular evening in Incarville, as if by chance, his eyes, those epistemological instruments which in medical practice mediate between the "general laws" and the individual "case," are singularly deficient because the learned doctor has forgotten his glasses. Necessary in the way that the metaphor is necessary, this forgetting combines with medical knowledge to constitute the epistemological particularity that generates the jealousy: the deficient sight that introduces the "secret" is conjoined with the "professional point of view" that brings the general laws to bear. Cottard fixes his warning first of all at the level of a misguided education. This casino, he says, is a particularly dangerous place for young daughters: "I should certainly never let mine come here." The prudent father continues, "Are they pretty, at least? I can't make out their features" (SK 2.823 / P 3.191). The "they" here refers not to his own daughters, but to women the medical specialist does not know, and this "they" is also the object of Marcel's desire, which immediately becomes much less confident.

The focalization brought into play here is particularly necessary: the knowledge is precise but it is derived from another source; the view is pointed but it is indirect. "There now look," says Cottard, who was unable to make out whether they were pretty or not:

> I've left my glasses behind and *I can't see very well*, but they are *certainly* at the climax of their arousal. It's not sufficiently known that women derive most excitement from their breasts. And theirs, *as you see*, are touching completely. (SK 2.824 / P 3.191)

The doctor's epistemological competence is quite astonishing, since even though he cannot see their features, he is nonetheless able to diagnose their internal states. The "certainly" functions as the epistemological cog that turns the perception into knowledge. "It is not sufficiently known" prepares the medical cliché, which can only be introduced because the doctor is present. The narration, thus, needs his "remark," the bearing of which has already been announced. But on another level, the level at which the visual prosthesis is lacking, this "it is not sufficiently known" also implies the verdict that makes the kindling of jealousy possible: where jealousy is concerned, one never knows sufficiently.

Formed from the combination of medical knowledge, which is the discourse of another, with deficient sight, which needs indirect language to sharpen its definition in order to constitute itself as knowledge, the ground on which this scene is built establishes the *lack* of knowledge with insistence, thereby preparing its well-known outcome. The narrator continues, "I do not know whether they heard or guessed Cottard's observation, but they slightly detached themselves while continuing to waltz." What they detach here is obviously their breasts. It should be noted that this arousal is defined precisely as a result of the breasts touching "completely." This can only mean that, taken literally, the climax of pleasure is defined as a flattening.

While the "cruel mistrust" is said to have been kindled by a remark—language-based—made by Cottard, the transformation that this remark creates in the hero's perception is connected to the laughter, the essence of which already contained all the important elements. The slight detaching of the breasts is also to be taken literally. Proustian breasts, like the bellies, have a tendency to be detachable. This detaching is not in any way reassuring here, since it is explained by something altogether more worrisome: the repetition of the "same deep and penetrating laugh":

> But the turmoil it roused in me this time was a painful one; Albertine appeared to be conveying by it, to be making Andrée share, some secret and voluptuous thrill. It rang out like the first or the last strains of some unknown festivities. (SK 2.824 / P 3.191)

It is hard to see why this laughter, which had previously the effect of inspiring the desire to stay close by Albertine, now is said to be *only* cruel. This suggests that the cruelty had already been present in the very effect of its voluptuousness. The difference is that now something else is added that eliminates the voluptuous pleasure but which is expressed nonetheless in similar terms: thrill, festivities, voluptuous, secret, unknown. That the difference between the first laugh and the second does not depend on these elements, which are, however, the "official" attributes of jealousy, is revealed in their repetition from one laugh to the next. Rather, this difference is situated equally in the sensual and the sensory register. In the first laugh there were flowers, scents, and particles with predicates that were so delicately necessary. In the second laugh all this has disappeared to be replaced by auditory perception. Marcel appropriated the first laughter; in the second the sensations that he mentions are attributed to Andrée. The "unknown festivities" are unknown to Marcel. The subtlety of the first description of the laughter is replaced by penetration and depth, that is, the auditory murmur inspired by the doctor's discourse. Perception is troubled by others' knowledge.

Why is it necessary for the jealousy to establish itself that there be this whole apparatus of complex collective perception that operates once again by means of a superimposition of mediations? The sight of the breasts is situated epistemologically in an uncertain zone between the distant vision of the swelling hillsides and the close-up vision of the detached belly. The narrator recognizes the limits of his perception in terms that are now familiar to us: "a phenomenon as seen by me, of course, from my side of the glass which was by no means transparent, and without my having any means of determining what reality there was on the other side" (SK 2.827 / P 3.194). This lack of seeing lays the foundations for the lack of knowledge that turns the jealousy into epistemology and the breasts into a site of otherness.

It is for these reasons that the scene of the dance is presented as ethnographic. Specific, specialized efforts in "fieldwork" attempt to compensate as much as possible for the inherently problematical status of this discourse. It is a collective investigation that is supposed to be dialogic, but which is sanctioned by official knowledge.[2] The matter at stake here is doubly impossible knowledge: internal knowledge of the other and particular interpretative knowledge that is mediated by general theoretical knowledge. Translated into Proustian terms, and in response to Lévi-Strauss, who characterized ethnography as "the view from afar," this double impossibility figures the gulf that separates distant vision and close-up vision.

The knowledge in question is defined by its status as generality and externality. The ethnographic master, the one who "knows," is only able to produce an external effect because he does not see well. For, as Marcel thinks much later, it was not because of his own presence at the casino, but because of Cottard that Albertine "had detached her breasts from Andrée's" (SK 3.51 / P 3.566). This is, indeed, only a weak effect, but without Cottard's assistance, the hero, who is even more blind than the doctor without his glasses, would have seen nothing. This is enough to reveal the mediated character of sight.

115

The "ethnographic" situation is characterized, then, both by a fundamental need to be two, a collaboration that enables the transmission of knowledge, and by an equally fundamental need for blindness. The two men settle themselves into the position of voyeur, and from then on they have no need to participate in the scene itself. The young girls dance together because they lack "male partners," but the men make no attempt to join them. Thus they are able together to construct a knowledge that is sufficient to enclose the ethnographic object. Albertine is taken prisoner in the same way that the peoples studied by ethnographers were colonized. But their position as observers proves radically insufficient for full understanding, which is the declared objective. This type of inter-male collaboration has been progressively theorized, beginning with Freud and passing through Claude Lévi-Strauss, René Girard, and Eve Kosofsky Sedgwick, ending in the latter's works with the concept of homosociality.[3]

The narrator says he is afflicted with a poison the effect of which begins only after a certain time (SK 2.825 / P 3.193). He leaves with Cottard, *absorbed in conversation*—like the man who fails to see the belly of a pregnant woman, a metaphor for Charlus's homosexuality—as if to mark more clearly the deficient nature of his knowledge. He thinks back to the master's remarks a little later, and

> As though it were possible for an invisible link to join an organ to the images of one's memory, the image of Albertine pressing her breasts against Andrée's brought a terrible pain to my heart. (SK 2.904 / P 3.268)

What we have here is an image, and this in a double sense: it is this visual image of the flattening of the breasts that establishes itself within the narrator's body, where, either by the intermediary of words, or by the equally auditory one of laughter, it is to have its long-term destructive effect. This effect depends upon the fundamentally unknowable character of the thing that was seen but only badly seen.

The flattened breasts remain the important image of the woman who is other, therefore, unknowable and, therefore, desirable. They are the objects of the flattened exploration, of the "pressing together." Both desire and jealousy become, by means of the breasts, enterprises in knowledge, the preferred method for the attainment of which is the flat-

116

tening out of its objects. One example will be sufficient to show this. A little later, while taking the train for Balbec with Albertine, the narrator is visually fascinated by the wet mackintosh that clings to the young girl's body like a supple suit of armor:

> And, looking at Albertine's mackintosh, . . . which, *close-fitting*, malleable and gray, seemed at that moment not so much intended to protect her clothes from the rain as to have been soaked by it and to be *clinging to her body* as though to *take the imprint* of her form for a sculptor, I tore off that tunic which *jealously enwrapped* a longed-for breast. (SK 2.894 / P 3.258)[4]

What we see at work here is the figure of "pressing together," the paradigm for which has been established in the "dance breast to breast." This pressing together, I suggest, constitutes the essence of the Proustian subject's epistemo-erotic enterprise, in which words such as "enwrapped" and "jealously" figure the integration of this enterprise into the visual-tactile dimension. This "pressing together" or "close-fitting-ness" is a result that can never be reached, but which nevertheless constitutes the Proustian subject's temptation, his desire and his permanent objective. The image and its ground are the embodiments of this result. The breasts that press against one another are the figuration of it.

If Charlus does not actually have breasts, he nonetheless possesses a rounded form, the equivalent of the kitchen maid's detachable belly. He quickly becomes a "powerful monster" that "navigates his way towards us with his enormous body," the weight of this body being constantly underlined. At other moments the ironic and homophobic descriptions of Charlus reveal an element of Proustian "truth": "He waddled along with his swaying paunch and almost symbolic behind" (SK 2.890 / P 3.254).[5]

The ethnographic scene of the dance of the breasts echoes, both in terms of its difference from and its similarity to, the other scene of voyeurism, during which Marcel discovers Charlus's homosexuality, and in which the rounded form is embodied in the latter's "big bum," which remains out of sight. The ethnographic idea even intervenes explicitly here, at precisely that moment when the association with the dance is also made almost explicit. As was the case for the observation of the dance, the position of the subject invested with sight undergoes an elaborate, improbable, and intertextually specified preparation. Trying to justify his eccentric and imprudent choice of the particular means of exercising his voyeurism, the narrator gives three reasons (SK 2.630 / P 3.10).[6]

The first is his impatience, which naturally foretells his implication in the scene. The second is his memory of another act of voyeurism. While at Montjouvain he spied lengthily on Vinteuil's daughter and he saw that before Mlle Vinteuil and her girlfriend made love, the latter tried to profane the father's photograph by spitting on it. The young narrator takes this act to be the essence of sadism, a sadism that, because of this primary scene, is to be essentially visual for him. But the narrator, who does not seem to feel the slightest guilt for either his voyeurism or his impatience, seems to have more difficulty in admitting the third justification for his risky and improbable choice. He even uses the words "unconsciously decisive" to assert its validity. This reason is an interest in voyages of discovery and exploration. Saint-Loup has been influential in creating this interest, which no doubt makes it less puerile than it seems, as he says himself. The aim of this interest, which is only derivative but is nonetheless not without importance, is to contradict, "to follow—and see controverted," Robert's knowledge (SK 2.630 / P 3.10).

The ethnographic character of this scene is of crucial importance to an evaluation of its place in the whole of the work and particularly in its relation to *Sodome et Gomorrhe II*, which critics have tended to consider separately. The problems it poses for a theorization of Proustian homosexuality have provoked a certain confusion among critics: it has been deemed sentimental and reductive.[7] But this scene can also be taken as a self-reflexive ethnographic exploration, that is to say, as a revelation not of Charlus, but of Marcel. It functions, thus, through the intermediary of bringing one person "out of the closet" in order that the other be drawn *into* the closet, in a quite literal sense. Read in this way, the meaning and tone of the scene change completely.

The voyeurism here is more complex, more theatrical, and, I believe, more important for the interpretation of the scene as a whole than has generally been recognized. The voyeuristic situation immediately establishes the scene as a spectacle.[8] The narrative that the narrator gives of this scene is detailed and saturated with events designed to produce suspense, thus showing that he is freer of the fairly elementary status he still had at Incarville. This is, indeed, a voyage of discovery, for which the narrator has first of all left the "comfortable" position he describes as "marvellous" and which "commands the hilly slopes." This descriptive detail underlines the abandon of the elevated position in the house at Combray from which he saw the swelling hillsides. In place of this favored but childlike position, he chooses the staircase. But this position in the staircase, both intermediary and provisional, presents many a danger.

On repeated occasions verbs of action introduce abrupt changes, and these changes constitute the frame for the account of the journey: "I went down to the ground-floor window," "I drew quickly aside in order not to be seen," "I again recoiled in order not to be seen" (SK 2.624 / P 3.4). Later, as if it were a parody of Julien ascending to Madame de Rénal's chambers in *Le rouge et le noir*, he ends up "stealthily" hoisting himself "up my ladder" (SK 2.631 / P 3.11). But before he makes this risky ascent, he first runs another absolutely unnecessary risk, for which he gives the three reasons already mentioned.

The risk is undergone because he chooses to avoid an itinerary that he has described in length, introducing it as just a trifling thing: "In order to get to it, I merely had to . . . " (SK 2.629 / P 3.9). Contrary to what this introductory phrase seems to suggest, as if it were intended to lead in the wrong direction, this itinerary, which is rejected because it lacks a risk element and because of the association with Montjouvain and his impatience, is extraordinarily complicated:

> In order to get to it, I merely had to go up to our flat, pass through the kitchen, go down by some service stairs to the cellars, *make my way through them across the breadth of the courtyard above*, and on arriving at the place in the basement . . . , climb the flight of steps which led to the interior of the shop. (SK 2.629 / P 3.9)

The alternative route that he takes is recounted in these few words: "Keeping close to the walls, I edged my way round the courtyard in the open."

At the explicit level the difference is both clear and straightforward: security versus danger of discovery. The narrative rhythm, the length of the first description, and the succinctness of the second, suggests a supplementary issue at stake, which can be seen immediately if we take the text literally. Indeed, although the interior itinerary is safe, it is slow and requires the negotiation of steps and stairs: it is a journey of penetration, which the narrator sums up as "the way through the cellar." By contrast, the outside route, which is said to be dangerous, is defined as being "in the open." Next to the dangers of the labyrinth recounted by Phedre to Hippolyte, those run by Julien Sorel seem quite insipid.

This attraction to the dangerous route, which the narrator proclaims to be both childlike and unconscious, characteristics we should take seriously, lies precisely in that which makes it dangerous: visibility. The narrator-explorer makes a point all through this scene of his position, not *in* the field of vision, but *as* this field of vision. He keeps close to the wall, flattening himself like a fully exposed image that is unseen precisely because it is an image. He loses his consistency as a person, as an autonomous body, to flatten himself against the thing seen. He does not open the fanlight[9] through which he watches and he does not tell us what he sees. Such is, then, the nature of this otherwise dangerous journey of exploration, the climax of which consists in Marcel pressing himself against a small window. The matter at stake is not the discovery of a secret, which had been guessed long before, that is, the external fact of Charlus's homosexuality, but rather the veritable revelation of this homosexuality. The important thing is that Marcel has visual access to it, that it is an image, which does away with the dangers of penetration that are presented as less formidable ("I merely had to . . . ") and, therefore, as less heroic.

The voyeur is alone. The vision acts neither as a poison that pains the heart, nor as a time bomb. And, most important—which explains the differences between the two scenes—the object of his voyeurism is not dear to him. This does not mean to say that he is not implicated in it. But it is Charlus, the object of vision, who, without knowing himself to be heard, expresses his desire for the voyeur even while he insults him.

This desire is situated in the present tense of the narrative, which complicates the voyeur's complicity and his fear of punishment, trouble, and implication:

At the present moment my head has been turned by a strange little fellow, an intelligent little cit who shows with regard to myself a prodigious want of civility. He has absolutely no idea of the prodigious personage that I am, and of the microscopic animalcule that he figures in comparison. But what does it matter, the little donkey may bray his head off before my august bishop's mantle. (SK 2.634 / P 3.14)

The last word provokes Jupien's utter incomprehension, which enables Charlus to begin a list of absurdities. This is of little note. And the narrator, poet of the detail, is no doubt not bothered by the "microscopic" or by the verb "to figure." The Baron's language never ceases to surprise, and we are left speechless at the repeated occurrence of the word "prodigious." But the patent absurdity of the last sentence quoted does not detract totally from the worrying character of this evocation of a "little" object of desire, expressed in the present tense and which is said to "bray"—as if he had already been caught in a blatant act of voyeurism.

The situation makes it quite clear that, far from being a simple scene of revelation by means of which this theatrically complicated voyeurism is invented, this scene is also "ethnographic." This is the case because it poses the problem of the epistemological subject's implication in the enterprise, and this implication leads to blindness. Ethnography as a situation of desire for knowledge of the other, which is essentially problematic, can be read as an implicit metaphor for what Sedgwick calls the "epistemology of the closet." Indeed, the apprentice ethnographer presses himself against the wall of the shop/closet in order to be part of, or to be in on, the revelation.

Sedgwick (*Epistemology of the Closet*, 235), who had already signaled the deficiencies of the translation of "soulever le coeur" as "to stir the heart," also points out another translation error that is very revealing as far as the "closet" is concerned. This mistake does away with the "rounded" nature of Charlus's body as an object of desire. Jupien's remark, "Vous en avez un gros pétard!" ("What a big bum you have!"), has been translated in a way that keeps the affectionately teasing tone but without reference to the form: "Aren't you naughty!" (SK 2.632 / P 3.12). This translation is, in our context, doubly mystifying, for it denies Jupien his temporary function as ethnographic professor and it pushes Charlus back into the "closet" from which Marcel had so carefully pulled him.

121

Here "flatness" fully assumes its double meaning. Flattening out the "big bum" by removing the concrete and specifically homosexual reference to the body, the translation flattens the body, the very roundness of which the text puts into sharp relief! Thus it flattens the specificity of the so-called discourse of "bad taste," and it flattens sexuality by reducing it to sentimentality.

The manner in which the epistemological investigation is carried out, that is, as we have seen, by pressing up against the wall, is significant for the apprenticeship of the narrator-voyeur. The rivalry at play in the apprentice's perception is not this time a rivalry between hearing and seeing, but rather between long-distant and close-up vision. These two visions are embodied respectively in the fat Baron, who is fixed in the distance, and the bumblebee, which is enlarged by the imaginary association. These are, so to speak, two figurations of roundness.

The elaborate parallel between the mimed actions of the homosexual couple and the failed perception of the "botanist" has been extensively commented upon by critics.[10] Our shameless voyeur has posted himself at the best-situated place for a quite implausible length of time in order to witness the fertilization of a rare orchid by a bumblebee, the appearance of which he expects for less than rational reasons. All these fine details combine to stage a vaudeville in which the narrator executes a dance designed to remain invisible to its object, but which associates the narrator with this object by means of its figuration. This dance certainly makes the narrator most visible to his reader. The scene spawns its own double: the scene of the watching meshes with that of the very revealing mime. But in the long discussion about hermaphroditism and self-fertilization, which oscillates between the rule and the exception—poles that are subsequently reversed when the exception becomes the rule that corrects the original rule, turning that which is initially called vice into the supreme law of nature (SK 2.626 / P 3.5)—the element almost overlooked is the "detail" of the partition.

122   There is, so one says, an impenetrable barrier between the sexes, and the famous bumblebee must help overcome this barrier. Between the voyeur and the primal scene below him there is also a barrier that is kept carefully in place—Marcel does not open the fanlight. But the fact that this fanlight remains closed does not prevent Marcel from participating

in the scene, since he does this by "pressing" himself against it, by becoming one with the image as he superimposes himself upon it. Moreover, taken literally, as it should be, the fanlight is less a hole or a small window, that is, an instrument of seeing, than a word that more specifically introduces a question, thus making it an instrument of knowing. The word in the French text is *vasistas*, which is formed from the German "Was ist das?" and refers to the question "What is it?" that the porter asks through the small window in the door. It is, thus, an epistemological instrument that encourages the combining of understanding with perception in order to produce knowledge, which can, in the last analysis, do without sight. Sight has resigned: at the very moment when Charlus and Jupien go into the house, Charlus "humming like a great bumble-bee," Marcel, who is "engrossed," loses sight of the real bumblebee that has just flown into the courtyard.

This scene is, of course, much longer than that of the dance at Incarville. Moreover, it does not involve a dance as such. The favored figuration here is the pose: mime, tableaux, a slow-motion film that contributes to the shocking effect by means of its successive pauses. In symmetry with the "dance breast to breast," this scene is also introduced by an anachrony, not proleptic this time, but analeptic. Although *La recherche* usually has no regard for "chrono-logics," in both these cases the temporal deviations are underlined. In the episode of the dance at Incarville the narrator announces that the scene in fact happened a few weeks later. In the case of the second scene, at the moment it happens the narrator contents himself with arousing the reader's curiosity by declaring that he has made an important discovery (SK 2.595 / P 2.861). He puts in place a very sophisticated decor that is somewhat fastidiously "artistic" with multiple references to painters, paintings, and towns that are overdetermined by pictorial and dream-related allusions. Delft, Haarlem, and Venice are evoked over a page and a half. This evocation is called upon to justify visually the narrative extravagance of his keeping watch when all he is waiting for is the Guermantes' return. The watch **123** began in the morning and is continued throughout the afternoon. At the beginning of *Sodome et Gomorrhe I*, when the scene is finally taken up again, the fastidious preparation of this scene is carefully brought back to our attention.

Given that he is sensitive to the depth of vision, the voyeur has some difficulty positioning himself. He says, "I rather missed my Alpine eyrie." This regret is compensated by the vision, which he describes without ambiguity as well and truly distant, of the footmen who are "converted by distance into minute figures in a picture, . . . behind the large, transparent flakes of mica which stood out so pleasingly upon its ruddy bastions" (SK 2.623 / P 3.4). This distant vision does not seem to have any other function than to contrast with the close-up vision, with the contemplation, of the botanist: "I was peering through the shutters of the staircase window at the Duchess's little tree and at the precious plant, exposed in the courtyard with that assertiveness with which mothers 'bring out' their marriageable offspring, and asking myself whether the unlikely insect would come" (SK 2.623 / P 3.4).

The metaphor of marriage, which is made necessary by the double context that it announces, heralds the imminent arrival of the bumblebee, whose function is to make this marriage happen. But the conscientious botanist fails to see it. After his patient and improbable wait of several hours, he is paralyzed by the shock of what he sees. This trauma means that he is incapable of applying the correct vision at the correct moment. The reconciliation of (visual) space with (narrative) time has failed.

The missed bumblebee nonetheless has an absolutely crucial function in this long episode of voyeurism. Like a magnifying glass, watching for the bumblebee adapts the voyeur's eye to close-up vision. It is the pretext given for the kindling of a desire to spy, and it not only imposes a tense stillness on the voyeur, it is also transformed into a double of the voyeur's experience in the following parenthetical remark:

> I decided not to let myself be disturbed again for fear of missing, should the miracle be fated to occur, the arrival, almost beyond the possibility of hope (across so many obstacles of distance, of adverse risks, of dangers), of the insect sent from so far away as ambassador to the virgin who had been waiting for so long. (SK 2.624 / P 3.4)

124

Finally, the bumblebee, the agent of fertilization linked to Charlus first ironically and then, in a surreptitious way, iconically, is also, because it is also a detail, a rounded version of the butterfly.

The scene is also accompanied by a running commentary, which underlines its theatrical character: "I was equally unaware that he was capable of improvising his part in this sort of dumb show which . . . seemed to have been long and carefully rehearsed" (SK 2.627 / P 3.7). This commentary specifies the very "color" or the nuance of this theatricality. Contrary to the "dance breast to breast," which had a wise and tragic air to it, this scene is said to be "not positively comic; it was stamped with a strangeness, or if you will, a naturalness, the beauty of which steadily increased" (SK 2.627 / P 3.7). This difference in tone would seem to be serious, given the relation of the two scenes to homosexuality.

It is during the dance that the rounded form asserts its crucial importance. Jupien "stuck out his behind" and he "contemplated with a look of wonderment the plump form of the aging Baron" (SK 2.626 / P 3.6). This plump form obviously constitutes the "supplementary" motivation for the comparison between Charlus and a pregnant woman. This comparison belongs to a series of comparisons and metaphors borrowed from the domain of nature, the function of which is to turn "vice" into nature. The repeated metaphor of the series is clearly the orchid and the bumblebee. Moreover, the explicit relation between Charlus and the bumblebee, that rounded detail so central to the whole operation, is not limited to their function in the fertilization process. The fact is that the fertilization takes place, so to speak, "on the flat," without any penetration being necessary, since the flower goes half the way and the bee has only to brush against it.[11]

The interweaving of the various gazes, that of the voyeur, the biologist, and the geologist, the latter first rejected (SK 2.623 / P 3.3) then recuperated during the voyage of discovery, brings to mind another scene. The overlapping of gazes that gives rise to the double image of the fertilization of the orchid, which is a visual failure, and the regulatory self-fertilization of Charlus's plumpness, recalls the scene of the Commices Agricoles in Madame Bovary, which is, then, a third literary intertext. The reader will remember that in this scene, which is permeated with Flaubertian idiocy, the illicit eroticism is inscribed by means of another parallel with animals. The view from on high—the one that Marcel gives up because he knows all too well its vertiginous effect—is

125

combined with a close-up view, which is that of the two actors (Emma and Rodolphe), who are in the middle of a lover's conversation. In Flaubert, the element that makes the liaison is the voice, which provides a background murmur, a meaningless accompaniment. In Proust, sound takes the form of a cry, and this functions as a worrying and criminal reminder of Albertine's laugh. But the importance of this sound has been displaced. It loses its importance as a sign to become an accompaniment, less revealing than comparative and serving to draw out the centrality of vision all the more.

My point is that the essence of this meeting is visual, that is, flat and capable of being flattened to the point of becoming natural, as the narrator says with such insistence. Natural fertilization is, then, the application of one on the other, the "pressing together" of two identical leaves. This is also the Saussurian metaphor for the sign.

The fact that this "dumb show" stands as a model, as a perfectly regulated silent visualization, could well be linked to the prominence of the Baron's plumpness. The Baron gives full rein to his nasty personality in a series of statements that exhibit vulgarity, sadism, and snobbery. All these aspects that make him extravagant, distinctly mad, and even dangerous,[12] disappear during the silent spectacle, which is "long rehearsed" to the point of perfection. Here nature intervenes to regulate and then to correct the excesses of its own laws, "as the thyroid gland regulates our tendency to plumpness" (SK 2.625 / P 3.5).

Plumpness and the belly of a pregnant woman, bumblebees and hillsides: the rounded form never ceases to haunt the text at precisely those moments when it poses the problem of visual access to the desired body. This is an acute problem, since it isolates the subject who is incapable of giving "shape and solidity," of participating in a capacity other than that of apprentice-doctor or of traveler who is kept at a distance, refusing to penetrate into the labyrinth. The disgust that threatened the "young man" who was sent off to the Louvre to cure himself by contemplating flat paintings also presides over the repeated figuration of objects and bodies, the rounded form of which frustrates their "flatness." In order to finish off with this spellbinding but dangerous and insufficient form, let us compare two other contemplations, the first of a quite disgusting object, and the second of a quite fragmented body.

The first contemplation has no subject; it is a comparison. Its object is soundless vision, or the suppression of sound. The narrator, temporarily sent to await Saint-Loup in his room, where he would like to remain, imagines that he has fallen ill in order that he may cosset himself in this cosy environment, which is closed off to all noise. To describe the delicious silence that encloses him as a body would enclose him, he evokes a deaf person who

> Cannot even heat a pan of milk next to himself without having to keep an eye open to watch, on the tilted lid, for the white hyperborean reflection, like that of a coming snowstorm, which is the premonitory sign it is wise to obey by cutting off (as the Lord bade the waves be still) the electric current; for already the fitfully swelling egg of the boiling milk is reaching its climax in a series of oblique upward undulations, puffs out and fills a few drooping sails that had been puckered by the cream, sending a nacreous spinnaker bellying out in the hurricane, until the cutting off of the current, if the electric storm is exorcised in time, will make them all twirl around on themselves and scatter like magnolia petals. But should the sick man not have been quick enough in taking the necessary precautions, presently, his drowned books and watch [would] scarcely emerge from the milky tidal wave. (SK 2.74 / P 2.376)

Several of the registers studied thus far intervene in this comparison, figuring its dynamic by means of their combination. To sum up these registers, rather rapidly perhaps, there is the sea-mother, the fixed image, violence, and disgust. We also recognize the terms involved in the figuration of the still life, which was so delicately invoked as a homeopathic cure for disgust. These are the terms that create an oscillation between a threatening violence (the hurricane) and a smooth, nacreous surface. The superimposed comparisons of snow, sea, storm, the violence of the elements, and the silence of the storm in the pan, combine to transform the (maternal) milk into the breast in a series of upward undulations that bring to mind the upward pressure of nausea.[13] The risk of being thrown off course, of twirling around, is averted by the petals of the magnolias, which are both large and mottled. The role of the description here is that of a mise en abyme of the dangers that the narrator attempts to avert through his ambivalence toward the rounded form and the sensuality it reflects, which leads him to fix on "flatness."[14]

Snow and sea, hurricane and Poe-like Maelstrom, a capsizing that only the Lord can prevent: these large-scale elements alternate with the minuscule ones of the small pan of milk. But these two different scales are the objects of fierce competition from the rounded and the flat form, the first being uncontrollable movement (the bellied-up spinnaker and the fitfully swelling egg) and the second being fixed (the hyperborean reflection and the magnolia petals). This contemplation is itself a detail that is subjected to the magnifying glass, and, as such, it installs the entire mechanism that causes whoever runs the risk of being swallowed up to feel quite ill.

Referring to the whole of *La recherche* as well as to its narrator, whom he does not distinguish from it, Gilles Deleuze suggests the image of a spider's web, which, for him, is characterized by its sensitivity despite an absence of organs. In this context, let me take from this image the reference to a web, a surface that is stretched out flat, as is writing, in the form of "the snail's trail." This image undoubtedly provokes mild disgust, and this is precisely one of the reasons why we have to come back to it.[15] When Emma Bovary vomits up the black milk of poison as she dies in an ultimate protest against the banning of her right to write that had weighed upon her life as a woman (Schor), her gesture prefigures the disgust that the Proustian young man feels before the breast, which is only acceptable if it is turned away, that is, if it is flattened or detached. Between a sensuality focused on the breast[16] and disgust, the difference is as radical as it is subtle. It hangs only by a thread as delicate as the snail's trail.

This is, in fact, one of the important meanings of the second contemplation I announced, the frequently interpreted passage in which the narrator contemplates Albertine's nudity, or rather, to use visual terms, he contemplates Albertine as a "nude." This passage has been most commonly invoked as a site of the Proustian narrator's sexual ambivalence:

> I would open her chemise. Her two little uplifted breasts were so rounded that they seemed not so much to be an integral part of her body as to have ripened there like fruit; and her belly (concealing the place where a man is disfigured as though by an iron clamp left sticking in a statue that has been taken down from its niche) was closed, at the junction of her

thighs, by two valves with a curve as languid, as reposeful, as cloistral as that of the horizon after the sun has set. (SK 3.74 / P 3.587)

This passage has given rise to speculations on the sexual and even personal identity of the "model" for the description. It has been made into a proof of the narrator's homosexuality, with the detachable breasts held up as evidence (Rivers, *Proust and the Art of Love*, 212). That these breasts are revealing I am quite prepared to agree, but revealing of what exactly? According to Rivers they betray the male body, and it would appear that this fits with the pictorial tradition in which, for lack of available female bodies, male bodies were used as models and imaginary breasts were added on afterward. Other critics[17] object to the principle of this argument and the specific terms in which it is elaborated. They criticize how precisely this scene has been made into an exception to the rules of common sense, to say nothing of the critical code of conduct. If one wants to understand how Proust figures sexuality, it is better to look at what he writes than at what others say he hides. This passage gathers together both the necessary ingredients and the traces of effort, in other words, all that is required to achieve the impossible, which Antoine Compagnon sums up as "to be both Racine and his princess in one person" (*Proust entre deux siècles*, 107).

As Kaja Silverman quite correctly says, the usual "mastectomizing" interpretation—the one that emphasizes the detachable nature of the breasts—raises insurmountable problems. It is enough to mention only three. First, this interpretation implies both a misogynist and a homophobic definition of homosexuality.[18] Second, it suggests a thematic of castration that is singularly absent, not only from this fragment, but from the whole of *La recherche*, with one exception that we will look at later. A third problem is the neglect of how the breasts, as they are described here, appeal distinctly to the mouth.[19] Added to this, of course, is the neglect, or the negative appreciation—as a last resort—of the strongly visual nature of the description. In a novel in which voluptuous pleasure is so deeply synesthetic, this is a sad neglect.

Many critics have been interested in this description because it is, indeed, sufficiently exceptional within the work to be taken as emblematic of the whole. We immediately expect it to say something essential

129

about Proustian sexuality, not as far as Proust's biography is concerned, but rather on a figurative level: it reveals the phantasmic mechanism of the novel. And, as previously, it is by taking it literally—as a surface rather than a hidden place—that we can see its significant aspects. Given that it is a "nude," that is, a visual description of a naked body, it is useless to ignore the eroticism of the description. Rather than calling it a description of Albertine naked, let us give this excerpt the title of "Albertine as nude" and regard the entire passage as the description of this image.

Indeed, as Kaja Silverman emphasizes, the eroticism of this description of breasts lies principally in the appeal to the mouth. Like an interdiscursive crossroads of many traditions, the metaphor of fruit suggests Combray-like freshness, health—the other's heath, given that Marcel's health is fragile—the innocence of the garden of Eden before the Fall, and, last, cannibalistic temptation. Far from introducing an artificially artistic character, the description underlines the fact that the breasts, although detachable or, at least, not integrated into the body, are nonetheless the product of a natural process—of a maturation. The fragmentation of the body is not, therefore, presented as being against nature. In terms of my purpose here, it is also important that the breasts appear both detachable and edible, not only because they seem to have matured like fruit, but also because of their spherical form, which makes them a perfect model of roundness.

In my view, we would do well to resist the temptation to import into this passage that cliché of psychoanalytic inspiration according to which "the breast" signifies "the maternal" in general. Even penned by an author whose hero is such a mamma's boy, these breasts have nothing maternal about them.[20] If we consider it important to evaluate this passage in terms of sexual identity, we have to take into account the fact that this characterization of the breasts is followed by that of the penis. It is impossible to ignore how this penis is inscribed in the text. It is distinctly negative, although there is no figuration of emasculation. Also impossible to ignore is how the penis is actively eliminated. It is aesthetically and, let us say, erotically eliminated, but it is not excised. Moreover, the penis, which is said to be disfiguring, has nothing phallic about it; quite the contrary, in fact.

If the narrator finds the belly without the iron clamp to be "repose-ful," this is also because the horizon is located at the very place of its closure. Nothing from beyond that horizon will come and disturb him. For once the long-distant vision is briefly in harmony with close-up vision. Neither disfigured by an iron clamp (that intruder from within), nor offering an opening that would have to be penetrated, this body is presented as a surface to be brushed against. This passage does not, in fact, describe the object of desire as sexually specific, be it a man or a woman. Albertine could easily be said to be neither one. The description, however, describes a very specific desire. The eroticism that is established here is of a rigorously oral order, and, as a result, the gender of the object of desire is not defined in the traditional terms of sexual difference.

Given what we have just established, what do we now see in this passage? A picture, representing a body that is orally enticing. The attributes of this body are not integrated into it, but this is not the result of a—violent—detaching, since it is the "fruit" of a natural process. The oral attraction to the surface combined with, and reinforced by, an oral thematic suggests a vision most closely related to that of the painting by Caravaggio (Fig. 10).[21] Proust does not, of course, give a faithful description of this particular image. The painting in question is not even of a nude. But the image nonetheless corresponds term by term, aspect by aspect, to that other image that the Proustian ekphrasis places before our eyes.

The oral quality of this figure's undeniable attraction depends in the first place on the fruits that the young man holds in front of his body, as if they were a substitute for it. But this quality also makes the face and the skin glow with that combination of light and the clean, smooth, and slightly soft surface that characterizes Caravaggio's sensuously appealing portraits of young men. In other words, it is by the painted surface, the painted matter, that sensuality is to be distinguished from other affective aspects of the representations in Caravaggio's art. The face is also 131 made erotic at the level of the performative force of the young man's gaze, with its particularly striking combination of submission and provocation, signified by the half-open mouth and eyes.

Although the lower half of the body, evoked in Proust's text, is ab-

Fig. 10. Caravaggio, *Young Man with Basket of Fruit*, 1593. Rome, Galleria Borghese.

sent from this picture, the sexual ambiguity that is foregrounded in the ekphrasis is represented by Caravaggio's use of means that are properly pictorial. This sexual ambiguity is to be found in the head, the face, and the hair, but also in the way the head is carried, and in the ever so slightly visible lines and surfaces of the body, particularly in the shoulder, the neck, the join between them, and the curve of the arm that tenderly grasps the basket of fruit. Suggesting both that it is taking possession and that it holds a precious gift, this last gesture also represents that other ambiguity, a thousand times more subtle, between "I" and the "other," an identification and a projection, which characterizes the homosexuality figured here and which goes far beyond the pertinence of the question whether Albertine was "in reality" a man or a woman.

However, this still leaves the question of how to reconcile the idea of the nude, foregrounded in Proust's passage, with this painting, the sensuality of which is established by other means. In order to understand how this virtual conflict is resolved, we must read the passage according to the genre that we have said defines this description, that is, the nude, bearing in mind the traditions and problems implied by this genre. In the second half of the nineteenth century the academy of the nude had run into problems of two sorts, both of which were stylistic. On the one hand, the nude had to be distinguished clearly from pornography. The cost of this distinction was the avoidance of any suggestion of movement, which led to rigidity. On the other hand, in order to prevent any discomfort for the spectator confronted with sexual difference—a difference that was the "source" of this genre but also its fragility—the nude had traditionally evolved in the direction of softness, of the censoring of any marks. It was this delicacy that Manet so scandalously rejected in his Olympia, and we all know what this cost him. The art historian T. J. Clark presents the problem of the nude and sums it up in these terms: "If [the naked body] is chaste, and it sometimes is, it is rigid and inanimate with its own decorum; and if it engages with sexuality, it does so in ways which verge on violence or burlesque" (*Painting of Modern Life*, 128). Proust was particularly sensitive to Manet's position, which, as Compagnon says, resembles his own (*Proust entre deux siècles*, 27). He is especially interested in the Olympia. He has the Duchesse of Guermantes say that with the passage of time there remains nothing of the scandal that surrounded the painting, which "looks just like an Ingres!" (SK 2.542 / P 2.812), a comparison that reflects the narrator's own opinion (SK 2.436 / P 2.713).[22] Something that looks just like an Ingres can be nothing other than the smooth, closed, harmless nude. Ingres's style is opposed to that of Manet: he produced images without a trace of that autonomous sexual subjectivity which is exactly what made Manet's painting scandalous (Clark, *Painting of Modern Life*, 133–35). By means of body hair, of openings in the body, and of a frank, active gaze,

133

Manet portrayed an autonomous subjectivity that could not fail to introduce an irreducible sexual difference.

Let us read the second half of the ekphrasis in the light of this problematic: "And her belly (concealing the place where a man is disfigured as though by an iron clamp left sticking in a statue that has been taken down from its niche) was closed, at the junction of her thighs, by two valves with a curve as languid, as reposeful, as cloistral as that of the horizon after the sun has set." By putting the male and female body in aesthetic competition, this description accomplishes two extremely difficult things at once. First, without denigration of any sort—the description is completely positive—it reactivates the nude, not by suggestively evoking in the manner of Manet what had been missing from the nude in the aftermath of Ingres, but rather by declaring that sexual difference is visible, but not important. Only the gaze and the desiring body to which this gaze belongs are important. Furthermore, taking as its basis this reactivation of the nude, which is, shall we say, made erotic without being sexually defined, the description finds a place for the male body. This is what, in a quite different context, Compagnon's pertinent analysis reveals when he writes: "Paradoxically, the fascination for Lesbos and Gomorrha is evidence of a will to give man back to literature: like a mirror that man holds up to himself, Gomorrha opens up his body to poetry" (*Proust entre deux siècles*, 107). And Compagnon continues by saying that rather than it being a question of "hermaphrodites," the novel reveals "fleeting metamorphoses and endless fluctuations that make every body both a masculine and a feminine body" (107).

It is important to state quite clearly that the point of my analysis is not to deny the homosexuality of the novel, but on the contrary to make the homosexuality more specific. This homosexuality is defined, however, not in terms of the object, and even less in terms of a supposed biographical model, but rather in terms of the focalizing subject and its engagement in the process of desire: the subject that sees this body.[23] It is by taking the lead from the focalizer that we can interpret not just the fact of homosexuality, but also its implied form.

In order to grasp this specificity, which, it seems to me is of major importance for *La recherche*, I turn to the typology that Silverman elaborated. She analyzes the description in question within the framework of a brilliant psychoanalytic theorization of male homosexuality, for which she distinguishes three models within Freud's work. First, there is "The Negative Oedipus Complex" when the subject identifies with the mother and desires the father. Second, there is the "Greek" model in which the subject identifies with the father and desires what he once was himself. And last, there is the so-called "Leonardo" model in which the subject can alternate between an identification with the mother and desire what he once was and an identification with what he once was and a desire for the mother (*Male Subjectivity*, 363–71). It is in relation to this last model that Silverman situates the description of Albertine (as nude).

As a result of the breasts' appeal to the mouth, the desire in question can be integrated perfectly into the "Leonardo" model of homosexuality. In this model, by virtue of the fundamentally oral character of the desire, the subject's position oscillates between an identification with the mother and an identification with what he was himself at an earlier stage. Inversely, this model finds the object of desire to be variable according to the same possibilities: the object is identified with the mother or with the earlier self that is loved "as if by the mother." This homosexuality is neither misogynist, since it is not based on the elimination of the female presence from the triangle of relations, nor castrating, since it declares the phallus to be unimportant.

In fact, this description does not represent Albertine's body in terms of a lack. While it may seem possible to remove the breasts from it, we are left, then, with quite empty hands, since the narrator has already taken it upon himself to reject the penis. The latter is not only described as "disfiguring"—a term that indicates its effect without making any pronouncement on its nature or its "aesthetic"—but also as something left over, as something that has no relevance for the desire that is created. Silverman says as much in these very terms: "The dominant trope of sexual differentiation here is not 'lack' but 'superfluity' or 'term in excess'" (379).[24] In this description, where the visual dimension is vital, the penis is superfluous because it reveals the inside (of the statue) that we are not supposed to see. We now know to what extent the Proustian text prefers the surface, at the expense of depth. Moreover, this inside proves that the statue is not autonomous, that it cannot stand alone. The penis is disfiguring because it creates a dependency.

135

We shall have more to say later about the erotic organ that is activated by this description. It offers a solution to the dilemma that the narrator poses for himself, with the only reservation that it is phantasmic: an imaginary organ that is superior to lips and which makes the ideal, olfactory, gustatory, and tactile kiss possible. As an extension, or rather as a less satisfying but more real substitute for this fantasy organ, there is sight, a final resort with which the narrator has to make do. The gaze is, thus, the instrument of an epistemological process, and we are now in a position to evaluate its inherently erotic aspect. These two aspects are inseparable in Proust: the desiring subject desires above all else to know, and knowledge is a function of desire. The flat surface, the partition against which the subject can press himself, the skin of the face against which he can lay his own skin, the body on which he can gaze—in all these cases this surface is the site of the Proustian subject's double desire.

Elsewhere, the erotic gaze is a source of danger:

> Her intense and silky gaze fastened itself, glued itself to the passer-by, so prehensile, so corrosive, that you felt that, as it drew back, it must tear away the skin. (SK 3.146 / P 3.656)

The point is that this gaze is directed toward another. The desired object locates her own desire elsewhere. The gaze then becomes an instrument of torture. Ontological otherness hurts, which is the reason for this work's massive subjectification. In the description of Albertine as nude, however, the gaze is applied by Marcel, who uses it to smooth out the body, to flatten it, and to remove anything that might give it volume, that might hide something underneath. The problem is that "beneath any carnal attraction that goes at all deep, there is the permanent possibility of danger" (SK 3.76 / P 3.589).

chapter nine

The Father Revised and Corrected

...had buried itself in the stone, which had softly
given way beneath it.

—Proust, *A la recherche du temps perdu* (SK 1.66 /
   P 1.61)

Alone in this room that is not yet a room but a
cavern of wild beasts, invested on all sides by the
implacable strangers whose privacy he has dis-
turbed, he desires to die.

—Samuel Beckett, *Proust*

The description of "Albertine as nude" and the interpretation of
it that was suggested in the previous chapter seem to have dispensed
with all need for a clearly "male" position in the work and in the desires
that animate it. Now we must look more closely at what this description of Albertine as nude rejects or ignores, and at what cost.

The first description of the father, who is so rarely described in *La recherche*, has already been evoked. This scene is in many senses "primal,"
the ramifications of which, for the value of the visual thematic in the
work, we have yet to explore. Of course, at this moment of supreme
gratification of desire, Marcel, whose eyes are no doubt dilated from
tension, perceives a visual image. It is significant that this image, far from
representing an immediate perception, functions instead as much by superimposition of representations as by a multiplication of paternal bene-
factors. But above all else it is significant that this image offers no clear
position of identification.

The father is both invested with absolute power and seen in drag; he
is sickly and represented in the white robes of an angel, with a scarf of
soft colors. Moreover, once this metaphoric machine has been put into
gear, he is replaced by Swann, who was responsible for giving Marcel
the image that serves as the point of comparison, an image that is, in
fact, an engraving based on a work that doesn't exist. The problematic
of indirect and pluralized visual representation becomes quite mis-

137

guided here, but for the moment it is enough to notice that the father, who has just been declared omnipotent, is now "taken" or "drawn away" by the image, and, thus, no longer seems very powerful. This drawing away is not to be ignored.

Not only is the paternal image unable to offer a position of identification to the child, other fragments also depict images that are tempting but ultimately unsatisfactory because they are too directly linked to the missing identification. We might think of the image of liquid power: the fountain, the torrent, and even, after the loss of power, the drip. Indeed, situated within the province of the masculine are also the scratch, the line, the asparagus, the tongue (or language),[1] and even, charged with at least as perverse an ambiguity, the valve. These objects form a network, but this network fails to establish an inhabitable position for the subject who desires at once to be, to be a desiring subject, and to define his being by his desire to write.

Again, the rhetorical status of the detail and its internal difference come up here: on the one hand the detail may be a detachable fragment and an inserted detail; on the other, it may be an overformed dis-figure and an unformed patch. Until now I have let these two figures float on the surface of the text and, more important, on the surface of what they represent. But is the detail not also the navel of the dream, that umbilical cord which Freud said is joined to the inner depths of meaning, which is most often of a sexual order? Thus, the question of penetration and the uneasiness it provokes is posed at the level of the poetics of *La recherche* itself, making possible the claim that Proust casts a taboo on depth that is equivalent to the taboo imposed on the name, which is fetishized at the same time that it is made taboo. In terms of the poetics of the detail, the basis for this taboo can be translated into the following question: how is it possible that, as Schor has said, the detail is inflated with meaning, while it is also just the residue of observation? The roundness is flattened out, the hollow is filled in, and the residues of observation are spread out.

Following directly from this taboo placed on depth, the visual detail becomes the site of an experiment into the possibility of finding viable alternatives to penetration. As is to be expected, this experiment leads to one form or another of "flatness," although the latter one, as an alternative to penetration, is now weighed down with the combined heaviness of sexuality and writing, those two Proustian enterprises that are henceforth inseparable.

The bedtime drama at Combray is a "primal scene" in that it reveals to the young boy relations between his parents that he does not understand. It is also a primary scene in its importance for the generating of the narrator's obsessions, and he mentions it at that crucial moment, which also generates the following novel, of the "desolation at sunrise," with which *Sodome et Gomorrhe II* ends and *La prisonnière* begins. It is also primary in that it inaugurates the work as a whole, and is the incipit for the first apogaeic moment, thus marking the first of the great dramatic movements of the writing, which stems from the scene with the fountain. And last, this scene is the primordial scene of seeing, that is, of the visual epistemology that is to lead the way to voyeurism.

The scene is, indeed, to be *looked at*, as the narrator makes quite clear. Let us, then, take another look at it:

> He was still in front of us, a tall figure in his white nightdress, crowned with the pink and violet cashmere scarf which he used to wrap around his head since he had begun to suffer from neuralgia, gesturing like Abraham in the engraving after Benozzo Gozzoli which M. Swann had given me, telling Sarah that she turn away towards [*se départir du côté de*] Isaac.[2] (SK 1.39 / P 1.36)

In fact, the obsessively visual character of the scene is clearer than its object. This passage is not particularly detailed as far as description goes. The only details mentioned are the scarf and the gesture. But the insistence on the visual is articulated through the mediated relation between the subject and the object of the vision. This relation between the subject who sees, that is, the focalizer, and the object seen, has been inverted. Whereas it is normally the case that the seeing subject is able to subject the fixed object to a detailed examination and an appropriation—that is the "essence" of the fixed image—here the subject is clearly described as transfixed, and it is the object that has the power to break the charm. Indeed, it is this possible break that makes the dumbfounded child tremble. The relation of identification, therefore, is also at risk of being inverted. Now, identification is one of the crucial matters at stake

139

in visuality, in which the compulsion to look tends to encourage an even greater absorption of the subject in the object because it operates at an unconscious level.[3]

Silverman suggests a distinction between two radically opposed forms of identification. The first, which is the more common, is a form of incorporation in which the subject makes the object of sight his own. The incorporation may remain figurative, in which case the other is transformed into an icon of the self. The otherness of the other is neutralized in a movement of appropriation that is based on an egocentric mimesis of the desire that is the real object of identification. This identification is called an idiopathic identification. The second form of identification is quite the contrary: it is a sort of going out of the self in which the subject exteriorizes himself in order to become "like" the other to the point of forgetting his own self. This is heteropathic identification, and it is a form of alienation. Freud writes of this identification: "The shadow of the object thus fell upon the Self, which could hence be judged by one particular instance like an object."[4] It is not the other that gets lost, but the subject himself who becomes an icon of the other. Proust opens his monumental work with a recognition of this risky identification: "It seemed to me that I myself was the subject of my book" (SK 1.3 / P 1.3).

So, while it is true that one of the first visual images of *La recherche* involves a classic opposition of a subject and an object, it strikes me as significant that these positions seem at first sight to have been inverted. If there is an identification here, it must be of a less classic type, that is, of a heteropathic type. Does this mean that Marcel "becomes" (like) his father?

In order to answer this question we also have to take into account the features of the object in the image itself, features that are like the conditions of possibility of such an identification. For the image, as such, is the product of the focalizer who is clearly paralyzed by the vision. The father-seen-as-image possesses characteristics that feminize him, such as his clothes (the "nightdress") and, in particular, the scarf, which sums up this feminizing effect: it is pink and violet. The reader will remember the extent to which pink is the color that marks the sexually alluring woman in Proust: Odette, the lady in pink, is the emblematic example of this aspect of the work.[5] The father is not only dressed in clothes that feminize him, he is also attributed features that undermine his power, such as his sickliness and his tendency to pamper himself. In his maternal attitude to himself, the father seems to become the mother. But his authority is summed up in the other descriptive visual detail, which functions by means of a superimposition of pictorial "layers." I am referring to his gesture.

We can well imagine how the type of image in question, the engraving after Gozzoli, with all the orientalism of the father's accoutrements, could create a link between the image of the powerful father and the image of the almost ridiculous father.[6] But that which is *seen* by the focalizing subject, the terrified, dumbfounded child, is already the product of a "secondary" elaboration that has passed through several stages of identificatory adaptation. This secondariness, the insistence on the mediated nature of the image as such, is the gesture's most "descriptive" predicate.

First, we must pay heed to the fact that the paternal position is doubly "diluted." It is mixed with feminine features and it is displaced. It switches from the real and present father to the absent and social father, Swann, whose role is twofold in this scene: he is the cause of the child's grief, since he is the reason for the refusal of the bedtime kiss; but he is also the giver of the gift—the engraving—that makes the kiss possible in the end. First an obstacle to the satisfaction of a desire, then the provider of the means of satisfaction, Swann is a combination of the two fathers, who makes access to the mother easier by representing a desire for her with which the child can identify heteropathically. The image serves as a base for such an identification, but it is not itself the object of this identification.

On the one hand, we have, then, the engraving by Gozzoli, which does not exist; on the other, there is the biblical story itself, which has been subjected to considerable distortion. According to Guillerm, it is not Sarah but Hagar who is sent off on the order of Abraham. Moreover, this is not an act of clemency, but an attempted murder. This interpretation has the advantage of drawing attention to the distortion and the ambivalence that it both suggests and censors. However, it is limited in its usefulness. First, it makes no comment on the pastiche of

141

biblical language, in which "to turn away towards" (*se départir du coté de*) has a specific sense of a sexual order. And second, the critic has only taken into account half of the intertext. It is Sarah who chases Hagar away, at first because of her jealousy of the other woman, and later because of her jealousy of Hagar's son.[7]

The biblical expression in question appears in a biblical text other than the one referred to here at an anecdotal level. That text is Judges 4, which tells the story of the murder of the enemy chief Sisera by Jael, the woman who had tempted Sisera into her tent with an invitation couched in these very terms. This is such a strong interdiscursive allusion that it acts like a foreign body in the discourse attributed to the child. The other limitation of Guillerm's interpretation is that it simplifies the intertext of the gesture itself. In one of these intertexts, Genesis 16, the positions are reversed: it is Sarah, who is sterile, who "orders" Abraham "to turn away towards" (*se départir du côté de*) Hagar, who is her slave. She gives him this advice in order that Hagar conceive the child that Abraham needs to "multiply" and, thus, to exercise the patriarchal role, which he is the first to fill, becoming thereby the model for all future patriarchs. This child also legitimizes Sarah's status within this patriarchal order, since she will literally own the child. Therefore, as a speech act, the verdict is a sexual order, the subject of which is the woman and the object the man, who has only to carry out the order, even though it is traditionally assumed that he took this upon himself quite happily. Biblical criticism has not sufficiently appreciated the extent to which Abraham, who is, so to speak, the father of patriarchy, is himself a weak character, lacking even in virility and, thus, containing within himself a questioning of his role. It is this aspect of his character that makes him so apt for the representation of the father in a work in which the paternal position is deeply problematic.[8]

In the other intertext, Genesis 21, which is interwoven with the first in this Proustian collage, it is indeed Abraham who sends off, not Sarah, but Hagar and her son, who has become superfluous and threatening since the birth of Isaac. Once again, this happens on Sarah's order, or at least on her insistence. In this case, however, there is no allusion to "turning away towards," in the sense that the biblical expression in question implies. The sexual charge has completely disappeared.

this visual image, which is described in detail and is central to the bedtime drama, which in turn generates an entire facet of the novel, the father's ambivalence bears the trace of that other, less easily admitted ambivalence, which is that of the mother.

This much we can say of the composition, of the meaning of the gesture. But there is more. We know that Rembrandt alone does not exhaust the affective charges related to visual art in Proust. For the coloring of the father's portrait we have to turn to Chardin. At the end of the essay "Chardin and Rembrandt," when Proust resigns himself after all to say a few words about Rembrandt, he does this through the intermediary of a reflection that is at first a bit too faithful to the other painter's self-portrait. He says of this self-portrait that:

> The negligence in Chardin's half-dressed state, his head already covered with a night-cap, made him look like an old woman.

The effect of this dress quickly takes on a more alarming aspect:

> For every detail of this formidable, careless state of undress, fully armed for the night, seemed as much as a challenge to correctness to be an indication of taste. (*CSB* 377)

The visual language then becomes a paternal language when the old man, in his effeminate dress, engages in a ferocious battle with a "young man," who is the double of the hero of this piece:

> It often happens to a young man faced with an old man, in a way that never happens to him in the company of a young man, I mean to say that he does not understand clearly this language that is figured like an image, but is rapid, direct, and surprising, like a rejoinder, and that we call facial expressions. (*CSB* 378)

The visual language, which consists in the simple exhibition of the sight of the paternal face in all its ambiguity, leaves the young man with the uncertain message of a threat that is turned against him: "Either our youth has injured him in his weakness, or he is rising up in an impassioned, useless challenge that is painful to watch" (*CSB* 378).

It seems to me, then, to be quite appropriate that next to Rembrandt's drawings we take another look at this self-portrait in pastels (Fig. 6). We find once more the striking colors of the cashmere scarf

147

that the father has tied around his head, although here they are seen around the painter's neck, his head being otherwise adorned with white and blue ribbons tied elegantly in a bow. The colors of Proustian sexuality appear in sharp contrast with those of virginity. Moreover, we understand easily how this eye could have inspired the oedipal cry from the heart that was quoted above ("impassioned useless challenge that is painful to watch"). The old man's eye does indeed present that strange mixture of indulgent softness and derived authority, secondhand authority we might say, that we identified in the image of the father and which stymied the son who so desired to get out of himself.

The figure of the young man reminds us of the disgust from which his twin suffered before going to the Louvre to feast his eyes on paintings by Chardin. This disgust now seems all the more important, given what we know about the predominance of oral pleasure in Proust's libidinal economy. In fact, this disgust, which is linked to the end of meals, is also related to the bedtime drama, in a turning away that takes us back to Swann's way. It is only at the end of *Sodome et Gomorrhe*, at the moment of desolation at sunrise, which is another essential moment generated by the voyeurism at Montjouvain, that the narrator makes explicit the rivalry at play in the scene of the bedtime kiss. The rivalry that has crept into his relationship with Albertine is brought to bear on his childhood memory, and the bedtime drama is juxtaposed to his memories of Albertine, both of which the narrator describes as similarly hostile. We are not, then, surprised to find that in this otherwise astonishing evocation of childhood rivalry the remains of a meal appear before us like the traces of everyday life that provoked the young man's disgust and brought about the appearance of Chardin:

> It was Trieste . . . that exhaled that hostile, inexplicable atmosphere, like the atmosphere that used to float up to my bedroom at Combray, from the dining-room in which I could hear, talking and laughing with strangers amid the clatter of knives and forks, Mamma who would not be coming upstairs to say good-night to me. (SK 2.1158 / P 3.505)

And although, if we are to believe Combray, these strangers must include the person who gave the paternal image, that is, Swann, who is invoked in a metalepsis as a brother in jealousy ("like the atmosphere that, for Swann, had filled the houses to which Odette went at night in search of inconceivable joys"). There is definitely an ambiguity between the different positions here, but this ambiguity affects not only the sexual positions, but also the generational positions. All we can make out now are distant traces of the classic triangles. We are faced with an inextricable mixture of intertexts and inter-images, as well as of psychosexual positions, since the one implies the other.

Despite the distance that separates the youthful essay and the mature novel, this reflection enables us to see better where the primal visual image might be situated. What we have here is not so much the diegetic figure of Abraham, as the diegetic visual figure of anxious uncertainty before a father who leaves the mother to the son. But this gesture is not carried out without a certain aggressiveness, which is due to a weakness imagined, in a fearful projection, as the only possible explanation for the father's renunciation. It is not surprising, then, that the child remains dumbfounded, struck with paralysis: this is the cost of heteropathic identification, the cost of the weakness attributed to the father.

chapter ten **The Fountain of Ink**

Armed with this image of the weak father, let us return to the passage in *Contre Sainte-Beuve* about solitary pleasure in the little room that smelled of irises. We had abandoned this passage just at the moment when the son pushed the father from his place as a means of curing the disappointment with the flat breasts of the hills and clouds, which are nothing but mere insubstantial reflections in the subject's gaze. Once the sun has disappeared from between the breasts / swelling hillsides and the subject, he is able to address the source of his pleasure directly to the former, without the father / sun being interposed. This pleasure takes a most recognizable form, the terms of which are scattered throughout the novel:

> Finally an opalescent jet rose up in successive surges, like the moment when the fountain at Saint-Cloud arches forth—which we recognize, since the endless flow of water gives it an individuality that is outlined most graciously in its firm curve—in the portrait that Hubert Robert left of it, while only the crowd admiring it had . . . which create little pink, vermillion or black valves in the old master's painting. (*CSB* / G 69; gap in the manuscript)

There is nothing surprising in the fact that the moment of climax is figured in the form of a fountain. The "successive surges" are not in the least surprising either. We have already seen how we must appreciate the coloring of this figuration, which is subtly introduced in "opalescent" and which we can easily supplement with the "mottling" from the passage on reading. But we encounter something more troubling in the pictorial nature of the comparison invoked here. This comparison is necessary to express the individuality of the fountain, but consequently, it turns this individuality against itself.

What can the fountain's gracious outline bring to the "unknown and original pleasure that is not the substitute for another" (*CSB* / G 68)? Despite the fact that it should be opposed to it, this outline in fact reminds us of the *figuration* of the absent woman, as it appeared in the "secondary" masturbation that was rejected in favor of this masturbation ("solitary pleasures, which later only serve as a means of deluding ourselves as to the absence of a woman, of *figuring* to ourselves that she is with us" *CSB* / G 67). Derived "flatness" is insinuated into the "original," sought-after pleasure. Hardly has the father/sun been removed than the "old master" takes his place. It is the painted fountain, and not the one that the little boy produces, that possesses a particular individuality. Moreover, it is the painted fountain that has an "endless flow."

Through the painting, which the "crowd" has already tarnished, individuality is nonetheless saved to a certain extent by the outline with which it is figured. A substitute that is inevitably secondary, the figuration rejected at the beginning of the passage is recuperated at the end. This is one possible explanation, which has its own logic despite being only a hypothesis, for the fact that this generative scene reappears in the novel in the "lightened" form of "secondary," substitutive masturbation (Doubrovsky, *La place de la madeleine*, 28).

Between these two "versions" there is a degree of divergence and of similarity, both of which are significant. The swelling hillsides / maternal breasts have disappeared for the moment (SK 1.172 / P 1.156). And the fountain, that same "individual," as Proust would say, the one attributed to Hubert Robert, has also lost its place in the passage in *Combray*. This fountain, however, rises up again at the Princes de Guermantes's home where it soils a maternal figure (SK 2.681 / P 3.56). This resurrection should be taken literally, since *Contre Sainte-Beuve* mentioned the *portrait* left by Hubert Robert. A portrait is the image, the faithful visual representation, of a unique individual. It is only once we take quite seriously the necessity of individuality that we can see the enormity of the contradiction: full individuality can only be attained by the narrator with the help of two superimposed mediating layers. What should be inner essence is rendered through visible, external layers of paint. The reader will remember Bergotte's self-criticism at the moment of his death: his last books were too *dry*; in order to remedy this "a few layers of color" would have been necessary; hence the "preciousness" of the "patch" (SK 3.185 / P 3.692).

In opposition to the pictorial mediation in the previous passage, the fountain itself, not its portrait, is attributed to Hubert Robert in *Sodome et Gomorrhe*. That makes for one less mediating layer. Indeed, in the more elaborate text of *Contre Sainte-Beuve* the subject rejects the "figuration" of the absent woman in favor of an attempt to integrate himself with her through heteropathic identification. In *Combray*, on the other hand, the narrator tries quite openly to accomplish this substitution. But in both cases he fails.

First and foremost the novel retains the "voyage" from the pre-text of *Contre Sainte-Beuve*. This "voyage" here takes the form of an attempt to integrate the seeing subject with the thing seen, whereas previously it had been a dangerous, if not suicidal, exploration out of himself. Second, at the end of this voyage, the two texts both propose the sole element that can properly be said to participate in the figuration. This element is neither metaphoric nor figurative. It is the trace / writing on the flat leaf. From *Contre Saint-Beuve* to *Combray* the sense of this trace is less stable than its form. In *Contre Saint-Beuve*:

> I had left on the leaf only a silvery, natural trace, like the thread of gossamer or the trail of a snail. . . . [I]t was in the guise of this almost interminably extensible silvery thread, which I had to spin out of myself by going against the natural course of my life, that for a while I pictured the devil. (*CSB* / G 69–70)

152

In *Combray*:

> I explored, across the bounds of my own experience, an untrodden path which for all I knew was deadly—until the moment when a natural trail

like that left by a snail smeared the leaves of the flowering currant that drooped next to me. (SK 1.172 / P 1.156)

But the power of the trace remains: it is the power to leave a trace on a leaf in defiance of mortality. The snail's trail, with all it evokes of the volute form of the animal and of the mother-of-pearl, mottled color of its trail, having previously been identified with the devil, is now simply "natural." The diabolical opalescent liquid—which is black in a figurative sense—has become natural, a source of life: ink.

In order to evaluate *La recherche* in its relation to questions of visuality, the literary difference, if we can call it that, between the two narcissisms is more important than the theoretical difference. We have seen that substitution is clearly present in both texts. In the novel, this substitution is simply assumed more openly. There is good reason for this if we take into account the fact that primary narcissism consists above all in a lack of clarity, differentiation, and delineation.[1]

The concept of primary narcissism signifies the state of being before becoming a subject, the state of the subject who is not yet formed because it has not yet realized the limits of the self. We saw how the masturbating subject had difficulty in this situation with integrating himself with the thing seen, with insinuating himself in between the two swelling hillsides / breasts like the river/fountain. In *Combray*, however, the woman-substitute is no longer problematic. She does not place the subject's integrity in danger, since her absence enables the subject to define his own limits clearly. It is this possibility which allows him here, as before, to leave his "natural" trace, but here there is no "devilishness" implied. It is, thus, by giving up on the parental identification, from whatever side it offers itself to be *seen*, that the subject is able to write, that is, to spread out on the leaf that absolutely individual liquid which comes from within himself. Without a master, whether he be old or not, without breasts in which he could lose himself or it, the trace, which disintegrates in the effort at integration, is to be infinitely stretched-out, but natural, original, and individual. This trace is writing that is essentially both individual and, in Proust's case, masculine.

The father, who is, on the one hand, displaced—"Beat it"—and on the other, feminized, is also the object of a third secondary elaboration

153

by the subject. It seems to me that the description of the Guermantes' fountain, which recycles the climactic element in the passage on solitary pleasure, participates in this third intervention made by the subject on this site of a possible masculine identity. The description is long, and it is not possible to analyze it in detail.[2] But once again we find the narrative mechanism that characterizes descriptions with a heavy affective charge.

The reader will recognize the descriptions of the sea from *A l'ombre des jeunes filles en fleurs*, which are again introduced in this context:

> It could be seen from afar, slender, motionless, rigid, set apart in a clearing surrounded by fine trees, several of which were as old as itself, only the lighter fall of its pale and quivering plume stirring in the breeze. The eighteenth century had refined the elegance of its lines, but, by fixing the style of the jet, seemed to have arrested its life; at this distance one had the impression of art rather than the sensation of water. (SK 2.680 / P 3.56)

The frame and the distance are deadening. The quivering does not possess the color that could transform it into a butterfly. Like the sea during the first stay at Balbec, the view from afar produces a vision that is neither freed from its frame nor vivacious. Seen up close, however, the disappointment is of a different nature, since time is inscribed within the space that is outlined and "it was a constantly changing stream of water that, springing upwards and seeking to obey the architect's original orders, performed them to the letter only by seeming to infringe them." The fall is scattered, whereas "from a distance it had appeared to me inflexible, dense, unbroken in its continuity." It is clear that the "endless flow of water" that had fulfilled the individuality in the masturbatory writing has been reduced to a misleading impression that is visible from afar but which disintegrates into "exhausted drops" when seen up close.

Without doubt the jet of water lacks vitality. But once it is seen up close by the reader, that is to say, as a textual figuration, it actually takes on a very peculiar vitality: it becomes feminine. After the mention of the pitiful drops, a feminizing discourse begins to insinuate itself. The drops are described as "passing their sisters on the way up, and . . . floating before being drowned in the basin." This reminds us of the boiling milk that was discussed earlier. I dare to call this the feminized side of the fountain as opposed to its "masculine" side:

> They [the drops] teased with their hesitations, with their journey in the opposite direction, and blurred with their soft vapour the vertical tension of the shaft that bore aloft an oblong cloud composed of countless tiny drops. (SK 2.681 / P 3.56)

Indeed, the fountain, so "slender, motionless, rigid" when seen from afar, ends up completely soaking a lady who is madly but vainly in love with the Duke of Guermantes, as if the oblique reference to an erotic rivalry between man and woman could only lead the narrative toward a disaster. Moreover, and this would please the Freud of *Jokes and their Relation to the Unconscious*, the poor, drenched woman becomes an object of ridicule when an Imperial Highness reacts uproariously to the spectacle as if it were a choice moment of wit: "'Bravo, old girl!' he cried, clapping his hands as though at the theater" (SK 2.682 / P 3.57), and Charlus joins in the hilarity.[3]

The figure of the fountain in the fragment from *Contre Sainte-Beuve* is, thus, misleading. It is true that the fountain is obviously a perfectly acceptable metaphor for the event in question, that is, masturbation. But this acceptability could, in fact, be excessive and, consequently, risk being the object of an ironic reversal or, in other words, the object of an internal hostility and a flattening that are both specific to Proust.[4] The individuality that is applied to it only makes its contradictoriness stand out all the more. As a "portrait," a superimposition of images, it has no substance. From afar it has no life, up close it has no force. Its attack on the woman, whose "maternal" age is underlined tactlessly by the Imperial Highness, seems to happen almost out of spite, as if it were because of her hopeless infatuation. It does not offer an image of hetereopathic identification for the Proustian subject. But, in the same way that the young boy in the little room that smelt of irises in Combray makes the initial and initiatory jet of water rise up, he continues to try to identify an object of desire that corresponds to what he once was, according to the identifications outlined in the "Leonardo" model. But for the moment this object lacks "shape and solidity." He is only left with drops—of water, semen, ink, and tea.

From the point of view of this study, the experience provoked by the madeleine is above all else a struggle to find a place to anchor, to attach, this heteropathic identification that is without an object. It is this objectless identification that characterizes the first sensation in the madeleine experience: "This essence was not in me, it *was* me."[5] This struggle involves the difficulty implied by depth:

> I feel something start within me, something that leaves its resting-place and attempts to rise, something that has been dislodged like an anchor at a great depth. (SK 1.49 / P 1.45)

Once again it is important to take metaphors literally, especially those that refer interdiscursively to the key passages for masculine identification. The thing that wants to *rise up* is within the self, at a great *depth*, and this inner situation is characterized by a dislodging of the anchor.

While this thing remains in the depths, the hero can do nothing about it, since he cannot see it:

> Scarcely can I perceive the neutral reflection into which the elusive whirling medley of stirred-up colours is fused and I cannot distinguish its form. (SK 1.49 / P 1.45)

That the sight of the madeleine brings nothing to mind for him, that he has to incorporate the object in order to recognize it, these facts must not be seen as important only in terms of the question of incorporation. It is also significant that the object had no base. The image was linked to too many other images. It is within this framework of the need for a base that I would read the little colored shells (*valves*) in the fountain described in the passage on solitary pleasure.

Of course, the diegetic action of involuntary memory happens through an incorporation, and Doubrovsky is right to insist upon the "infusion," the "magic potion," that releases the sensation. But next to this obviously important aspect of involuntary memory lies the massively visual nature of its product: the images, the theatrical scenery, the "sheared-off section," the exclusively spatial piece that has been detached and which must have inflated itself with Time with the help of the base provided by the "tiny drop," strangely formulated in the singular, that bears "the immense edifice of memory." The magic potion is not only the missing maternal milk, the poisoned tea, and the child's urine; this base, as the novel specifies, is also a drop, like those that gave form to the figuration of writing.

The visual character of the produced memory is again indicated by a metaphor. In this case the metaphor describes enlargement through contact with water and it reduces what has just been so magnificently and magically evoked to the level of a visual trick. All that is left is an amusing encounter between water (of the fountain) and (a "leaf" of) paper: Proust calls it the Japanese game. This game is mentioned as if to underline the fact that the success of the Proustian enterprise has to pass through parental identification by interposed objects, but that this passage is not sufficient. At the moments when these identifications collapse into one another, when the subject incorporates everything by going out of himself, by becoming that other who should become him, the flat image offers an alternative or, at least, a ground on which he can temporarily lay down his fantasies. The Japanese game does not offer flat images in a literal sense, but they are totally flat in the figurative sense of being banal in comparison to the enormity of the memory to which they are likened. This is metaphoric flatness that is metonymically motivated.

A tiny drop can, then, serve as a ground for a part of this memory's immensity. We were already prepared to some extent for this by the description of the cat, which walked on the solid drops of water left in the oysters, like a Christ-Venus on water. This cat was the emblem of Proustian Chardinism that replied to Chardin's Proustian side. Under the magnifying glass of its infinite tension, the jet of water becomes the matter of writing. The drops, contained within the porcelain bowl, stretched out in the teaspoon of tea, are at least as pregnant in their role as objects-bases as the rounded, plump form of the breasts and the little cake. These drops are crucially important in this passage, which Doubrovsky has justifiably qualified as initial, initiating, central, archetypal, and also narratively unplaceable in that it is dispersed in innumerable fragments 157 (*La place de la madeleine*, 23).

It is at the level of drops, at the level of "the detail" if ever there was one, that the masculine specification of Proust's visual libidinal economy comes into play. These drops lend themselves to this particularly easily. They are the detailed elements, visible only up close, of the hard and forceful jet of water that was deadened by distance. They figure the fountain's trace without maintaining its "hardness." Let us not forget that, at the quite simply explicit level, the father, who is the official bearer of the water jet, is presented as being too "distant." In this framework, I contend that Proust is not attributing his generosity in the scene of the kiss to an understanding of his child; rather, he consents to this indulgence from indifference. The mother and the grandmother, both of whom are closer to the child, knew how great his suffering was, but "they loved me enough to be unwilling to spare me that suffering" (SK 1.40 / P 1.37). The father receives credit for affection: "For once he had grasped that I was unhappy and he said to my mother: 'Go and comfort him.'" There is an underlying regret in this reproach: if the father had loved the child enough, he would not have spoken about him in the third person, thereby keeping him at arm's length, separating himself from him narratively. He would have come himself to comfort the child in an exchange of positions between the first and second person.

It is also by slight indifference that the father allows his son to choose a career as a writer. He defines this career as a "pleasure" in a comment that combines his indifferent laissez-faire attitude with his concern for happiness: "Don't worry, the main thing is that a man should find pleasure in his work" (SK 1.519 / P 1.473). Once again his indulgence is expressed in the third person as if it were a passive gift, which has the effect of differentiating himself from his son. This problematic of distance as the ground for the Proustian subject's masculine identification is called upon at least once to figure concretely the problem of visible virility. The tears shed for the father-writer appear just after a quite different passage in which distance and its problems are figured in a spectacular way, so to speak, while also being represented as a spectacle. The passage itself follows closely on the description of reading as a mottled screen.

158 Marcel's reading, which is used to measure the strangeness of time, is interrupted by the cries of the gardener's daughter, and Marcel replaces reading with spectacle:

> Françoise and I should run too and not miss anything of the show.
> That was on the days when the cavalry from the local garrison passed

through Combray on their way to their manoeuvres, going as a rule by the Rue Sainte-Hildegarde. While our servants, sitting in a row on their chairs outside the garden railings, stared at the people of Combray taking their Sunday walk and were stared at in return, the gardener's daughter, through the gap between two distant houses in the Avenue de la Gare, had spied the glitter of their helmets. The servants had then hurried in with their chairs, for when the troopers paraded down the Rue Sainte-Hildegarde they filled it from side to side, and their jostling horses scraped against the walls of the houses, covering and submerging the pavements like banks which present too narrow a river-bed for the torrents of a flood. (SK 1.95 / P 1.87)

Such is the show of virility, from which Saint-Loup, the military hero who is also a spectacle of masculine beauty, is later to be detached.

The flood that ends this passage recalls the "torrent of activity" that appears just before it in the text. The spectacle of masculinity, of which the military parade is the prototype, is "played out" here, however, with a certain awkwardness in the tension between near and far. The synecdoche of the glitter of the helmets constitutes the visual essence of the masculine show. The first detail that gives rise to the synecdochic splendor is of a voyeuristic nature: the gaze has to weave its way through a narrow gap in order to cut out the object-detail. Hence, the distance is established by an effect of the gaze, which also establishes the glitter in the same movement. The detailing and the visual overflow go hand-in-hand here. Moreover, the spectacle makes the voyeuristic position necessary, as is seen in the opposition between watching the show and the servants' "normal" habit of watching, which is communicative and bilateral, and which is interrupted by the show.

The synecdochic helmets, which are details as well as visual fragments, receive further elaboration in *La recherche*. They are associated with wigs—that of the false marquise at the public convenience in the Champs Elysées and those of the old people in *Le temps retrouvé*—and they end up spreading out, as "flatly" as possible, the physical deterioration caused by time. This association makes the false marquise on the Champs Elysées a horrible figure in contrast—a literary *contraposto*—to the young, beautiful virility that is displayed in the show at Combray. The marquise who guards her lair, thus, also becomes the Python of the threshold,[6] proclaiming the impossibility of the two sexual positions that are offered as models to the young apprentice. In his rewriting of this sort of detail, Claude Simon has brilliantly demonstrated this liaison between the two themes, which are to lead to a sexual vacuum.[7]

The show continues to be characterized by a visual problematic. Hardly has the spectator got close than he is too close. The troopers fill the whole breadth of the road, making visual communication impossible. The horses scrape against the walls. The show has "covered" everything, and the result of this "covering" is the "excess" of close-up vision. This excess is figured as liquid: as a flood that overflows a too-narrow riverbed. Thus its base is insufficient. The spectacle, which is squeezed between the "too-distant" that necessitates the synecdoche and the "too-close" that imposes the metaphor of the flood, remains essentially invisible. This invisibility is a function of both space, which is imagined as too narrow, and time, which provides the frame of reflection in which this passage is situated. Despite the length of the passage (that is, of the text relative to the rarity of descriptive details), it clearly conveys the quickness of the (troopers') passage through the town.

The torrent of a flood is a recurrent figure in the work, and it represents the final, strong, and climactic figure of a passage. It remains as the reanimated and enlarged trace of the fountain, which was reduced to a few drips. On one occasion only in *La recherche* is this reduction of the fountain associated with a figure of castration. On the previous page the focalizing subject who witnesses the spectacular show is deep in his reading or in his dreaming. He is dreaming of travel and of love:

> And so, if I always imagined the woman I loved in the setting I most longed at the time to visit, if I wished that it were she who showed it to me, who opened to me the gates of an unknown world, it was not by the mere hazard of a simple association of thoughts; no, it was because my dreams of travel and of love were only moments—which I isolate artificially today as though I were *cutting sections* at different heights in a *jet of water*, iridescent but seemingly without flow or motion—in a single, unbending, irresistible outpouring of all the forces of my life. (SK 1.94 / P 1.86; emphasis added)

Once again, the final comparison seems to reinscribe exactly that which the principal sentence appeared to eliminate. In this dream, in which time and space are only reconciled with difficulty, we see the temporal version of the irreconcilability of close-up and distant vision. The beloved woman is surrounded by spatial images, which are extensions of the loved one but which also function as metonymies that provide a ground for the imagination. Time is represented on two levels, which are at once semantic and iconic. The separation of moments, which is said to be artificial and which is made to seem even violent in the idea of cutting sections, becomes tangible in the very separation that occurs within the sentence itself.

The object that is operated on—in the medical sense—is the jet of water, which is iridescent and, therefore, mottled. The motionless appearance makes an obvious reference to the hardness and the distant perception of Hubert Robert's fountain, which was presented as a paternal image that dissolved before our eyes into feminized drops. Here the jet of water is isolated by dashes and "operated on" by the instrument of dissection that is the reader/dreamer's analysis. The jet of water is opposed to an attribute that belongs to the narrator, and this opposition is marked by the separation created by the dash that closes the parenthesis. This attribute does not introduce the irreconcilability in question. In fact, in contrast to the jet of water, the outpouring does not labor under a contradiction between the hardness associated with distance and the dissolution caused by proximity. It is described rather as a single entity, identical to itself and unbending. In other words, it is unified, individual, and endowed with "shape and solidity."

The passage, thus, presents its image at both a figurative and, therefore, hidden level, and at an overdetermined and, therefore, explicit level. We have, then, a double image of both the castrating gesture, which is a hapax in the work, and the rivalry with the father, which appears in the terms that are central to masculine identity and its specific pleasures. If we take the term "unbending," it is clear that, despite the fixation on the feminine forms that we saw earlier, and despite the temptation to feminize the fountain's drops, the sought-after identity cannot be mis-   **161** taken. This identity, the individuality of which had been proclaimed in the fragment on solitary pleasure, is definitely situated within the province of the masculine, but without the identification with the father as a ground.

The "outpouring of all the forces of my life" suggests among other things that the subject is at a formative stage, that this moment is decisive, and that he is ready to go out of himself, to risk a heteropathic identification. But the object, without shape or solidity, still fails to provide a base. Here the subject gathers together his forces in order to face up to this lack. It is in his reading, that emblematic activity of identification, that the subject tries to solve this problem.

Indeed, a few pages later we rediscover the aquatic image in the context of the experience of reading in the bedroom. Let us read this passage once more, this time focusing on what it says of the intimate relation between poetics, the image, and the phantasmic:

> This dim coolness of my room was to the broad daylight of the street what the shadow is to the sunbeam, that is to say equally luminous, and presented to my imagination the entire spectacle of summer, which my senses, if I had been out walking, could have tasted and enjoyed only piecemeal; and so it was quite in harmony with my state of repose which . . . sustained, like a hand reposing motionless in a stream of running water, the shock and animation of a torrent of activity. (SK 1.90 / P 1.82)

The paradoxes of this passage are not limited to the use of metonymy, which is itself paradoxical in a passage that recommends the use of metaphor. But it is important not to underestimate the significance of this paradoxical poetics in its relation to the phantasmic, which interests us here. There are at least two other paradoxes related to the first one. The reader will notice the paradoxical way in which close-up vision, which is imposed by the fact of being shut in the room, allows for a vision of the totality, whereas distant vision, which would have been possible on a walk outside, leads to a piecemeal perception. The imagination resolves these contradictions and makes up for the limitations of the senses. The second paradox is contained in the hand that sustains the torrent in the final metaphor. This hand provides a base for identification.

The relation between the dim coolness and the sun is presented as if it were a mathematical equation, that is, by the relative terms of shadow and sunlight. This relation figures exactly the relation between the father and the son seen from the angle of pleasure. If the sun can be said to be the paternal symbol, then the place of happiness is necessarily in the shade. The sun is on the other side of the wall-screen. They are forever separated: the father is to always remain at a distance. The son, who competes with the father, reverses the terms of their rivalry. He chooses the shady side. It is not necessary to qualify this shade as maternal. The point is that he is trying to get out of that dichotomy. Outside in the sun, pleasure—orgasm—is all broken up. The attempt at heteropathic identification is interrupted for lack of an image that is fully visible when seen up close.

The narrator finds the ground he needs in his state of repose. This is not a state of relaxation, since it remains "unbending." In Proust, repose always refers to something other than relaxation. It is related to the suspension of contradictions and oppositions that he is working to unravel. The metaphor of the hand is most striking to us because of the force that is attributed to this one part of the body. While it is in repose the hand is motionless, and it is because of this repose that it is able to gather sufficient force to resist the shock. In this description of shock, animation, and the stream of water, we see clearly that the attempts to go out of the self have not ceased, since the torrent of water continues to flow. But they have found the necessary ground, which was missing previously, in the image of the hand or the stillness, which counters the immediacy of the water's chaotic activity. Here the repose, which is so important to the hero, which is fetishized to the point of becoming the commitment of his life, if not of his writing, takes on "shape and solidity." And this happens in relation neither to the father, nor to the mother, but rather to the self. It is hardly a new revelation to say that the Proustian libidinal economy is essentially narcissistic.

The drop is able by itself to harmonize all the different poles that Proust wants to keep united. The "few drops of lustral water," which remained in the hollows of the oyster shells "as in tiny holy water stoups of stone" (SK 1.929 / P 2.224), have a distinctly sacred tone to them. Even the images of Charlus, which are full of sarcasm after the "discovery," seem to benefit from the sacredness of drops when his tears are transformed, by a means of a reference to drops of sweat, into drops of blood ("as if a sob were more serious than a hemorrhage"; SK 2.986 / P 3.344). Drops are always charged with meaning, whether they are an initial part of a fountain, as in the "solitary pleasure," or whether they describe feminized dissolution, as in the scene at the home of the Prince de Guermantes. They may appear to be both foreign to the subject, as in the oyster shells, and in opposition to him in intermale rivalry, as in the dream of travel and of love; the point is that these drops are always the individual and unbending raw material of writing.

For a novel that is so largely dedicated to love from a male subject's point of view, there is a singular absence of penetration in *La recherche*. Marcel's favorite lover's position is to lie against Albertine, especially when she is asleep. The most explicit description of an erotic
scene does not go any further than the famous kiss. Marcel's utmost
pleasure comes from pressing his lips against Albertine's skin, breathing
in her breath, and contemplating her sleeping body: "I felt at such moments that I had possessed her more completely, like an unconscious
and unresisting object of dumb nature" (SK 3.67 / P 3.581). But the kiss
is not perfectly satisfying, and the sight of Albertine asleep is not sufficient either to calm Marcel's anxiety.

The reader encounters no movement, no desire, as the narrator puts
it, to descend into "the depths of her being" (SK 3.67 / P 3.581). The
word "penetration" does appear now and again, but it is often in a negative sense or else in a sense that has no sexual connotation or that does
not involve depth. For example, the discourse on lies speaks of "penetrating what one's interlocutor knows or guesses—but does not say—a
penetrating of the situation that, exceeding or falling short of his, makes
one now exaggerate, now underestimate, the involuntary desire to play
with fire and the will to escape unburnt" (SK 3.210 / P 3.719).

The Proustian subject's ambivalence about penetration can be seen
in two passages, both of which are well known but are not often read

in relation to each other. The first of these two passages describes the "public convenience" in the Champs Elysées and the second, appearing just after the famous "real" but disappointing kiss, evokes a phantasmic organ that makes the experience of the kiss more sensual. The two passages are united under the sign of the kiss, which is the matter at stake in both of them.

The public convenience is a closed space presided over by a false marquise, whose pastiche of high-society conversation makes her appear ridiculous. This passage has also been linked to Marcel's sexual initiation as a preparation for his entry into art.[1] I am only concerned with one aspect of this initiatory reading, which is made significant by the immediate context of the passage. The most important point is that the last word preceding this passage is "despair."

First, Marcel is a child playing under Françoise's watchful eye; then, Marcel is an adolescent who is both in love with Gilberte and in regular correspondence with her father, Swann, who is, thus, both his father-in-law and his substitute father. The discrepancy in age is clearly defined here. Our narrator, who scorns all chronology except when he wants to use it rhetorically, makes no bones of portraying a supervised child and an initiated adolescent one after the other in less than a quarter of an hour in diegetic time. In my presentation of the following reading, I would also like to demonstrate briefly the relevance of the biblical subtext, which appears as a *ground*, understood in the precise sense used so far.

Marcel, who was intimidated before visiting the public convenience, comes back sufficiently revived and strengthened to be able to "take" Gilberte. Previously he had been preoccupied by a desire to appear in his best light in Swann's eyes, not Gilberte's. In other words, he was more worried about how to phrase a letter to Swann than he was about courting Gilberte. His worries were those of a writer rather than those of a lover. What, then, makes this visit an initiation in the concrete and effective sense of the term?

At an explicit level, it is made clear that the marquise is interested in young boys, although the nature of this interest remains vague. Hence the double status of the hero is repeated within this fragment: is he a child to whom one offers sweets and who refuses this oral pleasure because of a maternal command, or a young man at whom one rather "less innocently" makes sheep's eyes? But this young man is only the metonymic extension of the desires felt by the old woman, who is described in a manner that suggests no attraction whatsoever on the part of the young man. The old Python, who is presented in mythical terms that justify an initiatory reading, obviously serves to provoke a development in the hero in which she plays no part.

The reader will remember the phrase from the bedtime kiss in Combray that introduced the biblical discourse: "telling Sarah that she must turn away towards Isaac" (*"se départir du côté de"*). I mentioned that this phrase plays a crucial role in another text with initiatory resonances. I am thinking once more of the text in Judges 4 in which Jael invites Sisera into her tent. Sisera dies there because he proves to be incapable of understanding and accepting the initiatory rite to which the woman subjects him. The phrase is repeated in order to underline its importance: "Turn in, my lord, turn in to me; do not be afraid."[2] The discourse of initiation is invoked in this text as a way of mixing up two vocabularies, to the great confusion of the uncomprehending Sisera. On the one hand, the latter relies on military vocabulary with its dichotomy between honor and shame, and he has shown himself to fail on these terms when he cravenly abandoned his troops. On the other hand, he uses the vocabulary of hospitality, which is another important ritual for the story, since it enables the female character to trick him.

The significant feature of this initiatory text is that the person who is to be initiated is shut into a closed space. Sisera turns out to be unable to survive the anxiety of initiation. His failing is shown by a mistake in *tone*: he employs an authoritative tone for which he is not qualified any longer. He has lost his position of "authority," yet he gives an *order* as if he were not in the power of a woman. He is executed in a manner that corresponds literally to his own misplaced order:

> And he said to her: go to the opening of the tent, and it will be [thus], if a man comes to ask you and says: is there a man here? Say : no man [*een-ich*, literally "no-man"]. (Judges 4:20, my translation)

By giving this order to the one who has all power over him, by attempting to assure himself a safety that he does not deserve, Sisera de-

167

clares himself to be a non-man. Jael carries out his order by driving the peg that she had used to put up the tent into his temple. Thus she kills him with the very object that had served to create the closed space. Her act is a penetration, and critics have not failed to see the iconic relation with rape. Sisera becomes a non-man by being the object of penetration.[3] Let us avoid one stereotypical misunderstanding straightaway: there is no question here of the sort of homosexual imagery that would tend to attract the Proustian narrator.

Our young hero fairs much better. Far from allowing himself to be shamefully and tragically penetrated, he penetrates—the word is repeated—into the place itself, agreeing to be shut in and obeying the female authorities who are in charge there. The fusty smell fills him with pleasure. It penetrates him, thereby relieving him of the puerile anxieties that had bothered him before he entered this place. It has a strangely beneficial effect on him: "This antiquated emanation which invited me not to enjoy the pleasure which it was offering me only as a bonus, but to descend into the underlying reality which it had not yet disclosed to me" (SK 1.531 / P 1.483). This descent is not a penetration; it is a more subtle contact.

The passage has a ritualistic, initiatory aspect, which stems at once from its theme, from its language, and from the memories and narrative recollections of strategic moments in the work. A recollection of this scene occurs, then, right in the middle of the last great voyeuristic "ethnographic" scene that completes the hero's sexual initiation (SK 3.843 / P 4.392). Let us read the passage in its entirety. I numbered each of the five stages in the rite of passage:

> I was in despair. I was obliged to leave Gilberte for a moment; Françoise had called me. I had to accompany her into a little pavilion covered in a green trellis, not unlike one of the disused toll-houses of old Paris, in which had recently been installed what in England they call a lavatory but in France, by an ill-informed piece of Anglomania, "water closets." [1] The old, damp walls of the entrance, where I stood waiting for Françoise, emitted a cold, fusty smell which, relieving me at once of the anxieties that Swann's words, as reported by Gilberte, had just awakened in me, filled me with a pleasure of a different kind from other pleasures, which leave one more unstable, incapable of grasping them, of possessing them,

a pleasure that was solid and consistent, on which I could lean for support, delicious, soothing, rich with a truth that was lasting, unexplained
and certain. I should have liked, as, long ago, in my walks along the Guermantes way, to endeavour to penetrate the charm of this impression
which had seized hold of me, and, remaining there motionless, to explore
this antiquated emanation, which invited me not to enjoy it, which it was
offering me only as a bonus, but [2] to descend into the underlying reality
which it had not yet disclosed to me. But the keeper of the establishment,
an elderly dame with painted cheeks and an auburn wig, began to talk to
me. . . . This marquise now warned me not to stand outside in the cold,
and even opened one of her doors for me saying [3] "Won't you go inside
for a minute? Look, here's a nice clean one, and I shan't charge *you* anything." Perhaps she made this offer simply in the spirit in which the young
ladies at Gouache's, when we went there to order something, used to offer me one of the sweets which they kept on the counter under glass bells,
and which, alas, Mamma would never allow me to accept; perhaps, less innocently, like the old florist whom Mamma used to have in to replenish
her flower-stands, who made sheep's eyes at me as she handed me a rose.
In any event, if the marquise had a weakness for young boys, [4] when she
threw open to them the hypogean doors of those cubicles of stone in
which men crouch like sphinxes, she must have been moved to that generosity less by the hope of corrupting them than by the pleasure which all
of us feel in displaying needless prodigality to those whom we love, for I
never saw her with any other visitor except an old park-keeper.

[5] A moment later I said good-bye to the marquise, and went out accompanied by Françoise, whom I left to return to Gilberte. I caught sight
of her at once, on a chair, behind the clump of laurels. She was there so as
not to be seen by her friends: they were playing hide-and-seek. I went and
sat down beside her. (SK 1.530–31 / P 1.483–84)

The first stage consists in relieving the subject of the worries that
weighed upon him so much that he was in despair just previously. The
second introduces the pleasurable sensation of being in this closed world
in which he can only descend, not into hell, but into reality. For a secu-
larized, Lacanian subject, hell is replaced by a reality that must preexist **169**
the subject, but of which he is not yet aware. It is a voyage of discovery
into the order of the world. In the middle phase of the rite, the marquise's proposition is made. She shows him her favor. For this young

man is chosen: "I shan't charge *you* anything." The cleanliness seems to mark the absence of danger; but is it not, in fact, the trap on which the criterion of selection is based? We must tread carefully: Jael had indeed told Sisera "do not be afraid." By giving him more than he asked for, she passes sentence on him.

When Sisera requests water, Jael offers him milk, and this milk sends him to sleep like a sleeping-potion, thereby abandoning him to the woman's powers. It is Marcel's weighing-up of the possibilities, his prudence in his evaluation of the offer, that constitutes the very examination to which he is subjected. The boy is seen to mature into a man in the wisdom of his evaluation. After what seems to be a last childish impulse ("which, alas, Mamma would never allow me to accept"), the text changes tone to begin the final phase of the initiation. Unlike Sisera, the hero does not fall prey to the woman's initiative; he refuses the supplement that condemns.

The theme of the excessive and, therefore, dangerous gift reappears, as if to underline the similarity between Gilberte and Jael, when, a little later, Gilberte makes Marcel drink too much tea and eat too much chocolate. This stimulant takes the form of a cake, an anti-madeleine not unlike the wedding cake in *Madame Bovary*, and it emphasizes the ritualistic aspect of childhood friendship that is sliding toward adolescent love (SK 1.545 / P 1.497).[4]

The reader senses quite clearly that the initiation has moved from one phase to the next with the description "she threw open to them the hypogean doors of those cubicles of stone in which men crouch like sphinxes." As Doubrovsky has so rightly said, "Whoever says 'sphinx' says 'Oedipus'" (49), but he also links this strangely solemn word to "sphincter," thereby reading the passage as a drama of cleanliness. According to this reading, then, the hero is the pre-oedipal child. The theme of cleanliness is certainly present here. But reading the passage solely in terms of an oedipal drama is to remain deaf to its full accomplishment. It is also to remain blind to the motionless men crouched there.

A little earlier in his commentary, Doubrovsky adds the word "suddenly," which appears nowhere in the sentence about the descent into reality. This addition enables him to understand the scene as a screen-memory. While I am quite prepared to admit that "whoever says 'sphinx' says 'Oedipus'" I would add that whoever says "no" quite politely to the sphinx-woman escapes from the prepared schema, from the "reality which it had not yet disclosed to me." The sphinx is a metaphor; it is, moreover, a metaphor of a woman with "rounded breasts." The sphincter is a metonymy—an instrument in the drama of cleanliness—and a hollow space. The stage of defecation mastery consists in knowing how to empty this digestive tube at the right moment. The primary feature of the space into which the initiate is invited to penetrate is precisely its hollowness. The cubes of stone are much reduced repetitions of the closed space into which the hero enters to begin his initiation. These spaces contain the sphincters that are both content and container; they remind us of the opaque glass jars.[5] Entering by a "hypogean" door, in other words, by an underground doorway, constitutes another version of the descent into reality. The men who are crouched there are even more confined than the narrator is within the four damp walls. The keeper who carries the key invites the young man to line up alongside these men who have penetrated into these cubes where they have lost all stature and mobility.

To penetrate into this place, with these men, would also be a deep commitment, a conformity to the prescriptions of the order of men. For the hero of this novel of initiation, however, extreme heroism and ultimate danger do not lie in adapting oneself to normality. During the voyeurism scene at the Guermantes' home we saw that venturing into the labyrinth, into which Phedre tried to drag Hippolyte, is not as risky as confronting the "flatness" of the visible wall in full sunlight.[6]

The young man, thus, turns the invitation down. He has passed the first test and, faced with the binary choices between his position as child under his mother's wing and that of the man fastened into the "normal" oedipal structure, he is ready to leave, knowing what he wants. He has avoided the trap that was set for Sisera. He did not turn away toward the false marquise who promises the forbidden oral gratification that would make him into a non-man (*een ich*) fixed in the pre-oedipal stage. The refusal to join the ranks of the closed-in men would also have furthered the hero's development into the very man that this text does not let him become: a man like any other. His status is suspended. The ex-

171

traordinary libidinal identity that characterizes the Proustian subject is constituted by this double refusal and the risk of suspension thereby entailed.

The fifth phase of the initiation is the departure. Leaving the closed space, the narrator has changed age-group. This results in him seeing his sweetheart immediately, even though she is hidden. No obstacle can hold him back now. He takes his place at her side, takes her in his arms, and, then, takes the initiative in the battle of force from which he is to come out the winner. He who had just before been a child in despair, behaves now as a strong, unbending seducer who chooses his sexual behavior with certainty:

> I felt myself so irresistibly attracted by her body that I said to her: "I say, why don't you try to stop me from getting [the letter to Gilberte's father]; we'll see who's the stronger."
>
> She thrust it behind her back; I put my arms around her neck, raising the plaits of hair which she wore over her shoulders, . . . we wrestled, locked together. I tried to pull her towards me, and she resisted; her cheeks, inflamed by the effort, were as red and round as two cherries; she laughed as though I were tickling her; I held her gripped between my legs like a young tree which I was trying to climb; and, in the middle of my gymnastics, when I was already out of breath with the muscular exercise and the heat of the game, I felt, like a few drops of sweat wrung from me, my pleasure express itself in a form which I could not even pause for a moment to analyze; immediately I snatched the letter from her. (SK 1.532 / P 1.484)

His pleasure here is only just disguised by means of a metonymically motivated comparison: the drops of sweat are metonymically related to the drops of pleasure. These drops are the mark of writing, the signature that the narrator-writer leaves on the leaf at the window in that other "place of convenience," the little room at the top of the house in Combray that smells of irises.

172 The libidinal identity that the subject has chosen for himself, as opposed to that offered to him by the false marquise, is an undeniably masculine identity, except that it does not involve penetration. The basis of the libidinal identity, which is the fruit of the initiation, is not without parallels to the passage that describes Albertine as a nude: Gilberte's

cheeks are red and round like cherries. The oral gratification, which would remain infantile if it involved only the sweets forbidden by the mother, becomes "fruitful," produces "drops," when it takes the form of the autonomous solution chosen by the young man. The contact that enables this production of drops is, above all else, epidermic, and the hero, who became a man in just five minutes, can now make it on his own. "I held her gripped between my legs": far from trying to penetrate her, he encircles the object of his desire. Content-container: we always come back to the same dialectic of the glass jars.

The narrator is trying to invent a sexuality that does not exist. Two of his *alter egos*, Swann and Charlus, are also struggling with the same creative challenge. Charlus, who is the object of an identification through spying, offers only surface images. Here is another of those sentences from the end of a paragraph, at the end of a voyage of discovery, in which the twists and turns of the ethnographic investigation are compensated for by a revealing image. This time it comes at the high point of the last scene of voyeurism. This is also, if we can put it thus, the high point of libidinal "flatness":

> Stealthily in the darkness I crept as far as this window and there in the room, chained to a bed like Prometheus to his rock, receiving the blows that Maurice rained upon him with a whip that was in fact studded with nails, I saw, with blood already flowing from him and covered with bruises which proved that the chastisement was not taking place for the first time—I saw before me M. de Charlus. (SK 3.843 / P 4.394)

"I saw before me": this visual image, for which we are prepared by the suspense created by its final position in the sentence, is placed *before* the hero and *for* the hero. And Swann, the very Swann who on first appearances seems so conventional in his love, also attempts to be innovative in this domain. Here he is the object of a tale that is supposedly learned thirdhand, but that is told in such a way as it seems like a preparatory version of the autobiographical novel to be written in the third person, which was destined to be rejected. The words taken up by Camus in *La chute* in reference to "physical possession"—"in which, by the way, one doesn't possess anything"—belong originally to Swann (SK 1.255 / P 1.230). The narrator speculates whether the expression "to do cattleya" means "the same thing as its synonyms," and Swann hopes that "it was the possession of this woman that would emerge for him from their large mauve petals; and the pleasure which he had already felt . . . seemed to him . . . a pleasure which had never before existed, which he was striving now to create, a pleasure—as the special name he gave it was to certify—entirely individual and new" (SK 1.256 / P 1.230).

To invent one's own sexuality is not easy, especially when one is a man and the basis for this sexuality is precisely the rejection, the negation, of the masculine model. This rejection is everywhere, infecting numerous memories with a repulsive negativity. The act of sexual pleasure that is most often described is the kiss. But it is never a great success. It whets the subject's appetite—in a literal way. The paradigmatic kiss is that of the grandmother; it is a surface kiss that nourishes: "When I felt my mouth glued to her cheeks, to her brow, I drew from them something so beneficial, so nourishing, that I remained as motionless, as solemn, as calmly gluttonous as a babe at the breast" (SK 1.718 / P 2.28). This kiss of the suckling baby is to remain his model. Thus he refuses Albertine's attempt at an adult kiss (SK 2.863 / P 3.229), and this refusal is evoked later in a recollection.

The retrospective account places the two types of kiss in a revealing contrast. The contrast is just slightly attenuated by a concessionary "even when," but the final comparison leaves us in no doubt:

> I could feel against my lips, which she would try to part, her tongue, her maternal, incomestible, nutritious, hallowed tongue, whose strange moist warmth, even when she merely ran it over the surface of my neck or my stomach, gave to those caresses of hers, superficial but somehow administered by the inside of her flesh, externalized like a piece of material reversed to show its lining, even in their most external touches, something like the mysterious sweetness of a penetration. (SK 3.508 / P 4.79)

The kiss is, then, the center around which the narrator deploys his creative imagination in the service of pleasure. The notion of penetration takes on a particularly idiosyncratic meaning in this context.

174

It is when the narrator allows himself to dream of the construction of a totally phantasmic organ of pleasure that we see how he understands ideal erotic pleasure and the significance of penetration in this ideal. Here is how he would like the body to be built:

I told myself this because I believed that there was such a thing as knowledge through the lips; I told myself that I was going to know the taste of this fleshy rose, because I had not stopped to think that man, a creature obviously less rudimentary than the sea urchin or even the whale, nevertheless lacks a certain number of essential organs, and notably possesses none that will serve for kissing. For this absent organ he substitutes his lips, and thereby arrives perhaps at a slightly more satisfying result than if he were reduced to caressing the beloved with a horny tusk. But a pair of lips, designed to convey to the palate the taste of whatever whets their appetite, must be content, without understanding their mistake or admitting their disappointment, with roaming over the surface and with coming to a halt at the barrier of the impenetrable but irresistible cheek. . . . for in that desolate zone in which they are unable to find their proper nourishment they are alone, the sense of sight, then that of smell, having long deserted them. (SK 2.378 / P 2.659–60)

For our apprentice, supreme pleasure is of an epistemological nature. It is not for nothing that he undergoes the various initiations, a crucial element of which is the acquisition of knowledge. Before the disappointing experience of the kiss, he still believes in "knowledge through the lips," which would enable him to integrate oral pleasure, that is, pleasure that pertains to both the sense of taste and touch, with sight and smell.

The self-inflicted irony, which is accentuated by the comparison with the sea urchin and the whale, does not succeed in obscuring the "serious" intent of his own procedure. Looking beyond the two species of animal, the sea urchin and the whale each represent one end of the scale that the narrator has such difficulty in reconciling. The infinitely small sea urchin is a detail decomposed into nasty, hard, even poisonous elements, like the grain of an enlarged photo or of a neck seen up close. In other words, it is completely lacking in subtlety and softness. The whale, which is smooth because it is large and, thus, distant, is totally lacking in flexibility, in that "life" represented by the yellow butterfly. The irony has fully prepared us for the following comparison: "if he were reduced to caressing the beloved with a horny tusk." This tusk follows from the hardness of the sea urchin at the same time as it introduces the much larger whale. But nevertheless, a horny tusk taken iconically resembles most markedly the instrument of penetration that was used by the men shut up in the sphinx's stone cells. Here, however, this instrument is presented in a totally negative vision: it is blind, hard, large, unfeeling, and it hurts.[7]

What is the relation between this imagined, mythical kissing organ and the attributes of the men whom the false marquise puts into cubes, perhaps even "incubates"? Can we perceive a word-for-word opposition? It is true that this organ is supposed to be the solution to the "barrier of the impenetrable but irresistible cheek." This suggests a desire for penetration that seems easily to be modeled on male sexuality. But by identifying this penetration with the genital version normally associated with such a notion, we are forgetting that the organ for kissing is above all else designed to come to the aid of a synesthesic sensuality.

The aim is to absorb smell, taste, essence, and contact through all the orifices of the body by gleaning all these qualities from the cheek's surface. These cheeks have retained less the rounded form of the peach than the velvety surface of the fruit, that is, if we are to believe Caravaggio. Blocked by the closure of the cheek, the hero would like to descend to a deeper level, to descend to a reality he is not able to explore for want of the necessary organ. But once there, he would desire no more than to "remain still." This desire is a palimpseste of the male organ, which, despite its diffuse state, remains the mark that differentiates male homosexuality, even in this "democratic" version, which offers other desires and other sexual positions. The desire to go further in, to know more intimately, the closed body of the other can be neither ignored nor assimilated to a male identity based on phallic privilege. For the hero does not go any further in. Before he joins the men in the sphinx's cubes, he stops short. Rather than an appendage or an instrument of localized penetration, the organ seems instead to be like an extremely sensitive and perfected skin, an instrument for the penetration of subtleties.

Even though it is fictitious, this organ does seem to accomplish its purpose on one occasion: it appears in the passage quoted earlier, as if called upon to demonstrate a non-phallic voluptuousness (SK 3.508 / P 4.79). Once again it is Albertine who is required to perform according to this fantasy. It is a little after her death that the narrator recollects the sensation produced by her, or by him, and this novelistic artifice is designed to lead to the conclusion of her story. It is striking that the only mention, unless I am mistaken, of the word "penetration" in the context of sexual pleasure is used to establish a metaphoric equivalence between "their most external touches" and penetration.

This phantasmic organ fills in the gaps of Proustian desire in another way: it enables the gulf between close-up and distant perception to be closed. Without such an organ, the much-desired kiss leads to inevitable disappointment. This disappointment is formulated in visual terms:

> At first, as my mouth began gradually to approach the cheeks which my eyes had recommended it to kiss, my eyes, in changing position, saw a different pair of cheeks; the neck, observed at closer range and as though through a magnifying-glass, showed in its coarser grain a robustness which modified the character of the face. (SK 2.378 / P 2.660)

The kissing organ is a substitute for a masculinity that is unacceptable and an object-less heteropathic identification. But it is also a descriptive detail that is inflated or produced by an imaginary magnifying glass that allows us to *see* the nuances and the subtleties through which the high drama the novel claims to narrate is played out.

This phantasmic and fantastic organ is both so strange and so "necessary" at the time of its intervention it could be called dreamlike. As far as dreams are concerned, according to Naomi Schor, the detail is also the unexplained, the excess of interpretation that, like the famous "navel" of dreams, resists interpretation and sinks into the depths of the dream's meaning, which is most often of a sexual order. And Schor continues by asking the following question: how do what Freud in *Michelangelo's Moses* calls "the unimportant details of waking life," which he describes as "the refuse of observation," come to be inflated with meaning? (*Reading in Detail*, 70).

The residues of observation clearly mean that the kissing organ is invoked in relation to knowledge, in relation, that is, to the desire for an observation that is impossible, subtle, essential, and in which all senses would collaborate. Instead of the lips, which remain limited to the desolate outer zone, this organ must go beyond the limits of the real in order that the subject can know another reality, the secret of which the false marquise had neglected to reveal to him. This impossible organ paradoxically assumes the function of reconnecting the dreamer to reality. So how does this navel, the trace of the umbilical cord that reconnects the wildly inflated writing to the individual essence that rises up in the text from *Contre Sainte-Beuve,* swell up with meaning?

With Proust the deepest secrets are not to be found in the depths. The umbilical cord, which is drawn from itself in the little room that smells of irises, is written like a trace (from a snail), like a line (in the flutes on the valves of a scallop shell), like a figure, and like a drawing. It is a signature (like Gilberte's illegible signature). The signature thus traced contains the secret of the hidden identity of the self that is projected onto all the others in whom this "I" discovers himself. Hence, also, the taboo placed on the first name of the "I." The navel of dreams points toward the outside, toward the future of writing, as opposed to the inside of the maternal body and the time passed by the child in this inside. To write, by drops—of ink, milk, semen, oysters, sweat, and blood—is an act that introduces "flatness," an act of "pressing together," of applying the essence of the self onto a flat leaf-base.

In this conception the valve becomes masculine, since it figures the base by means of the self-identification that is necessary for our apprentice-writer. Even the church at Combray, which would seem to lend itself so well to being imagined as a feminine valve, evokes a valve-base, as in the following passage, which is most revealing in this respect:

> The tomb of Sigebert's little daughter, in which a deep valve, like the bed [*trace*] of a fossil, had been dug, or so it was said, "by a crystal lamp which, on the night when the Frankish princess was murdered, had detached itself, of its own accord, from the golden chains by which it was suspended on the site of the present apse and, with neither the crystal being broken nor the light extinguished, had buried itself in the stone, which had softly given way beneath it." (SK 1.66 / P 1.61)

In this description of the tomb, which is a traditional valve, the Proustian valve is a trace that is superimposed upon the cavity. This figuration of a valve upon a valve has been carved out by one of the hardest materials possible—crystal—in the context of a violent action that eliminates the woman, who is, metonymically speaking, the bearer of the traditional valve. The peculiar final image, as always, says everything:

"had buried itself in the stone, which had softly given way beneath it."
Stone, crystal: softly?

This is an inscription as opposed to a penetration, and the hardness
becomes voluptuous on the condition that it remain on the surface. The
plump sensuality of the madeleine (SK 1.48 / P 1.46) could not exist if it
were separated from its other side, the fluted valve of the scallop shell.
The glass jars in the Vivonne again come to mind: the content and the
container are reversible. Whereas heterosexuality, as it was reflected before him by the crouched men of the false marquise, is based upon a
clear distinction between these two positions, Marcel's search (*recherche*), the itinerary of which is traced by *La recherche*, is seeking, not an
absence of distinction, but reversibility.

This trace-writing is dangerous, as is the reversibility of which it is
the image. Its figuration is superimposed, in this case, on the tomb,
which is not a fortuitous situation. The reader will remember the association, at the time of Bergotte's death, between Vermeer's masterpiece
and the banality of the newspaper, an association that caused the narrator to read the announcement "as though traced in mysterious lines
inopportunely interpolated there. They had sufficed to make of a living
man someone who could never again respond to what one said to him,
to reduce him to a mere name, a written name, that had suddenly
passed from the real world to the realm of silence" (SK 3.199 / P 3.705).
It is the capacity to reply, to carry out the linguistic act of reversing the
subject positions, that differentiates the living from the dead.

After all, the Proustian subject draws his images in language. It is in
language that the bitter struggles, in which the subject engages in order
to constitute himself, are played out. By speaking of him in the third
person, the father of Combray does not offer him an obvious starting
point, which is ultimately all for the good, since this refusal entails the
necessity of the almost interminable search for an alternative, which has
to be invented.

The trace of writing is, thus, constantly associated with vital forces, **179**
the essence of the self, the spurting outward that make this male, indi-
viduated subject a subject who writes the reversible surface onto which
he applies himself in successive layers. It leads to the infinite spreading-
out of this immense work, the base of which is provided by the book.

This book is flat, but it is inflated with meaning by means of these residues of observation, of which the description of the tomb-valve that I have just quoted is an example. The tomb stone gives way softly beneath this trace: the book is "a huge cemetery in which on the majority of the tombs the names are effaced and can no longer be read" (SK 3.940 / P 4.482). Effaced, indeed, but at least it is on the surface of the stones that the names were written.

part three **The Flatness of Photography**

The point, then, is not to heal the split between words and images, but to see what interests and powers it serves.

—W. J. T. Mitchell, *The Language of Images*

I must therefore submit to this law: I cannot penetrate, cannot reach into the Photograph. I can only sweep it with my glance, like a smooth surface. The Photograph is *flat*, platitudinous, in the true sense of the word, that is what I must acknowledge.

—Roland Barthes, *La chambre claire*

chapter twelve **Positive-Negative: The Visual Rhetoric of Capture**

Although it may appear somewhat paradoxical, the most successful way of bringing about the "prodigiousness" toward which the entire poetics of *La recherche* tends, is visualization, or in other words, the externalization of sensation in space rather than over time as one might expect from the title of the novel. If we can characterize Proust's poetic practice as being above all else located within the province of negativity—the negativity of refusal and denial, from which the possibility of prodigiousness stems—we can expect the most successful type of detail, and the one that is therefore favored, to be the dis-figure. As a doubling-over of form, the dis-figure is able to multiply the negative quite prodigiously and thereby transform it into a positive. It is the preferred strategy because it is indispensable to the capture of time in an art of spacing-out.

The simplest and most obvious strategy is the temporal synecdoche. But a first example demonstrates that even this becomes immediately more complicated. In terms of a limited rhetoric of the detail, it is the rhetorical use of the fragment that ought to meet the narrator's needs:

But in my dreams of Combray (like those architects, pupils of Viollet-le-Duc, who, fancying that they can detect, beneath a Renaissance rood-screen and an eighteenth-century altar, traces of a Romanesque choir, restore the whole church to the state it must have been in the twelfth cen-

183

tury) I leave not a stone of the modern edifice standing, but pierce through the Rue des Perchamps and "restore." (SK 1.181 / P 1.163)

Let us make no mistake about it: the rather heavy-handed irony directed at the architects and the dreamer only partly hides the rhetorical anxiety of the passage, which goes beyond the investment in the fragment. First, the fragment is inscribed negatively; the traces discovered by the architects are replaced by an absolute negation in the "I leave not a stone." This negates all possibility of synecdoche. The present space offers no help in the search for lost time. But it is the absence of the spatial fragment that constitutes the lack here. The point of comparison is already inscribed on the fragment negatively: the architects, apprentices like the narrator, find nothing; they only *fancy* they find something.

The narrator continues:

And for such reconstruction memory furnishes me with more detailed guidance than is generally at the disposal of restorers: the pictures that it has preserved—perhaps the last surviving in the world today, and soon to follow the rest into oblivion—of what Combray looked like in my childhood days; pictures which, because it was the old Combray that traced their outlines upon my mind before it vanished, are as moving—if I may compare an obscure portrait[1] with those glorious works, reproductions of which my grandmother was so fond of bestowing on me—as those old engravings of the *Last Supper* or that painting by Gentile Bellini, in which one sees, in a state in which they no longer exist, the masterpiece of Leonardo and the portico of Saint Mark's. (SK 1.181 / P 1.164)

It is the image that meets the narrator's needs by turning the lack (of stones) into a fragment (of time), thereby enabling him to restore time. The architectural comparison is to be taken literally.[2]

But the image is not a metaphor, invoked by the narrator to meet this particular need. It is not an icon, that is, a similarity, but rather an imaginary image. As such it is defined as a trace, which is the ultimate index of time, the only lingering sign of what was but is no more. Moreover, as the text says, and we can only believe it, the space that no longer exists does indeed produce a trace. The Combray of today, fixed in time, has nevertheless inscribed in the narrator's memory the fragments that are indispensable to a loosening of the fixedness of the present lack.

184

These images are said to be moving; in other words, if we continue to read literally, they are successful as performative synecdochical actions of retotalization, even if this means that they may be doubly at fault. Although they are portraits, with a pretense to iconicity, as such they are obscure, that is, both "minor" in the sense of banal and invisible. What saves them in their function as fragmentary traces is the fact that, when recuperated by the comparison, they are once again doubly "flat" images: that is to say, banal because they are reproductions and two-dimensional because they are printed on paper.

Furthermore, the narrator insists on the nature of the condition necessary for this double "flatness": it is through these reproductions alone that one can see in present time those masterpieces *in a state that no longer exists*. If art is historic—if the history of art has meaning—this history can only be grasped through poor reproductions, flat images, or fragments, the value of which is their negative relation to the real thing. The poetics of the magic lantern continues to be fruitful.

To be sure, it is not by chance that these masterpieces of great art are so often evoked at the crucial poetic moments of the text. But this does not mean that they figure only as prestigious aesthetic models. For it is no more a matter of chance that they are placed in the eminently modest position of being the point of comparison, that is, in a secondary and subservient role. Great art, like the kitchen maid, is used on behalf of the flat image. Flatness becomes magnificently productive as a result of the help provided by art. And it is the necessity of this visualization for the project of presenting time spatially that incites the narrator to use the visual image, which seems at first sight to be so badly suited to his needs. This visualization of time is the second strategy that is developed in the face of the fixedness of the image against which the narrator collides.

It is perhaps rather paradoxical to read the principal vectors of the poetics of *La recherche* through the detail. Indeed, a lot has been made of the strategy of distantiation in Proust's novel, which is opposed to de- **185** tailing. It is, however, through this distantiation, in some sense against the grain, that we can best measure the importance of the poetics of the detail as the very foundation for the endeavor of searching for lost time.

It is precisely this strategy that Marcel adopts when he is overcome by disgust at the banality of everyday life, provoked perhaps less by its ugliness than by the repellent inexorability of present time ("that sordid moment when the knifes are left littering the tablecloth among crumpled napkins"). He finds respite in fixing his gaze on the distant sea (SK 1.746 / P 2.54). This fragment is paired with the prototypical detail of the dis-figure, since once again Marcel borrows Mme de Villeparisis's gaze in his process of learning to see.

The carriage in which they ride together effectively thwarts any possibility of close-up vision: "Mme de Villeparisis's carriage moved fast. I scarcely had time to see the girl who was coming in our direction" (SK 1.765 / P 2.72). These two movements, like two negations, cancel one another out. But the paradox is resolved when distantiation proves to be helpful to the process of detailing, which it does through "flatness." The long-desired views of the sea do not function in the way the narrator had expected:[3]

> Before getting into the carriage, I had composed the *seascape* which I was going to look out for, which I hoped to see with the "radiant sun" upon it, and which at Balbec I could distinguish only in too *fragmentary a form*, broken by so many vulgar *enclaves* that had no place in my dream—bathers, cabins, pleasure yachts. But when, Mme de Villeparisis's carriage having reached the top of a hill, I caught a glimpse of the sea *through the leafy boughs of the trees*, then no doubt at such distance those *contemporary details* which had set it apart, as it were, from nature and *history* disappeared, and I could try to persuade myself as I looked down upon its waters that they were the same which Leconte de Lisle *paints* for us in his *Orestie*, where "like a flight of birds of prey, before the dawn of day" the long-haired warriors of heroic Hellas "with oars an hundred thousand sweep the huge resounding deep." But on the other hand *I was not near enough to the sea*, which seemed to me not alive but *congealed*, I no longer felt any power beneath its *colours*, spread like those of a *painting* between leaves, through which it appeared as insubstantial as the sky and only of a darker blue. (SK 1.760–61 / P 2.67–68)

186

Here we see the passage from the desire for a seascape to the discovery of a painting. Why is this visual experience a failure when it seems to succeed so well in coming full circle?

The seascape was too fragmentary when Marcel was close to it; it is

In order that the detail function other than by detailing; in order that it help enlarge or insert—rather than detach—the infinitely small into general laws, there must also be a certain delicacy of form and quivering, of flatness and mobility, of light and fragility. It is visual, it is an image, but it is also something else. This something else we find in the realm of photography: an art that is both flat and banal, that is able to enlarge the detail, to capture the past, and to figure movement.

In the scene from the Duchess of Guermantes's salon in *La fugitive / Albertine disparue*, at the moment when the narrator, suffering from amnesia, is to be introduced to the very person who was the great love of his youth, he reflects on the deceptive and disappointing nature of both writing and photography. In the 1954 Pléiade edition of *La recherche*, the sentence is as follows:

> Our mistake is to present things as they are, names as they are written, people as photography and psychology give an unalterable notion of them. (3.573)

Or according to Tadié's Pléiade edition:

> Our mistake lies in supposing that things present themselves habitually as they really are, names as they are written, people as photography and psychology give an unalterable notion of them. (SK 3.585 / P 4.153)

This reflection is offered as an explanation for the bizarre fact that the narrator had "mis-corrected" the name that the concierge had already misheard and written incorrectly. The fact that Gilberte had stared at him, and that he had brushed up against her, taking her to be a tart without recognizing her, appears in no way strange to him. For this reflection to take place, it is forgetfulness, rather than the contrary, that is necessary. In the first Pléiade edition, the verb *présenter* was not reflexive, making it a question of presentation, that is, of photography as a means, as a medium of communication. In the Tadié edition it becomes a question of the belief that the frequent use of the medium has established as a routine element of culture. Between these two versions we can see the difference between a behavioral pattern and a conviction, between a culture and a religion.

191

Roland Barthes wrote the following on the subject of photography: "The Photograph does not call up the past (nothing Proustian in a photograph)."[9] If photography does not call up the past, what else is it doing so insistently in *A la recherche du temps perdue*? As art, as a medium, as a technique, photography contains within itself the two sides of the notion of "flatness."

Barthes was not wrong: the photograph, which according to him has nothing Proustian about it, is fundamentally implied in one of Proust's endeavors, but this endeavor is quite different from that of trying to recover lost time through sensation. Rather, photography is the art of paradox, of the positive-negative. On several occasions Proust calls it "sick," if not deadly. At the beginning of the work, in *Un amour de Swann*, it is already presented in this manner in a reflection on Odette:

> He would say to himself, almost with astonishment, "It's she!" as though suddenly we were to be shown in a detached, externalized form one of our own sicknesses, and we found it bore no resemblance to what we are suffering. "She"—he tried to ask himself what that meant; for it is a point of resemblance between love and death, far more striking than those which are usually pointed out, that they make us probe deeper, in the fear that its reality may elude us, into the mystery of personality. (SK 1.336 / P 1.303)

This reflection is very Barthesian, not so much because of its meaning, or its effect, but as a result of its status as a sign. It weaves a web or a network around the loved one, in which the photograph, unable to find or capture this loved one, is itself caught. The externalization does not imply immobility. The referent for "those" eludes us, recedes beyond grasp, just as that sentence says; love goes hand in hand with death; the resemblance is defined as an evasion. This constitutes precisely the first part of Barthes's study. It is an example of Proust's "philosophy of the novel," in which the semiotic first principle is that the sign is a sign precisely because it re-presents an absent, elusive referent.[1]

Here the semiotics of the image is just as negative as it is in the theory of the American semiotician Peirce, who, incidentally, was Proust's contemporary. It is widely recognized that this philosopher's ideas, which are today so popular, have suffered considerable distortion, to the point that the important subtleties of his thought have been forgotten. Thus his concept of the icon, for example, has been reduced to the same banal idea of a positive mimetism, which is equivalent to the vulgar conception of photography. It is perhaps worthwhile, therefore, to quote Peirce's definition of the three categories of the sign, according to its relations to meaning, then compare that definition to the passage on Odette's photograph:

> An *icon* is a sign which would possess the character which renders it significant, even though its object had no existence; such as a lead-pencil streak as representing a geometrical line. An *index* is a sign which would, at once, lose the character which makes it a sign if its object were removed, but would not lose that character if there were no interpretant. Such, for instance, is a piece of mould with a bullet-hole in it as a sign of a shot; for without the shot there would have been no hole; but there is a hole there, whether anybody has the sense to attribute it to a shot or not. A *symbol* is a sign which would lose the character which renders it a sign if there were no interpretant. Such is any utterance of speech which signifies what it does only by virtue of its being understood to have that signification.[2]

The formulation here is essentially negative. According to these definitions, Odette's photograph fits into all three categories, which is characteristic of Peirce's theory. The photograph is an icon, but in the negative sense ("even though its object had no existence"). It is also indexical (Proust: "externalized") and symbolic ("a sign which would lose the character which renders it a sign if there were no interpretant"). This fundamental negativity of the sign is the basis on which Proust builds his work. The photograph, commonly assumed to be a pure icon, an absolute and inescapable resemblance, is in fact the visual image that poses this negativity in its most acute terms.

194

We have seen that Proust's interest in the image is not of a simple aesthetic order, but rather reflects a central need of the very project of *La recherche*. The image is subjective, even "psychological." But we can now see that it relates to a psychology of the textual subject, not the biographical subject. It is also semiotic, that is, it is an instrument called upon by the need to "invent," to create new perceptions in order to say them. Given this double use of the image, it is necessary to explore its twists and turns as a literary agency: "flatness," not simply *in* the work, but *at work*.

"I must therefore submit to this law: I cannot penetrate, cannot reach into the Photograph. I can only sweep it with my glance, like a smooth surface. The Photograph is *flat*, platitudinous, in the true sense of the word, that is what I must acknowledge," writes Barthes in *La chambre claire* (164). Proust inscribes the very innovation of his writing within this realization.

Photography in Proust is centered most of all around the grandmother, that object of lost love, the forgetfulness and then recollection of which constitute the paradigm for the hero's love. The meaning of the photograph is elaborated in several stages through the grandmother's relation to photography. To begin with there were the photographs the grandmother bestowed on the young Marcel—photographs of Hubert Robert's *Fountains of Saint-Cloud*, of Turner's paintings of Vesuvius, "which offered a degree more of art" (SK 1.43 / P 1.40). For the grandmother, struggling with the loss of aura that Walter Benjamin so deplored, these photographs constitute a way of outsmarting the vulgarity of mechanical reproduction and commercial banality.[3]

Over and above the pedagogical significance of the photograph, the grandmother also provides the pole around which the device of the photograph is established diegetically in *La recherche*. The reader will remember the plot surrounding the photography session at Balbec. In order that her grandson might have a beautiful image of her to keep after her death, which she knew to be imminent, the grandmother asks Robert de Saint-Loup to take a photograph of her. Thus we see the same interweaving of the photograph with love and death that Barthes describes. Marcel, who does not know that his grandmother is dying, is extremely irritated by what he perceives as her coquetry. This irritation provokes him meanly to extinguish the expression of joy from the old woman's face that she wanted to have preserved for him (SK 1.844 / P 2.144). They engage in a blind struggle for power over the image, for the power to determine what the image is to be, and for the power to control the brief click that immortalizes that which nonetheless only slips away: the past.

The photograph in question reappears often in the novel, both as the object itself and as a memory of the event that produced it. In each instance it changes meaning. It is also the object of choice around which the plot that opposes Marcel to his doubles is developed. The reader will recall these doubles, whose misleading identity Marcel discovers during his "ethnographic" enterprise, that voyage of discovery that he makes without leaving home. This discovery has the effect of advancing his self-discovery. In the episode of the grandmother's photograph, Saint-Loup, the photographer, is in retrospect described as being "a stranger to himself" once the narrator discovers that he used this opportunity to feel up the hotel lift-boy in the darkroom, which becomes through this revelation a "camera lucida" (SK 3.699 / P 4.259).[4] The grandmother's photograph is also indirectly a photograph of Robert.

The narrator reflects often on his impulse to spoil all pleasure and happiness, which he reveals on this occasion. His reflection begins during the involuntary recollection that overcomes him on the first evening of his second stay in Balbec. He considers the photographic session as part of a more general tendency that gives him cause to believe that he killed his grandmother:[5]

> I . . . had striven with such insensate frenzy to expunge from it even the smallest pleasures, as on the day when Saint-Loup had taken my grandmother's photograph and I, unable to conceal from her what I thought of the ridiculous childishness of the coquetry with which she posed for him, with her wide-brimmed hat, in a flattering half-light, had allowed myself to mutter a few impatient, wounding words, which, I had sensed from a contraction of her features, had struck home; it was I whose heart they were rending, now that the consolation of countless kisses was forever impossible. (SK 2.786 / P 3.155–56)

Words which struck home. Since Barthes one might say that words have taken precedence over the photograph, but this precedence is "photographic." The very mission of the photograph is to strike home: "A photograph's *punctum* is that accident which pricks me (but also bruises me, is poignant to me)." It is in this way that Barthes elaborates his concept of the punctum before the discovery of the photograph from the Winter Garden (*La chambre claire*, 49).

The reflection continues by cruelly opposing the failure of the photograph to a nonexistent truth. Despite Françoise's remark, "Poor Madame, it's the very image of her, down to the beauty spot on her cheek," this visual detail is no more capable in this case than it was in that of Albertine of bridging the gap between the part and the whole (SK 2.803 / P 3.172). This incapacity has significant consequences: the photographic "it's the very image of her" fails to establish the link between the subject and the object of the vision that is the only means of saving the subject. Barthes writes: "If he cannot . . . supply the transparent soul its bright shadow, the subject dies forever" (*La chambre claire*, 169). Proust's narrator is well aware of this: "We had not been created solely for one another; she was a stranger to me. This stranger was before my eyes as I looked at the photograph taken of her by Saint-Loup" (SK 2.803 / P 3.172).

There is an irreducible divorce between the subject who looks, the object that is "fixed," and the operator. Between the three positions of this linguistic or love triangle, there is the movement of the merry-go-round that hides an emptiness in the center. This is the problem that the image poses, and even more so the photograph. Unable to immobilize, it is just as slippery as the object it is supposed to fix. And in its slipperiness, it acts, it strikes home, without the subject being able to control it: "All of a sudden I thought once again: 'It's grandmother, I am her grandson,' as a man who has lost his memory remembers his name, as a sick man changes his personality" (SK 2.803 / P 3.172). By way of the memory born from its negation (its loss), we once again encounter the association between photography and sickness. This sickness is warded off—but only just—in the enunciation of the identity of the subject in his consecutive relation to the object of the photograph.

The grandmother's photograph continues to obsess Marcel until the end of this chapter. The recovery from this sickness, which has developed around the photograph, is announced by the simultaneous upswing in interest in both Albertine and the sea. But during this time, the photograph has had a rival in the form of another photograph. It is this other photograph that sets in motion the real photographic figuration in the narrative discourse of *La recherche*. It operates as the shifter from the visual represented to a visuality that represents. This visuality is produced, not by Robert, who is Marcel's double and intermediary, but by Marcel himself. This is an important passage: it reviews in detail the significant aspects of the image in Proust, defining it as the place where affectivity and cognition, epistemology and aesthetics, the subject and the object, are inextricably mixed. Thus we see that the raw material of this novel consists in an interweaving of the external, "true," and objectifiable image with the mental image.

It is in this passage that we discover the phantom that haunts the narrator throughout the work, constituting the metaphoric counterpart to the first photograph, the essence of which it describes better: the nonreciprocal gaze. Entering the room without announcing his presence, the narrator writes, "I was there, or rather I was not yet there since she was not aware of my presence, and . . . she was absorbed in thoughts which she never allowed to be seen by me" (SK 2.141 / P 2.438). Here we have a pure example of that heteropathic identification, which is associated with a risk of alienation. This identification never stops appealing to the narrator, even while it exposes him to obvious risks.

This passage is made all the more significant by the fact that it presents another aspect of the narrator's tendency for voyeurism. The voyeur is constantly in danger, since alienation robs him of his self when he is not interacting with the other. This danger determines the extent to which the voyeur, whom we have seen in action, must "flatten" himself in visual identification onto his object, finding himself unable to avoid participation in the spectacle. This is the reason why I said earlier that pulling Charlus "out of the closet" is also for Marcel a way of going into the closet himself. The contemplation of the spectacle afforded by the other is a photographic act, in the serious sense of the term, both existential and formative. This is what Barthes is referring to when he speaks of the "flattened" presence of the referent in any photograph: "Light, though impalpable, is here a carnal medium, a *skin* I share with anyone who has been photographed" (*La chambre claire*, 127; my emphasis). The phantom of the grandmother, which reveals her illness, is, thus, also the phantom of Marcel, who is devoid of all substance (of "shape and solidity") when he sees without being seen or known to be there. The *specter*—both spectacle and phantom—which leads Barthes to define photography in terms of lost time, in other words, in terms of death, is exactly what the subject inevitably is himself.

> Of myself—thanks to that privilege which does not last but which gives one, during the brief moment of return, the faculty of being suddenly the spectator of one's own absence—there was present only the witness, the observer, in travelling coat and hat, the stranger who does not belong to the house, the photographer who has called to take a photograph of places which one will never see again. The process that automatically occurred in my eyes when I caught sight of my grandmother was indeed a photograph. (SK 2.141 / P 2.438)

The passage continues in the longest and most sustained reflection on photography in the entire work. Here photography is seen as an art, or an "automatic process," that cuts and slices, transforming life and the past, destroying the "animated system, the perpetual motion of our incessant love for them, which, before allowing the images that their faces present to reach us, seizes them in its vortex and flings them back upon the idea that we always had of them, makes them *adhere* to it, coincide with it." Describing oneself in the third person amounts to describing the uncanniness that results from heteropathic identification. As the photographer here, Marcel *is* Saint-Loup. He has gone out of himself in his acceptance of the complete cutting-off from self that sight produces on those occasions when it allows the other to be him- or herself. The grandmother is a specter to the extent that she is herself.

The photograph that makes the photographer a stranger to himself differs from the one that is described implicitly as its negative. The word "automatic" reappears and it is said to be "some cruel trick." The passage gradually develops a more hostile, if not violent, language, leading at the end of this worrying amplification to the description of the mental photograph that is always with the narrator:

> I saw, sitting on the sofa, beneath the lamp, red-faced, heavy and vulgar, sick, vacant, letting her slightly crazed eyes wander over a book, a dejected old woman whom I did not know. (SK 2.143 / P 2.440)

The "truth" of photography is this stranger, this unknowable person. The image is to be applied to that of Mamma at the station in Venice, in another phase of the hero's cruelty. The association suggests that the cruelty he revealed in Balbec, which only led to a slight contraction of the face, is less than the diegetically imperceptible cruelty of seeing without being seen. This second photograph will always remain with the narrator, and it will supply a certain constitutive strength for his sense of self. It is the work of a "photographer" who is a stranger to himself, the product of a voyeurism that an identificatory "pressing-against" is unable to redeem, the effect of a realization of what is involved in the objectifying gaze.[6]

The photograph, such as it appears in this absolutely central role in *La recherche*, is modeled in this way. The material photograph of the grandmother is combined with the mental photograph, both of which are disseminated throughout the work. An eye for an eye: the eye that is veiled by habit, tenderness, the continual affective adjustments that we make to our field of vision, is opposed to that other eye, which is mercilessly "to one side," that is to say, the lens of the camera. Here we have, then, another visual prosthesis, but this time it serves less to see better than to see differently, elsewhere, to one side. It is the art, not of mimesis, nor of direct indexical contact, but of deviation.[7]

In the very middle of the passage on the mental photograph of the grandmother we find this strange comparison, which both explains the photographic effect and embodies it in its localized precision:

> But if, instead of our eyes, it should happen to be a purely physical object, a photographic plate, that has watched the action, then what we see, in the courtyard of the Institute, for example instead of the dignified emergence of an Academician who is trying to hail a cab, will be his tottering steps, his precautions to avoid falling on his back, the parabola of his fall, as though he were drunk or the ground covered in ice. (SK 2.142 / P 2.439)

The comparison mercilessly dramatizes what remains of the puppet that is the other divested of the protection of perceptual and affective routine. Does the photograph make the subject sick, does it kill him, or does it reveal the sickness or the immanent death within life? As we know, Roland Barthes came back to this question.

Given the importance of the photograph and its appearance at the crucial moments of this work, it seems to me to be worth exploring *La recherche* with the help of photography as a mode of figuration. As an art of flatness, it underpins numerous evocations, tentative descriptions, and reflections, at times named, at others present in its terminology, and sometimes even under silence but activated by a certain narratorial "focus." Indeed, photography's presence in Proust's work goes beyond its explicit or thematic evocation. The photographic mechanism can be seen at work in the cutting-out of details, in the conflictual dialectic between the near and the far, and in certain "zoom" effects. It can also be seen in the effects of contrast, which prevent or enable the under- or overexposed image to be seen. It appears in the focusing, when the image oscillates between clarity and indistinction, an effect that I relate to what I called Proust's Chardinism. It also insinuates itself into the problematized perspective in which visual depth leads to "flatness," which is both less satisfactory and less revealing than the vision of the surface. Photography is more revealing than anything else because it offers the possibility of a rapid, broken succession of different images of a same object. Such a succession can lead to the production of a series of snapshots that write the trace of movement. This movement is not cinematographic, but recalls rather the effect of a "contact sheet."[8]

Photography has to be taken as a figure, as a repeated theoretical metaphor that helps to describe an aspect of this work that is more specific than the more general word "visual" would suggest. These are effects of language, which remain irreducible, but which enlighten another unexpected feature of this writing. By considering them as photographic, these devices, which appear to be so different, in fact unify the work under the auspices of "flatness," the poetic impact of which can, therefore, be assessed.

Situated on the surface, unlike the archaeological fragment, the detail tends to take on an insistent visual appearance, which gives it a quasi-photographic aspect. The kiss Marcel bestows on Albertine exemplifies this effect. In this case, the coarse grain of the image has important affective consequences:

> At first, as my mouth began to approach the cheeks which my eyes had recommended it to kiss, my eyes, *in changing position*, saw a *different pair of cheeks*; the neck, observed at closer range and *as though through a magnifying-glass*, showed in *its coarser grain* a robustness which *modified* the character of the face. (SK 2.378 / P 2.660)

We can see more clearly now how the magnifying glass can act as a zoom lens, closing in on and thereby adjusting the image until the woman's neck becomes a man's neck: "a robustness which modified the character of the face." The modification, like the photographic print, is permanent. Albertine's neck is mentioned on several more occasions and always in terms of this robustness that is here "produced": "Albertine's neck, which emerged in its entirety from her nightgown, was strongly built, bronzed, grainy in texture" (SK 2.1162 / P 3.508). Thus photography is capable of transforming "reality," and close-up vision, far from closing the gap between the image and the focalizer's subjectivity, has rather the effect of widening it. The estrangement or alien-

ation effect, which is suggested by phrases such as "in changing position," "a different pair of cheeks," "as though through a magnifying-
glass," "modified," is precisely the photographic effect achieved by a
zoom lens.

The fundamental characteristic of photography is that the bond between subjectivity and vision is broken. This break is primarily temporal, but it is also visual. It enables one to see not only what was and is
no more, but also the "coarse grain" that cannot be seen by the naked
eye. It casts an uncanny gloom over what we know to be inescapable reality; the close-up gaze, like the photograph, separates the subject from
the object.

The establishment of this distance between the subject and the object is the metaphor for, or an extreme example of, the more radical and
worrying distance that separates the subject from himself. As
Doubrovsky says,

> That the subject is "split open" by his discourse, that an absolute cleavage
> separates for him the order of Being and the order of Logos is neither
> Freud's "discovery" nor Lacan's, but Proust's; his whole book consists in
> the setting in place of the transparent and unbridgeable distance that di-
> vides "I" as referent from "I" as reference, subject of existence ("hero")
> from subject of discourse ("narrator"). At stake here is not a temporal dis-
> junction but an ontological break. (*La place de la madeleine*, 120)

This ontological break poses a difficulty for literature that writers attempt to resolve in their own ways, each thereby leaving his or her in-
delible mark. This split needs figuration; it needs the abyss, or the negative, of the trace in writing to accommodate it. In Proust it is photography that provides this accommodation.

Split, yes; but also "cover," or "pressing against": the photograph ad-
heres to its object. This "cover," or "pressing against," is as important
for Proust as the "split." As we know, the kiss is both the most "daring"
act of voluptuous pleasure and the one that marks most clearly its failure. This is why the narrator creates the imaginary organ that should
offer a solution to this failure. But the organ is not really put to use.
Paradoxically, it is the failed kiss at Balbec, the one that is refused, that
provides the model of the most successful attempt. This success is due

203

to the fact that, as a result of the refusal, the kiss remains entirely visual. We must also take into account the intoxication of the desire that acts like a close-up, thereby presenting this kiss as the effect of a zoom lens. The effect is one of a to-ing and fro-ing between close-up and distant focus. This movement alone is able to prevent the disgust that is caused by close-up perception, which spoils the clarity and blurs the image. This was the central issue in the references to Chardin's still lifes, which were relevant beyond their thematic of everyday life.

From a realist point of view, which is so massively ambiguous for this novel, the zoom effect in the failed kiss can be explained in terms of focalization. The hero looks at the object of his desire, moves closer to it, and ends up too close. This excess of proximity is indicated at the level of the diegesis by Albertine's warning: if he does not stop, she will ring the bell. It is at this moment that he lifts his eyes to look into the distance, to heal his eyes, which are tired by the effort made in trying to keep a degree of clarity in such close-up perception. But the to-ing and fro-ing becomes much more significant in terms of the rest of the passage, for its affective charge as well as its epistemological questioning, if we attribute it to the slight but crucial discrepancy that establishes itself between the object and the self in the form of a lens. The mobility of the gaze is not, in fact, indicated anywhere in the passage. The close-up and distant images follow one another as if on a screen, and the subject, quite still, submits himself to their parade.

The passage recycles the vocabulary and the fantasies of the fragment on solitary pleasure. We find the same Pascalian reversal of the large and the small, the same sense of immortality, the same "swelling hillsides." Here is an example:

> Her cheek was traversed by one of those long, dark, curling tresses . . .
> the valley lay bright beneath the moon. The sight of Albertine's bare
> throat, of those flushed cheeks, had so intoxicated me . . . that it had de-
> stroyed the equilibrium between the immense and indestructible life
> which circulated in my being and the life of the universe, so puny in com-
> parison. The sea . . . , the swelling breasts of the first of the Maineville
> cliffs, the sky in which the moon had not yet climbed to the zenith—all
> this seemed less than a featherweight on my eyeballs, which between their
> lids I could feel dilated, resistant, ready to bear far greater burdens, all the

mountains of the world, upon their fragile surface. . . . I should have smiled pityingly had a philosopher then expressed the idea that some day, even some distant day, I should have to die, that the eternal forces of nature would survive me, the forces of nature beneath whose godlike feet I was no more than a grain of dust; that, after me, there would still remain those rounded, swelling cliffs. (SK 1.995 / P 2.285–86)

But, after this exaltation, which is produced by the mobility of the zoom, when the gaze tries to fix on the large-scale focus, things go wrong:

Albertine's round face, lit by an inner flame as by a night-light, stood out in such relief that, imitating the rotation of a glowing sphere, it seemed to be turning, like those Michelangelo figures which are being swept away in a stationary and vertiginous whirlwind. (SK 1.996 / P 2.286)

On first sight, this passage seems to belong to the references to art history. I detect a Rembrandtism in the evocation of inner luminosity, and Michelangelo is mentioned explicitly for the whirlwind effect—for the baroque "madness of seeing."[1] But the mobile vertigo, which "turns the stomach" and makes the subject sick with disgust, is also the result of an excessive and overambitious close-up. It is very clearly the lens that refuses all relief, and this refusal corresponds to the reference to the swelling forms in the distance. The externality of this lens, distinct from the subject, is signified by Albertine, who seems hardly human at all, as if she were only useful in this respect. She is reduced to this external state; she is too close for the relief of her form to be acceptable; thus she is both a flat image produced by the narrator and a stranger to him.

The "zoom effect" is produced by the lens's mobility; it is not a stable detailing, but rather an end point, beyond which one cannot get closer. The other end point is distance. The zoom extended into the distance fixes the seagulls, which thus become flat images, like white water lilies (SK 2.836 / P 3.203). The lens freezes and records an image: "Indeed they did seem to be offering a lifeless object to the little waves." **205** The zoom effect alone can explain how the seagulls, seen from afar, at a distance that immobilizes and flattens them, can at the same time resemble water lilies, which would be minuscule or even invisible at such distance. This is, of course, the result of an effect of focalization, but we must avoid adding an excessive psychological dimension to this focalization: the focalizer is provided with a visual prosthesis, which is in turn a productive extension of the discrepancy between the subject and his vision.

The importance of photography as an epistemo-erotic device for Proust's writing is quite obvious in Marcel's relation with Albertine. If this relation is above all else a visual one, it is even more specifically a photographic one. Moreover, it is generated by a zoom effect. Just as it happens in Antonioni's film *Blow-Up*, the first image of the band of young girls is a group photograph, from which, after successive enlargements, Albertine gradually emerges, like a print that has developed its own individuality. But whereas *Blow-Up* used the metaphor of enlargement in the darkroom, Marcel enlarges during the photographic session itself.

Sometimes it is not (yet) the photograph that matters, but rather the seeking of the "exact" shot by means of the zoom lens. The exact shot is a close-up that is not overwhelming. This search is described in minute detail, for example, in a passage in which the hero, at the beginning of the summer season, seeks out the young girls who had so enraptured him before. In the following fragment, the gaze, distant at the beginning of the sentence, moves in closer toward the end:

> But I could not arrive at any certainty, for the face of these girls did not fill a constant space, did not present a constant form upon the beach, contracted, dilated, transformed as it was by my own expectancy, by the anxiousness of my desire, or by a sense of self-sufficient well-being, the different clothes they wore, the rapidity of their walk or their stillness. (SK 2.867 / P 3.232)

The focalizing subject transforms the correct grammatical form for a singular noun ("face") accompanied by a plural predicate ("these girls") into a zoom effect. This combination is maintained right to the end of the sentence. It is partially neutralized by the more and more rapid succession of nouns ("clothes"—in the plural—"rapidity," "stillness"). A bad pupil of the impressionist Elstir, the narrator appears here as quite a good apprentice photographer. If only the model would pose for him, he would be able to fix the lens at the right distance, that is, at the distance necessary to hold the image still.

The lens with multiple focus points, which produces the zoom effect, poses the paradox that draws the fine line between modernism, the contours of which are defined by an absolute subjectivism, and another aesthetic, which is both indebted to the nineteenth-century fascination with flatness and a precursor to the postmodern questioning of the subject's ontological status. This paradox is, according to Ann Banfield's persuasive interpretation, the very one that Barthes perceives in photography: the paradox of a subjective vision that is inhabited and that is inhabitable because it is set off in a thousand different ways, temporal, spatial, mimetic, and figurative. Manipulated by the focalizer, varying the possible accommodations by means of its very instability, the lens inserts itself between the subject and the object of vision. As a result it produces an irremediable estrangement between the two instances that are often considered to form the basis of visual epistemology. Thus Proust explores a mode of vision that is traditionally prestigious and well established, but his narrator contests this reputation. According to this traditional mode of vision, the subject's place in the center is fixed and safeguarded forever. This is the object of Proust's critical experimentation. The paradox resulting from his experiment calls into question the massive egocentrism of this work and the nature of this "egophany,"[2] which has received such considerable critical attention.

Even more important than the zoom effect, the effects of contrast, of chiaroscuro, and the contours that delineate the images are all basic to photography, which is the art of exposing things in varying ways to light. Overexposed, the object is invisible; underexposed, it is invisible again. Contrast takes on an extraordinary signifying and affective value in the key experience of reading, which is intended to establish the "I" through heteropathic identification. We have already encountered this sort of equation of relations: "This dim coolness of my room was to the broad daylight of the street what shadow is to the sunbeam" (SK 1.90 / P 1.82). I have also already mentioned the Rembrandtism that **207** serves as a vehicle for the references to this paradoxical chiaroscuro, in which shadow is more revealing than light. Proust uses this emulation of the master-painter to overcome the father.

The effective density of how photographic contrast works can be seen very clearly in one page from *Le temps retrouvé*, where four instances of it occur, each one adding a nuance of meaning to the chiaroscuro and all functioning by means of the link to memories that are here "corrected." Diegetically the page is situated during the hero's evening walk, which is later to take him to Jupien's hotel and the final scene of voyeurism. The hero is reflecting on the war and the soldiers who are suffering in the trenches. It is a quite exceptional page, as much because of its touching tone of serious compassion as because of the insistence with which it refers to the photographic, which helps to express the compassion. The affective charge of the first implies an extraordinary density of reference to the second.

The passage begins after a space that marks the end of the ironic description of the platitudes that the Verdurins and friends pronounce about the war. This space contributes to the change in tone and highlights it. It is, thus, a diagrammatic icon of the contrast, which is precisely the basis of its effect. At the beginning of the evening, according to the narrator, one could see "little brown dots which one might have taken, in the blue evening, for midges or birds," and, delving into his stock of images with an emotional investment, he compares this deceptive effect to that of a mountain that looks like a cloud. "But because one knows that this cloud is huge, solid, and resistant, one's emotions are stirred." On top of this optical illusion he superimposes the zoom effect: "And I too was moved by the thought that the brown dot in the summer sky was neither midge nor bird but an aeroplane with a crew of men keeping guard over Paris" (SK 3.756 / P 4.313). The shots of airplanes that he had "taken" previously, first near Balbec and later with Albertine during an outing in Paris, are mentioned, but the reader knows not to attribute any importance to this. Except, that is, in terms of the visual poetics, for which these references are like an advance warning that the following photograph is part of a series of prints.

Next comes dinner time. The photographic image is fed by the light coming from the inside. In this way it becomes one of the most striking evocations of an earlier image:

208

> If, passing in the street, I saw a wretched soldier on leave, escaped for six
> days from the constant danger of death and about to return to the
> trenches, halt his gaze for a moment upon the illuminated windows, I suf-

fered as I had in the hotel at Balbec when fishermen used to watch us at dinner, but I suffered more now because I knew that the misery of the soldier is greater than that of the poor. (SK 3.756 / P 4.313)

The memory of the poor people at Balbec has already been mentioned in *La fugitive / Albertine disparue*, as it was earlier in *A l'ombre*. This memory reveals the nature of this visionary attitude which I have chosen to call here flatness. It expresses how flat vision and even banalities can sometimes become sublime through photography. Since the medium in question becomes in this case the principal way into an integrated knowledge which remains emphatically flat, I shall quote all three of these passages before continuing my reading of the page.

Here is the recollection from *La fugitive / Albertine disparue*. It occurs at one of those moments when the smallest "nothing" is capable of setting off Marcel's jealousy:

> But the latter [jealousy] suddenly revived at the thought of Balbec, because of the vision which all at once reappeared (and which until then *had never made me suffer* and indeed appeared one of the most innocuous in my memory) of the dining-room at Balbec in the evening, with all that populace crowded together *in the dark on the other side of the window, as in front of the luminous wall of an aquarium* [watching the strange creatures moving around in the light but] (and this I had never thought of before) in its conglomeration causing the fisher-girls and other daughters of the people to brush against girls of the bourgeoisie envious of that luxury. (SK 3.531 / P 4.102)

(The passage in brackets does not appear in the Tadié edition.) This "nothing" that sets the jealousy off is a visual image that is figured according to the paradoxical chiaroscuro that we have already encountered. Here the narrator denies having suffered from this image, and the "I suffered as" mentioned in the previous passage suddenly rings hollow in terms of this one. But this would be to underestimate the productive, generative quality of the superimposed images from which this novel is built. For it only rings hollow if we adopt a banal realist stance. Far from being hollow, the image, once it has been recycled, never loses its capacity to modify the meaning, to reveal new meaning and even to create meaning in every new "print" that the narrator makes. But in order

209

that this production of meaning be set in motion, the reader has to accept that the novel transgresses the subjectivist limit that defines its modernism. This modernism would be limited to an epistemological questioning. By going beyond this frame Proust's work crosses into a prophetic postmodernism and runs the risk of ontological doubt.

My point is that the occurrence of this memory establishes another effect that, as a visual metadiscourse, expresses the extent to which the photograph is a "skin" (Barthes) that cannot be shed. For the heteropathic identification with the poor people extends to the phantasmic evocation of the subject as the object of vision. The narrator sees himself as the object of "ethnographic" vision, as a strange being in an aquarium. This vision has been prepared by the mental photograph of the grandmother, which was also a photograph—a representation "in the third person"—of the "I." The reversal is made possible here by the plate of glass against which the double-sided image is pressed. Of course, this "pressing against" has the lateral effect—like a false center to the passage—of evoking that other "pressing against" of the female bodies that brush against one another, remaining hopelessly out of his reach. Thus he suffers from jealousy, which appears clearly here to be rooted in the visual.

The first passage, of which these two are the recollections or, rather, the new prints made under different conditions, shows even less compassion than the second. It is preceded by a true voluptuous delight in chiaroscuro ("I knew that from the chrysalis of this twilight, by a radiant metamorphosis, the dazzling light of the Rivebelle restaurant was preparing to emerge") which leads to the contrasting vision of the poor people:

> Its windows stood open no more, for it was night now outside and the swarm of poor folk and curious idlers, attracted by the blaze of light which was beyond their reach, hung in black clusters, chilled by the north wind, on the luminous sliding walls of that buzzing hive of glass. (SK 1.864 / P 2.164)

No compassion here; no suffering either. The poor people are not only the object of vision, they are also very badly seen. Our photographer has yet to perfect the balance between the light and the opening of the aperture,[3] and as a result there is a lack of contrast.

If we follow these three descriptions through the development of the novel it becomes clear that the poor people are gradually liberated as the narrator becomes more proficient. Here they are once again reified into insects, which are cruelly kept in their place, and no suffering is associated with them. But they are to be transformed into human beings endowed with an active subjectivity, then into individuals who deserve compassion, and finally into heroes. The word "compassion" should be taken literally, as an etymological synonym of "sym-pathy." Such compassion is made possible by a change in the ontological status of the hero, who briefly "presses himself" against the soldiers, just as a chemical liquid fixes light on a sheet of paper. From one passage to the next the vision improves with the help of a more competent manipulation of the contrast between light and shadow, which in the page from *Le temps retrouvé* gives the photograph, like lost time, a new and unimagined dimension.

Let me continue, then, my reading of this page from *Le temps retrouvé*. The dinnertime rush is in full swing when the blackout regulations take effect and everybody jostles against one another, creating a scene that "took place in a mysterious half-darkness which might have been that of a room in which slides are being shown on a magic lantern, or of the auditorium, during the exhibition of a film, of one of those cinemas towards which the men and women who had been dining would presently rush" (SK 3.756 / P 4.313). So we rediscover the magic lantern: the narrator leaves the reader the trouble of recalling the memory from the beginning of the novel, which was the primary experience of contrast and continues to be the recurrent source of the chiaroscuro effect.[4] Here, for example, is one such experience: "as suddenly one sees a huge shadow which ought not to be visible obliterate the figures on the screen of a magic lantern, a shadow which is that of the lantern itself, or that of the operator (SK 3.549 / P 4.119).[5] Or this one from the very beginning, in which it is not the machine but the screen that adds the strange, unwelcome element that spoils the illusion: "I could still distinguish Golo's horse advancing across the window-curtains, swelling out with their curves and diving into their folds" (SK 1.10 / P 1.10). The lantern is properly magical: "It substituted for the opaqueness of my walls an impalpable iridescence, supernatural phenomena of many colours, in which legends were depicted as on a shifting and transitory window"

211

(SK 1.9 / P 1.9). The transparency of the spectacle, added to the mysterious half-darkness, constitutes the frame from which will appear the shadow, which in SK 3.549 / P 4.119 is the shadow of the subject, the operator turned into specter.

Finally, as a fourth instance of this photographic effect, there is on this same page a contrast effect that is as necessary for vision as memory is for the restoring of lost time, for which it is, in my interpretation, the spatial figuration:

> Ah! if Albertine had been alive, how delightful it would have been on the evenings when I had dined out, to arrange to meet her out of doors, under the arcades! At first I should have seen nothing, I should have had the pang of thinking that she had failed to turn up, when suddenly I should have seen one of her beloved gray dresses *emerge from the black wall* then her smiling eyes which had already seen me. (SK 3.757 / P 4.314)

The four consecutive images here share both the contrast *in the image* as the condition of visibility and the minimal, reversible contrast between the subject and the image as the condition of subjectivity. This is the form assumed by the magic of visual contrast on the written page.

But contrast is not only the primary condition of photographic visibility, which in turn generates subjectivity; it is also the means of fixing the blur, that other problem for vision. Thus, in the evening at Combray, the grandmother used to teach the young Marcel to watch the sky and spot the crows that carried the announcement of his own death. Here is the vision produced by this chemical bath:

> Then, having crisscrossed in all directions the violet velvet of the evening air, they would return, suddenly calm, to absorb themselves in the tower, baleful no longer but benign, some perching here and there (not seeming to move, but perhaps snapping up some passing insect) on the points of turrets, as a seagull perches with an angler's immobility on the crest of a wave. (SK 1.68 / P 1.63)

The comparisons intended to represent immobility function like the shadow and the sunbeam, that is, by means of a paradox. For immobility is not really the first association brought to mind by an angler "on the crest of a wave." But by means of this visual image, by means of the photograph that it is able to snap, instantaneously, the immobility becomes all the more intense.

The focus is, thus, not only a simple technical process to get the "right" effect, but also the very production of an image that would otherwise remain invisible and, therefore, nonexistent as an image. As we have seen, the photograph also reveals a deep complicity with the art of serialization. The evocation of the poor people constituted a series of increasingly sharp prints, which were produced by an experiment linking the visual and the moral. The most successful method of focusing is that which generates the next photograph. The serialization, which we might say functioned paradigmatically in the example of the poor people—and also in those of the airplane and the magic lantern—by means of a progressive adjustment of the same image, also functions syntagmatically in the production of consecutive images, each of which announces the next. This technique makes the photograph more and more cinematographic without ever losing sight of the distinction that separates these two media. We are dealing with something like an avant-garde photograph, which appears prior to cinema. This photograph calls into question diegesis as the founding principle for a succession of images. It reveals an experimental desire to further the possibility of producing images by sight alone, that is, of creating a visually based "diegesis." The avant-garde rediscovers its military meaning in a breathtaking seizure of power by the image.

This seizing of power takes place within the domain of photography. Framing and focus are both prior to the very possibility of serialization. The passage that makes this point on the priority of framing and focusing has already been mentioned in the third part, since it picks up the theme of solitary pleasure in a phantasmic evocation of masturbation, qualified by Doubrovsky as secondary. We are still at the beginning of *La recherche*, where all the important mechanisms of the work are established. In terms of the production of images, however, this scene could not be more primary. For in an almost chance movement of the camera, it produces what is the first, the primal, and the primary scene of voyeurism. The staging produces a photographic setup, and at its very center, like a mise en abyme, we see a photograph.

The passage containing the collage that I want to look at and which must be read in its entirety begins with "Alas, it was in vain that I implored the castle-keeper of Roussainville" (SK 1.172 / P 1.156) and ends with "the most terrible and lasting form of cruelty" (SK 1.180 / P 1.163). The image of the castle brings back to mind the vision from "the little room that smelt of irises" from which Marcel "could see nothing but its tower," framed as if by a well-focused lens "in the half-opened window." Again, the solitary pleasure of bygone days is here presented as a very dangerous voyage of discovery: "With the heroic misgivings of a traveller setting out on a voyage of exploration or of a desperate wretch hesitating on the verge of self-destruction, faint with emotion, I explored, across the bounds of my experience, an untrodden path which for all I knew was deadly" (SK 1.172 / P 1.156). The castle is no help whatsoever to the photographer who is wrestling with the problems of framing and long-distant vision: "In vain did I compress the whole landscape into my field of vision, draining it with an exhaustive gaze . . . "; "I would stare interminably at the trunk of a distant tree"; "I scanned the horizon, which remained as deserted as before"; and the trees remain as inert as "trees painted on the stretched canvas background of a panorama" (SK 1.173 / P 1.156).

The frustration with the inert quality of these images, the failure to produce beings with "shape and solidity" by means of vision, is described in strong terms of impotence, illusion, and subjectivity. "Flatness" then intervenes, quickly provoking an investment in a quite different type of creation:

> They [the desires] no longer had any connection with nature, with the world of real things, which from then onwards lost all charm and significance, and meant no more to my life than a purely conventional framework, what the railway carriage, on the bench of which a traveller is reading to pass the time, is to the *fictional events* of his novel. (SK 1.173 / P 1.157)

And it is straight after this evocation of fictional events that the following image is called forth and produced, an image that is doubly photographic. The transition is rationalized by the spatial contiguity ("another impression which I received at Montjouvain"), and the narrator suggests a change in subject, introducing the voyeurism scene with reference to "the notion I was to form of sadism."

But the contiguity is more fundamental than the simple spatial localization suggests, a localization that is deceptive in any case if we take the spatial inscriptions literally, since "Roussainville" is not "Montjouvain." The visual motivation for the association is the trees in the evening light, trees from which he had vainly hoped to see a magical action produced. He has more luck here, simply because the magic is of a visual order. The image is highlighted by a fictional setup that belongs to fairy tales in which the hero falls asleep and then wakes up in wonderland with a magic mirror ("having gone as far as the Montjouvain

215

pond, where I enjoyed seeing again the reflection of the tiled roof of the hut"). Equipped with his zoom lens, the hero suddenly sees Mlle Vinteuil "standing in front of me, and only a few centimetres away." This sight, which is so close up that only a zoom could make it possible, is described like a well-framed photograph: "The window was partly open; the lamp was lighted." And our hero, who just happens to be there, just happens, that is, because of the previous image with its voluptuous dimension, justifies the following voyeurism with this half admission: "If I had moved away I would have made a rustling sound among the bushes, she would have heard me, and she might have thought that I had been hiding there in order to spy upon her." Which is, of course, narratively speaking, exactly what he is doing (SK 1.174 / P 1.157).

The zoom enables him to get even closer, gradually enlarging the image, thereby adding "a layer of fiction more," to paraphrase the commentary on the grandmother's presents of photographs. The object this time is the photograph within the photograph, that is, the photograph of the father, which is profaned under the eyes of the voyeur: "At the far end of Mlle Vinteuil's sitting-room, on the mantelpiece, stood a small photograph of her father" (SK 1.175 / P 1.158). The theatrical aspect of the scene has often been noted, and this dimension links it to the other scenes of voyeurism: to the one in which Marcel is waiting at the Guermantes' home, and to the one in which he observes the girls dancing at the casino, and to the one at Jupien's hotel. For my purposes here, it is enough to say that the theatrical aspect contributes to the visual fictionalization of this view, which is a true primal *scene* that generates the construction of lived reality by means of a visual image. Everything is fake, pretense, theater: according to the logic of textual contiguity, the traveling reader of novels had clearly announced the nature of things to come.

One of the multiple functions of this fictionalizing theatricality is to establish the dialectic of the spectator. On the one hand, this spectator is comfortably settled in a darkened room, in his "seat," invisible to the actors, behind the "fourth" wall of conventional theater. On the other hand, this ethnographer, a voyager in search of the secrets of life, is constantly in danger of exposing himself. Mlle Vinteuil plays her part. After the mention of danger for the narrator himself, who, therefore, stays put under his bush, trembling with fear, she pretends to want to close the shutters, thereby depriving the spectator of his vision, and heightening even further Marcel's fear: "People will see us," which also means "we will see them." Adding another layer of pretense, she says: "When I say 'see us' I mean, of course, see us reading" (SK 1.177 / P 1.159). Reading: like the traveler reading his novel. Reading and vision are bound together.

It is after these fictionalizing comments that the voyeur finds himself sufficiently well placed to be able to "press himself" against the view. This pressing-against takes place through an identification by means of which the narrator projects thoughts into Mlle Vinteuil's mind: "With an instinctive rectitude and a gentility beyond her control, she refrained from uttering the premeditated words which she had felt to be indispensable for the full realisation of her desire" (SK 1.176 / P 1.159). In this comment fiction is fully at work: the narrative mode according to which the "first-person" narrator restrains himself from, so to speak, "entering into another character's head," is bypassed in favor of the implausibility of the fairy tale.

The distant tree, rather than producing a woman, has produced first an image, which is fictional, then a voyeuristic situation, and last a second image, this time of Mlle Vinteuil, who in turn has produced a third degree of image in the photograph of her father. The profaning of this third image produces, not only the declared notion of sadism, but also the whole mechanism of jealousy. However painful jealousy may be, it is also, according to this logic, a voluptuousness of the gaze. Mlle Vinteuil's friend could not have put it better, despite herself, when she "instructs" the apprentice voyeur: "All the better that they should see us" (SK 1.172 / P 1.159).

This invitation to participate is repeated at the level of the father's photograph, when the father is invited to participate by means of his photograph in the theatrical act of pretended denial: "Oh! There's my father's picture *looking at us*; I can't think who could have put it there; I'm sure I've told them a dozen times that it isn't *the place for it* [for its/his place has been taken by the (other) voyeur]" (SK 1.177 / P 1.160; emphasis added).[1] It is in reference to these remarks that the theatrical representation can be considered ritualistic. These remarks are said to come from

217

the discourse of the father (Vinteuil) addressed to the father (of Marcel) in relation to his art. This is, in fact, the beginning of a whole series of acts that are said to be "liturgically" centered around the photograph of the father, onto which Mlle Vinteuil's friend spits.

The young boy that, according to a realistic calculation, Marcel should be at this point—he needed permission from his parents to stay out late—shows a profound wisdom in his disabused moral and aesthetic assessment of this exercise in sadism:

> It is behind the footlights of a Paris theatre and not under the homely lamp of an actual country house that one expects to see a girl encouraging a friend to spit upon the portrait of a father who has lived and died for her alone; and there is nothing like sadism to provide a foundation in life for the melodramatic aesthetic. (SK 1.178 / P 1.161)

What is said here in terms of the theater can also be understood, by means of the insertion of the diegetic photograph into the scriptural photograph, as a discourse on photography. By becoming a mise en abyme, the photograph of the father underlines and expresses the photographic poetics of this work. And the melodramatic aesthetic is the other side of "flatness: banality."

The flatness does not depend so much on the avowed content of this scene, namely sadism. In fact, the novice voyeur starts with sadism, then "progresses" onto homosexuality, and finishes, in *Le temps retrouvé*, with masochism. Inasmuch as the narrator himself declares the influence of this vision of the two lesbian lovers on the rest of his life, it is also a revelation of his female homosexuality. This cannot fail to complicate the image: if we look no further than the visual mechanism of this scene, that is, the "pressing together," then the conjunction of the hero and the vision makes him into a lesbian through heteropathic identification.

But this is not to be taken in a "realistic" sense either. The point is not that Marcel, the young (?) hero of the novel, becomes a double homosexual. The point is that he becomes a double photographer and that this is an "identity"—or equipment—that he needs in his ethnographic journeys at the casino in Incarville, then at the Guermantes' home, and finally at Jupien's hotel. Rather than his initiation into sadism, this scene establishes a way of making the image produced by the internal click effective, "pressing" the narrator in his function as focalizer onto what he sees. This "pressing against" is necessary in order to question better the traditional epistemology in which subject and object are clearly distinguished and, further, to explore the alternatives opened up by this questioning.

Marcel, a lesbian?[2] Of course not, if we take this subject as a character in the full, "dense," realistic sense; but such a reading would be inappropriate. Yes, if we consider him as a written form that writes. In one sense, this primal "pressing against," which is the figuration for all exploration of knowledge and of the jealousy that it generates, poses the pressing together of two smooth bodies, without a disfiguring iron clamp, as an "ideal." It is an ideal in which voluptuousness, aesthetics, knowledge, and writing are all bound together. In this sense, this aspect of *La recherche* will be recycled and turned around a little later by Djuna Barnes, who, in her 1936 novel *Nightwood*, makes lesbian love into the ideal of the ultimate realization of the "loss of self." In this respect she appropriates the poetics of Proust's novel, in which lesbianism, defined by the pressing together of two bodies, is the ideal of a loss of substance, of the "shape and solidity" of self in flatness.[3]

We saw quite clearly in this scene that the realism of the "plausible" focalization has no relevance for this visualizing narrative. If a close-up view is necessary, the subject places himself a few centimeters away, enabling the "pressing together." And, in order that the photograph in the photograph become a dramatic agent, the zoom lens comes to its assistance. The close-up scene is called forth, produced, by the gaze fixed on a distant tree. Then the subject, like Alice in Wonderland, crosses the mirror of the pond and finds himself, as if by chance, asleep, then awake, just where he needs to be. All of this takes us far, not only from narrative realism—with its consistent focalization and its restricted field—but also from visual realism, of which the most characteristic tool is linear perspective. The latter is not absent; on the contrary, it is invoked, defied, and transgressed in order to express better the degree of transgression and to emphasize further the visual alternative that is opposed to it in the form of an "optical illusion." **219**

This emphatically visual relation, which is profoundly subversive in terms of perspective, is also established at the beginning of the novel in one of those visual descriptions that confirm the visualizing potential of a linguistic text: the description of the church steeple at Combray. There would be nothing striking about this passage, which would appear like an explanation of cubism for children,[4] if it were not for its insistence:

> Some doors away, on the left, raising abruptly with its isolated peak the ridge of housetops; . . . one let one's eyes follow along that ridge which had now become low again after the descent of its other slope . . . ; it appeared obliquely, showing in profile fresh angles and surfaces, like a solid body surprised at some unknown point in its evolution; or if, seen from the banks of the Vivonne, the apse, crouched muscularly and heightened *by perspective*, seemed to spring upwards with the effort which the steeple was making to hurl its spire-point into the heart of heaven—it was always to the steeple that one must return, always the steeple that dominated everything else, . . . raised before me like the Finger of God. (SK 1.71 / P 1.65)

The reader is alerted by the ironic hyperbole in "like the Finger of God," preceded by the personification of "spring upwards with the effort," the connotations of which we now recognize, and by words such as "dominated."

Perspective only serves to deceive, to create optical illusions, of which there are, according to the narrator, temporal versions ("There are optical illusions in time as there are in space"), which is described in a manner that corresponds point by point to the following:

> It was its [the memory of Albertine] fragmentary, irregular interpolation in my memory—like a thick fog at sea which obliterates all the landmarks—that distorted, dislocated my sense of distances in time, which became contracted in one place, distended in another, and made me suppose myself now further away from things, now much closer to them, than I really was. (SK 3.606 / P 4.173)

220 In fact, the difference between the first passage and this one is not simply one between space and time. In the description of the steeple at Combray the narrative situation was fragmentary, broken up by the plurality of focalizers. Even if a mad stroller, who were to run from one place to the other, could actually "take in" these different views of the

steeple, it is clear that a photographer could do it much more easily. The result would be, of course, not one photograph, but a series of snapshots. It is for this reason that the description is not necessarily cubist. In contrast, in the passage on the temporal optical illusion it is not the subject-photographer who moves, but the object, the view taken.

Despite this fundamental difference, the spatial and temporal optical illusions are sometimes integrated. Photography is explicitly mentioned in one description—a mental photograph—of an apparently anodyne spectacle. It is brought into view immediately after the description of the mythical kissing organ and is introduced by the phrase "having taken out of its distant frame the blossoming face that I had chosen from among all others." It appears just before the description of the "real" kiss. This is a breathtakingly dense description, signifying by iconicity at once its density, how it piles things together, and how it serializes the image that it produces:

> Apart from the most recent applications of photography—which huddle together at the foot of a cathedral all the houses which so often, from close to, appeared to us to reach almost to the height of the towers, drill and deploy like a regiment, in file, in extended order, in serried masses, the same monuments, bring together the two columns on the Piazzetta which a moment ago were so far apart, thrust away the adjoining dome of the Salute, and in a pale and toneless background manage to include a whole immense horizon within the span of a bridge, in the embrasure of a window, among the leaves of a tree that stands in the foreground and is portrayed in a more vigourous tone, frame a single church successively in the arcades of all the others—I can think of nothing that can to so great a degree as a kiss evoke out of what we believed to be one thing with one definite aspect, the hundred other things which it may equally well be, since each is related to a no less legitimate *perspective*. (SK 2.378 / P 2.660; emphasis added)

The matter at stake in this fantasy about the ideal kiss is, thus, the question of framing, which is posed so acutely by perspective. Here we have **221** successive attempts to frame successfully, which leads to a serialization of the image: "to include a whole immense horizon within the span of a bridge, in the embrasure of a window, among the leaves of a tree that stands in the foreground."

What is the fascination generated by these "most recent applications of photography"? It cannot be perspective, which was already naturalized in the description(s) of the steeple at Combray. Nor can it be the effect of depth, which, far from being favored by the Proustian narrator, is insistently discredited. We have also seen the seasickness caused by the attempt to see the sea "in perspective."

Here, in this phantasmic description of all that photography can achieve, perspective is used mainly to falsify the vision, to fictionalize it, as is already indicated in the personification of the beginning of the passage ("which huddle" that reactivates the catachresis "at the foot of a cathedral"). The framing is used to pluralize, or to serialize, the image, in order to turn it into a "contact sheet." The kiss itself, which follows immediately, is presented rather like a series of enlargements, which, as in *Blow-Up*, end up dissolving the image into invisibility, even if it produces a fabula on the way.

What seems to me to be important here, in the confusing whirl created by perspective, is the fundamental instability of the subject that classical perspective is intended precisely to control. In the case of *La recherche*, this instability is made more serious because the subject projects himself outward in a heteropathic identification in order to press up against the object. But the latter is no more stable than the former, and thus—running the risk of madness—the "I" and the "other" are set adrift in the form of the photograph and its referent, those double surfaces which are pressed together to make up the two-sided image.

This brings us to the photographic form that represents one step further in the direction of cinema, that is, toward the irreducibly pluralized and moving image. But the limit is never transgressed. Rather than adventuring into cinematographic writing, Proust explores photography's productivity to the point of absurdity: framed and focused, the photograph is serialized, but not according to a pluralization of the focalizer or the object, rather according to a process of offsetting that produces marginal changes in visibility, which become the object of the quest.

222

The photograph's primary quality, which is its most banal quality and, therefore, its flattest, is its ability to freeze momentarily an object that exists in a temporal flow, thereby producing snapshots. These are photographs that, in an album, give the impression of having been taken "on the spur of the moment," just as they insist upon the stillness that belongs to the medium rather than to the object itself. These images are like those taken from a film that is frozen. Here is an example, from *Un amour de Swann*, that gives a good sense of this strangeness or estrangement and the focalizer's feeling of externality:

> And by keeping the pipe firmly in his mouth he could prolong indefinitely the dumb-show of suffocation and hilarity. Thus he and Mme Verdurin (who, at the other side of the room, where the painter was telling her a story, was shutting her eyes preparatory to flinging her face into her hands) resembled two masks in a theatre each representing Comedy in a different way. (SK 1.286 / P 1.258)

The whole of the scene, which is theatrical like so many scenes from the various salons, presents the habitual combination of ruthlessly ironic conversations and caricatural gestures. But here we have two masks that isolate two faces—framing—and stop the movement in an imaginary click that makes this description into two snapshots.

In order to measure the poetic importance of the snapshot, here are the two twin descriptions of the view the narrator has from his position in the stairway when he is waiting for the Guermantes in the voyeurism scene that opens *Sodome et Gomorrhe I*. The first description is made up of a series of views like an imaginary museum of paintings from the Dutch school. It consists in the operator's (Barthes's term) primary act, namely framing. The view is related to painting ("and framing silent gestures in a rectangle placed under glass by the closing of the windows, with an exhibition of a hundred Dutch paintings hung in rows"; SK 2.594 / P 2.860). The kitchen girl is daydreaming, elsewhere the young girl is having her hair brushed by an old woman with a face like a witch: both of these images do evoke paintings. But there are moments when the collection of views looks more like a series of rather arbitrary and not very successful snapshots ("nothing but blocks of buildings of low elevation, facing in every direction, which . . . prolonged the distance with their oblique planes" SK 2.595 / P 2.860). And when the hero returns to his vigil in the afternoon the description of distant views alternates with the more detailed one of the orchid, and then, in the middle distance, with the snapshots of Charlus and Jupien taken on the spur of the moment. These snapshots capture them and immobilize them in a series of gestures, the description of which reminds us of the series of images made by the American photographer Eadweard Muybridge that were designed to "write" movement.

The narrator theorizes explicitly the transition from, or the difference between, the "museum" effect, which juxtaposes a collection of picturesque or pictorial images that bear an obvious intertextual relation to painting, and the snapshot effect. The Duchess of Guermantes is the mouthpiece for the "stupidity" that remains blind to this difference:

> "What? You've been to Holland, and you never visited Haarlem!" cried
> the Duchess. "Why, even if you had only a quarter of an hour to spend in
> the place, they're an extraordinary thing to have seen, those Halses. I
> don't mind saying that anybody who caught only a passing glimpse of
> them from the top of a tram without stopping, supposing they were hung
> out to view in the street, would open his eyes pretty wide." This remark
> shocked me as indicating a misconception of the way in which artistic im-
> pressions are formed in our minds, and because it seemed to imply that
> our eye is in that case simply a recording machine that takes snapshots.
> (SK 2.544 / P 2.813)

The difference between the two visual domains, painting and photography, is made all the more acute here by the Duchess's tendency to exaggerate. In order to transgress the limit between the two domains she has to have recourse to a most implausible circumstance—"supposing they were hung out to view in the street"—which is defined principally in terms of movement: "from the top of a tram without stopping." Nonetheless, the imagined situation requires a change in social class, and the use of the indefinite pronoun, "anybody," implies a depersonalization. This combination in turn represents the banality, the common character, of the photographic snapshot: unlike painting it produces a record of everyday life. The misconception of artistic impressions is also a misconception of the different visual domains.

Then we have the case of a reflection on the changing nature of people, during a walk with the rediscovered Gilberte, which ends with a reference to the snapshot as a metaphor for this fleetingness: "In so many people there are different *strata* which are not alike: the character of the father, then of the mother; one traverses first one, then the other. But, next day, the order of *superimposition* is reversed" (SK 3.710 / P 4.268). All that is needed in order to end up with a family album is to juxtapose the "strata" rather than superimposing them. Albertine in particular is a fleeting being because she leaves only snapshots behind her.

Indeed, in *La prisonnière*, Albertine, who has now lost the aspect she had in the photograph on the beach, consists in nothing but a series of snapshots:

> A person, scattered in space and time, is no longer a woman but a series of events on which we can throw no light, a series of insoluble problems. (SK 3.99 / P 3.612)

This dissolution into a flat, visual series only gets worse, becoming eventually the base on which the images of jealousy fix themselves:

> For I possessed in my memory only a series of Albertines, separate from one another, incomplete, a collection of profiles or snapshots, and so my jealousy was restricted to a discontinuous expression, at once fleeting and fixed. (SK 3.145 / P 3.655)

The last words, "at once fleeting and fixed," define very precisely the nature of photography and, in particular, the nature of the series of snapshots. It is clear, then, why the snapshot's vocation is to become the mise en abyme of that aspect of the novel which can be defined as photographic. These words explain the specific use Proust makes of the photographic mechanism.

The narrator composes "an album of Albertines" in the vain hope of fixing this inaccessible being. The "flatness" of the photograph, however, has an additional quality that frustrates this attempt: it invites pretense, masks, and playacting. It only fixes the external aspect, thereby hiding all the better the inner being, which, in the case of Albertine, we are justified in saying does not actually exist. While the series of snapshots provides the subject with an epistemological way out, the pressing together means that the photograph also affects the object, and, consequently, all is lost:

225

> And before she pulled herself together and spoke to me, there was an instant during which Albertine did not move, smiled into the empty air, with the same feigned spontaneity and secret pleasure as if she were posing for somebody to take her photograph, or even seeking to assume before the camera a more dashing pose. (SK 3.146 / P 3.656)

The series of snapshots functions at its best, revealing what this medium is capable of, in the representation of Robert de Saint-Loup, when it offers to the narrator, somewhat paradoxically, a mode of representation that is both unique and successful.

Robert is the most "photographic" character in *La recherche*. By this I mean that his luminous beauty makes him the most photogenic and, thus, the ideal photographic object. But he is a subject of photography as well; indeed, he is the most active photographer. It is he who takes the photograph of the grandmother and who develops it in order that the text can say what he did in the dark room. But most of all, he is constantly photographed in movement. He is one of those figures that Etienne-Jules Marey recorded in movement, or one of Muybridge's serialized figures (Figs. 13, 14). This rapidly moving character is a fleeting being, but not in the same way as Albertine.

The latter is characterized by her indolence and her systematic adaptation to the narrator's wishes. The reader will recall how Marcel obliges her to move from place to place on the day of the gathering at Mme Verdurin's home, where Mlle Vinteuil was expected to appear. He sends her elsewhere, only to discover that Lea was supposed to go to that very place that he had believed to be a safe haven for his loved one. So finally he sends Françoise to get her and bring her back home. All this is madness, but Albertine, lacking any autonomy as a character, like a puppet who submits to the needs of the story and its subject, adapts to all that is imposed upon her. Faced with the "collage" that the narrator is desperately trying to create, Albertine takes her place in the "picture" as well as she can. The snapshots only reveal all the more clearly and, therefore, all the more painfully, the essential impossibility of "fixing" her down.

Robert, on the other hand, escapes being fixed in a different, more active, and fundamentally more visual way. From the beginning of their friendship the visual rapidity of Robert's movement has been a leitmotiv that functions as a permanent feature that identifies the character,

Fig. 13. Etienne-Jules Marey, *Jump from a Standing Position*, ca. 1882. Paris, Bibliothèque Nationale. See François Dagognet, *Etienne-Jules Marey*.

that is, as his infallible characteristic. However, this feature is much more than a simple label or an index of identity. It is "inflated with meaning" (Schor, *Reading in Detail*). In the last voyeurism scene this rapidity seems literally to identify Robert, but it is not its only function. Here is the description:

> Too far off for me to be able to make out clearly in the profound darkness, I saw an officer come out and walk rapidly away.
>
> Something, however, struck me: not his face, which I did not see, not his uniform, which was disguised by a heavy greatcoat, but the extraordinary disproportion between the number of different points which his body successively occupied and the very small number of seconds within which he made good this departure, which had almost the air of a sortie from a besieged town. . . . This military man with the ability to occupy so many different positions in space in such a short time disappeared. (SK 3.838 / P 4.389)

227

This is what the photographer Muybridge and the scientist Marey were trying to capture, both for different reasons. It shows the passing of time

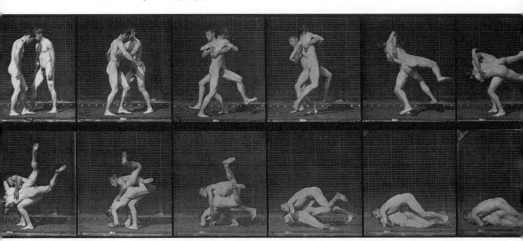

Fig. 14. Eadweard Muybridge, *Wrestlers*, 1887, part of the series *Human and Animal Locomotion*. Private collection.

in a subjectivity whose center is empty and whose senses are overruled. Without saying so explicitly, the passage identifies Robert visually as a visitor, if not a client, of the sordid establishment that the narrator is about to discover. I am referring here to Jupien's hotel where the hero-ethnographer finishes his voyage of discovery by encountering himself. Thus Robert is one "of them" as well. And although at the precise moment when the contact sheet passes before his eyes the narrator does not yet know what this group is all about—espionage, horrific crimes—he soon finds out: not only homosexuals, but also masochists who allow themselves to be bound to beds to be completely flattened out.

The psychological explanation for this characteristic rapidity was suggested much earlier. It is, in fact, quite "logical": "the fear of being seen, the wish to conceal that fear, the feverishness which is generated by self-dissatisfaction and boredom" (SK 3.717 / P 4.276). These reasons are supplemented later with the symbolic reason of the brevity of Saint-Loup's life. Fleetingness fits perfectly with this. It is by means of this characterization of Robert, who is the other side of Albertine, that the crucial epistemo-erotic question of *La recherche* is posed. This rapidity opposes Robert to Albertine, who is as dark as he is blond, more than it opposes him to Morel.

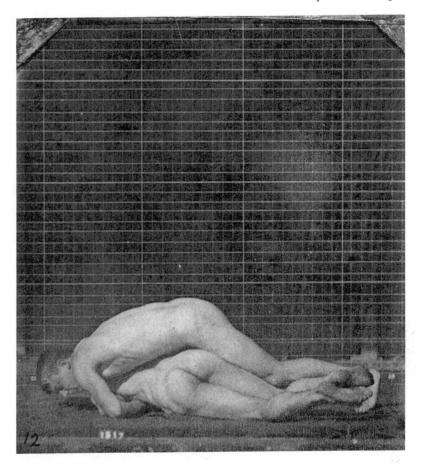

Fig. 15. Eadweard Muybridge, detail from *Wrestlers*.

In our passage the description has a clear diegetic function. It enables the narrator to mention the quite astonishing fact that this handsome aristocrat is taking part in the homosexual sadomasochism that is staged in Jupien's disreputable hotel. But the description allows this to be revealed under the cover of the darkness of night. Paradox upon paradox: this darkness is indispensable because it enables the vision of the contact sheet that records Robert's movement to shed the definitive light on the ethnographic investigation of sexuality.

This darkness also enables the inscription of complex intertextual relations between this episode and several literary genres, for which it can be viewed as the catalog. The passage brings to mind the realist adventure novel—the scene is a blackout during the war—and the espionage novel; it fits easily into the detective novel genre, as well as the novel of coming-of-age, and even the "strange" novel such as Maupassant's *Horla*.[5] This scene is more elaborate in its preparation than the earlier voyeurism scenes, and it calls the position of the onlooking subject definitively into question. The "pressing together" is almost complete this time. The description of the officer is part of this preparation, and the detailing of the snapshot in almost geometric terms underlines its importance. To put it simply, this scene from the final volume of *La recherche* is an important stage in the process toward the writing of time, which is the end, in both senses of the term, of the work.

The serialized snapshot comes even closer to the cinematographic sequence in a little scene that happens much earlier in the course of the discovery that the narrator is finally to make in Paris that night. It is, thus, separate from the one we have just discussed, but it is closely linked in epistemological and libidinal terms. It contains all the elements of the photographic poetics, and it displays their various meaningful aspects as well as the particular epistemology that underpins Proustian visuality. The scene in question describes the encounter between Robert and the "impassioned loiterer" as it is witnessed by the narrator—as the focalizer sees it.

Robert is accosted in the street by a man who propositions him; he responds with his fists. This event happens just after their outing as a threesome with Rachel, Saint-Loup's mistress. The narrator is reflecting on the illusory nature of Robert's love for Rachel. This reflection is founded upon a visual base, the pear trees in flower that he had contemplated earlier that day (SK 2.170 / P 2.459). In the diegesis this reflection justifies the fact that Marcel is walking behind Saint-Loup, which in turn justifies the distant vision he has of Robert. It is not so much a motivation (Hamon, *Introduction*) for the insertion of the description at this point, as it is for the specific way in which the vision is made into an image. In other words, it justifies the "discrepancy of the object-glass" (Banfield, "L'imparfait"), in the sense of both temporal and spatial disjunction.[6]

230

Then we have the strange description of this contact sheet:

> I saw that a somewhat shabbily attired gentleman appeared to be talking
> quite closely to him. I concluded that this was a personal friend of Robert;
> meanwhile they seemed to be drawing even closer to one another; sud-
> denly, as an astral phenomenon flashes through the sky, I saw a number of
> ovoid bodies assume with a giddy swiftness all the positions necessary for
> them to compose an unstable constellation in front of Saint-Loup. Flung
> out like stone from a catapult, they seemed to me to be at very least seven
> in number. They were merely, however, Saint-Loup's two fists, multiplied
> by the speed with which they were changing place in this—to all appear-
> ance ideal and decorative—arrangement. (SK 2.186 / P 2.480)

The theme of speed, which creates an association with cinema, is once
again, as in the passage analyzed above, represented by a drawing of
movement that is reduced to a series of fixed points. As such the passage also brings to mind the principal of the magic lantern. Muybridge's
work shows the extent to which the graphic representation of movement is difficult and "loquacious" (Fig. 14). Marey also dedicated a large
part of his career to the visual representation of the *continuous* trace of
movement, as opposed to its decomposition on a contact sheet as in
Muybridge. But the emulation between time and space, between movement and visuality, has a much longer history. The number seven from
the passage gives Robert seven arms, which is the sacred number of
pairs of arms that the god Shiva possesses in Hindu iconography.

In one of the enclaves of "essayistic" discourse from the end of *Le
temps retrouvé* in which the narrator reflects on literature, he presents
the following objection to cinematographic writing:

> Some critics now liked to regard the novel as a sort of procession of
> things upon the screen of a cinematograph. This comparison was absurd.
> Nothing is further from what we have really perceived than the vision that
> the cinematograph presents. (SK 3.917 / P 4.461)[7]

This statement fits perfectly with the device of the "contact sheet." **231**
What the narrator rejects is the procession, and most particularly the
procession of things. For such a presentation would be situated beyond
the realm of perception.

If the photographic mechanism suggests cinematographic possibilities, it only does so if the cinema in question is avant-garde and self-reflexive, like a succession of images spread out in space, each one held still. It would have nothing to do with the illusion of "real" movement created by the rapid projection of images. In other words, the technique in question here is crucial because it enables the production of not only a visual writing that is the trace of movement, but also a movement that is the trace of writing.

By remaining a little behind, Marcel-as-focalizer guarantees himself a view through a telephoto lens. The discrepancy of the lens motivates the distance, the framing, the reduction of all perception to sight alone, and consequently, the narrator's incomprehension. The reader will recall the Academician deprived of his perceptual routine. As is often the case, the incomprehension only enables the narrator to understand better, since it enables him to see better. This is rather like the intellectual equivalent of the shade in Rembrandt's paintings. Moreover, it is an important lesson in visual epistemology, and specifically in photographic epistemology: the senses lose their power over perception, the subject's center is evacuated, and the so to speak automatic notation—the writing—is the trace of the movement, of which it captures the essence. What we see here, in an absolutely pure way, is the shock wave, or rather the deep bond, between rapidity spatialized like writing in time, on the one hand, and perception of desire in all its purity because it is purely visual, on the other.

For it is indeed a question of desire in this system of vision that is presented as an aesthetic. The revelation of this desire happens in progressive stages, the first of which is the transition from distant to close-up vision:

> But this elaborate display was nothing more than a thrashing which Saint-Loup was administering, the aggressive rather than aesthetic character of which was first revealed to me by the aspect of the shabbily dressed gentleman who appeared to be losing at once his self-possession, his lower jaw and a quantity of blood. (SK 2.186 / P 2.480)

The comic effect of the zeugma only poorly disguises the more serious issue here. The gentleman has the same visual status as the narrator; the distance of one and the proximity of the other in this silent dance figure the "unstable constellation." The anonymous and fleeting character embodies the poetics that shifts Proust's work beyond avant-garde modernism toward a prophetic postmodernism.

The revelation of the meaning of this strange evocation is limited first of all to the level of the anecdote, and the reader, who is desperate to "understand" (as readers should be able to in any readable novel), is given an explanation. Then, at the discursive level, this revelation is reported by the narrator. But he does not present this revelation in free indirect speech, as one might expect: "It was an impassioned loiterer who, seeing the handsome young soldier that Saint-Loup was, had propositioned him" (SK 2.186 / P 2.480). This sentence defines the limits of the realist logic in which diegesis and discourse collaborate peacefully. Here, however, the attribution of subjectivity poses a problem. Although this explanation should "logically" come from Saint-Loup, since the narrator has voluntarily placed himself in a position of being able only to see, it is, in fact, the narrator who takes responsibility, again "logically," for the evaluation of Saint-Loup's military—virile—beauty. There is, therefore, a third "logic" to this explanation, which stipulates that the narrator share, at least visually, the photographed desire. Significantly, the verb that acts as a shifter is "seeing."

Indeed, the explanation for the event is followed immediately by a further explanation that is inspired by a sort of unfettered psychology, which is quite difficult to understand if one fails to take seriously the photographic epistemology that is at issue here:

> And yet the recipient of his blows was excusable in one respect, for the trend of the downward slope brings desire so rapidly to a climax that beauty in itself seems to imply consent. (SK 2.186 / P 2.480–81)

Here we see the downward slope, as we saw it on the contact sheet ("they seemed to be drawing even closer to one another"). But it is also a metaphor for the essential flatness of this scene, which only reemphasizes the importance of this very particular way of learning to know desire.

Three aspects of this scene make it both central to the work and transform it into a mise en abyme. First, the pure desire is a figured writing of time, which is visually accessible, at the risk of having to distance oneself to see it and at the cost of giving up on ever satisfying it. The reader will recall the kissing organ that enabled sight to be integrated with the other senses. But this organ described precisely a fundamental lack.[8] Second, the desire fixes itself visually on Saint-Loup as the military figure. The military "category" had already been shown as a virile spectacle in the parade at Combray. His presence in the last voyeurism scene, which completes the ethnographic hero's knowledge by revealing the flatness of homosexuality, is thus essential, beyond the level of the anecdote or of the distribution of roles among the characters.

Third, and this aspect brings us to the important point about photography, this work in which desire occupies such an important and structuring place reveals here that desire is in turn subordinated to the possibility of writing. The writing is magically situated between space, which flattens it, and time, which spreads it out. The contact sheet of seven ovoid bodies figures the work, which, abandoning linear sequentiality in favor of an architecture of "unstable constellation," is happening, spreading itself out, before us. But like photography, the contact is only the "positive," the result of contact between fleeting light and the sheet of paper or base, of which the "negative" is the "shape and solidity," in other words, loss. Here the loss is localized in the unknown gentleman, who is shabbily attired and who is a fleeting but indispensable figure in the scene.

The triple loss—of all self-possession, his lower jaw, and a quantity of blood—is the ultimate dis-figure of the work. On the contact sheet, which is full of Saint-Loup's astral rapidity, one can imagine that there is only one image of this sad puppet. He is dripping blood—but falling down a downward slope he won't soil his shabby clothes—and disgusting,[9] and Robert's indignation marks the transition to a moralism that is necessary for the epistemological adventure to continue. But this moralism is irrelevant for the contact sheet, which concludes the passage. Thus the triple loss as a whole is a detail, but nonetheless such a dis-figured and dis-figuring one.

The loss of self-possession is situated at the level of "realism," of psychological explanation, where Proust's characters seem to have a traditional literary existence. The loss of the jaw, which is quite implausible, inscribes the dis-figuring of the character's face into the series. Mise en

abyme en abyme, for this loss dis-figures the very figure of the man.[10]
The loss of blood, which adds an obscene, violent, and "colorful" detail, dis-colors him. This subject of the triple loss, who is nothing but a
marginal object in the serial photograph, is nonetheless the exemplary
subject of desire, who, on a downward slope, comes closest to, and all
but accomplishes, the operation of "pressing against" pursued throughout the text, all the while remaining visible.

The triple loss is a dis-figure in a further way. It figures the loss of
knowledge undergone by the subjects implicated in the work: the narrator, focalizer-photographer, character, and critic. This loss is caused
by a strange device brought to play here in order to display and to know
that which is not supposed to be known. By remaining at the required
distance for this view of the scene, Marcel refuses to hear the loiterer's
proposition and, thus, to participate in this "impassioned" encounter, of
which he only sees the downward slope. Saint-Loup, in turn, refuses to
say it. After the thrashing, however, he sends Marcel away, adding that
he will meet him later, thereby leaving open the possibility of meeting
up with the loiterer. Here homosexuality becomes unspeakable. The
reader or the critic who theorizes the downward slope (here Bouazis, *Ce
que Proust savait*) in turn participates in this taboo on homosexuality as a
literary "act." The "flatness"—covering the homosexual encounter over
with a generalizing theory—thus repeats and thereby contributes to the
refusal to know "intimately" by participating in the act. This is also a
loss of "self-possession." The pressing against, that epistemological tour
de force, has almost succeeded, but the trace that remains is the contact
sheet on which is inscribed, almost illegibly, the movement of drawing
closer in which the briefest passage of time is spread out in space.

The reader no doubt remembers the beginning of *La chambre claire*
when Barthes describes his surprise, which he says no one will share.
On seeing a photograph of Napoleon's brother he says to himself: "I am
looking at the eyes that looked at the Emperor" (13). Photography, as
Barthes defines it, is already there: it is the sight, by definition in the present, of an irretrievably past vision. No exchange of eye contact, but
nonetheless two gazes that confront one another, one dead, the other
alive. Between these two gazes a gulf of past time has carved itself out.

We know how Barthes develops his wonderful essay on photography from the basis of this first vision. As a means of fixing the visual and the spatial, the photograph becomes the instrument of irrecoverable time and of death. Between the eye and the other many things can happen: Barthes uses the word "punctum" to sum up all the tiny events that he describes, modifies, criticizes, circumscribes, and specifies all through his work, until it no longer designates anything but his experience faced with his mother's death.[11] Along the way he mentions the photograph taken by Saint-Loup of the grandmother, but he compares the Tuché, the photograph of the Winter Garden which was his encounter with the real "that was," to the involuntary memory of the grandmother at Balbec.[12]

The amazement that photography provokes is never-ending: what are the effects of that glass eye that slips in front of the operator's eye? And it slips not only in front of Saint-Loup's eye, as in the anecdote about the photograph, but also in front of the narrator's eye throughout the sections in which the photographic governs the text. Photography enables the inscription of an essentially fleeting vision, which is both purely subjective and purely objective, fixing it like writing. As Ann Banfield has shown in her in-depth analysis of Russell's epistemology read through the optic of Barthes's essay "L'imparfait," the photograph is centered, but its center remains empty. Although it is private, it is completely lacking in any subjectivity. It is a flat image that is infinitely reproducible and allows endless alteration, thus offering an objectified image that is nonetheless circumscribed by a full subjectivity that does not inhabit it. This paradox of photography enables the seizure of the punctum, which is not constituted by form but by intensity (Barthes, *La chambre claire*, 148). The punctum is an effect generated by an irremediably "flat" image, in all senses of the term, and it touches the spectator.

"This something has tipped forward, has provoked in me a tiny shock, a satori, the passage of a void," wrote Barthes (81).[13] Tipped forward: we rediscover the downward slope, which made the impassioned loiterer, at another level again, into the mise en abyme or the dis-figure of the photography that underpins Proust's work. The downward slope is the ultimate attempt to fulfill the unsatisfied need to press up against the other, like light on a sheet of paper. Barthes was able to give such a good account of this effect, if not of photography in general, which he denies most forcefully has a general effect, then at least of the photograph of the Winter Garden, precisely because he was wise enough not to show this photograph. It remains as fictional as the photographs in *A la recherche du temps perdu*. He also maintained the flatness of the photograph. Sometimes, in order to explain its effect, he uses the term "umbilical cord," but this "flat" or banal expression is literalized or reanimated because it is used in the context of the emanation of light that "links the body of the photographed thing to my gaze" (126–27). The effect that makes the photograph into a semiotic "index" is also what makes it iconic. The referent sticks to it, as similar to it as two peas in a pod.

However, faced with the eye/lens, the impassioned loiterer has to beat a retreat. The slope is dangerously steep, but touch remains impossible.[14] That particular flatness can never be. This is why Marcel has to be one "of them"; but in order that *La recherche* explore all the dark corners of "life"—knowledge, pleasure, beauty, time, writing—Marcel has to stay in the closet where the unmentionable is played out. In order that desire be maintained throughout this immense work, it must remain untouched by any attempt to satisfy it.

Conclusion

I believed there was such a thing as knowledge
through the lips.

—Proust, A la recerche du temps perdu (SK 2.377 /
  P 2.659)

Proust's work offers, represents, and constitutes a theory of
knowledge. It is a "work-theory" that deals with a type of knowledge
that does not separate the domain of the mind from that of the body,
in other words, that does not separate the cognitive, the affective, the
aesthetic, and the sexual domains. Rather it explores all avenues, however unusual they may be, that lead to the discovery of new aspects of
the real by means of sensations, experiences, and the very pores of one's
being. It is for this reason that we can treat Proust as a philosopher and
even view him in the same light as the greatest philosophers of this century.[1] The novel does not present this knowledge in the form of a theory; rather it makes us suffer it, feel it, and experiment with it.

At the end of this analysis we may once again ask ourselves this question: should we believe Proust?[2] The trap lies in what I have termed the
essayistic side of the work. For should we take the author's word as his
law when he is capable of writing elsewhere that "a work in which there
are theories is like an object which still has its price-tag on it" (SK 3.916
/ P 4.461). To take Proust at his word would be a serious misapprehen-
sion of his writing and of the theory that it implicitly contains. The the- **239**
ory appears, then, as a bonus earned by a disobedient, perhaps even ir-
reverent, reading. This study has offered a reading of A la recherche du
temps perdu that is developed from a concept that features nowhere in
Proust's own theoretical reflections. The concept in question comprises

the conjunction of the two meanings of "flatness," which are apparent in all sorts of ways in Proust's use of the visual image. This critical perspective originated in a conviction that was inspired in me by a "visual" reading of the work, a conviction that "flatness" is an important and constitutive—but not exclusive—dimension of the Proustian theory of knowledge.

The novel is a theory of knowledge, and this theory is generated in part by the mechanism of jealousy, which works backward. Jealousy is a desire for knowledge, and the experience of the impossibility of this knowledge is both severe and fundamental. It adopts the disaffected and exasperating form of imprisonment. But the object that the subject wants to know through possession, or to possess through knowledge, is a fleeting being, since it is other. Albertine vanishes into a puff of smoke, and if she has really existed, she certainly was never really in her prison. The impossibility of keeping, possessing, and knowing Albertine is what motivates and propels the exploration of a knowledge of the other that would result in another knowledge. Since this other knowledge has to be invented, it cannot be described. The image enables us to think an imagined version of such a knowledge.

Albertine has to be asleep, silent, with her eyes closed, in order to "offer up" her beauty. She also has to die so that the subject can attain his understanding. The fundamental knowledge attained is the realization that the other cannot be known according to the model of subjection, which is the interpersonal mode of objectification. The Cartesian model of knowledge, which is based on the radical separation of the subject and the object, and the vertical, "penetrative" relation that shapes this knowledge are both rejected from the very beginning. This model of knowledge has two paradigms: in close-up perception the paradigm is physics, in long-distant perception it is astronomy. The figures that define its rejection are precisely those optical instruments, those microscopes and telescopes, which are both necessary and deficient, and which provide an endless reflection of this central idea, as if it were seen in a mirror or read in a mise en abyme. That no conclusion is reached in this work is due, then, to the fact that it is inscribed from the very beginning to the very end of the novel by all that is contained within.

Each of the preceding reflections was designed to explore a particular aspect of Proustian "flatness." It is perhaps helpful here to see how these different aspects intersect and fit together to *figure* a problematic that is both characteristic of the literature of the time, which "straddled" two centuries, and, I believe, specific to Proust.

In the beginning there was the attempt to see, from afar and up close. Close-up vision splits the subject through its relation with the object, which is made invisible because minutiae and clarity are incompatible and cannot communicate with each other. This causes a feeling of vertigo, which provokes disgust and leads to the search for a homeopathic solution. It seems clear that this search first turns toward visual art, which it will make into a central and unavoidable problematic. The visualization of this problematic takes the form of a display of flatness, which becomes the configuration of the said problematic. Moreover, it seems "logical" that the art that works best in the search for a poetics that accommodates this problematic is not so much grand history painting, but the art of the detail, the art of still life, with all the disgust it implies.

Still life must not be understood here in terms of a thematic definition, but rather as a setup that inscribes this thematic in a figuration that is situated at the level of enunciation. Writing as it is figured by Chardin's *Skate* is a writing that spreads itself out flatly in order to encompass all the contradictory and paradoxical aspects of "life," or, in other words, all the facets of sensualist vision for which the subject and the object are reversible.

The spreading-out in a visual image of that which is fleeting in time leads Proust's writing toward a process of detailing, of enlarging the infinitely small so that each thing becomes "a world in itself." The figuration operates by means of an optical instrument that enlarges the image. The focalizer calls upon such an instrument to fill the gap between long-distant vision, which gives access to the recognizable whole, but which deadens it by flattening it, and close-up vision, which frames, isolates, deforms, and clouds. This instrument functions as a poetic instruction. It is in the piece of glass that is inserted into Mme de Villeparisis's ordinary eyeglasses that we see most clearly the process of detailing undertaken in this work. It focuses on the very problematic in question here and reveals the creative productivity that is released once one is reconciled to its presence. The surface of the enlarged image represents and embodies the surface of the text, and the magnifying glass indicates to us that we should contemplate this surface intensively. The "patch," a theoretical concept that attempts to specify the process of detailing, designates that which misleads a perception that is "too" attentive. In the manner of a decoy, the change in visual scale informs and makes invisible. The exemplary patch is Albertine's cheek, which is invisible.

The patch that informs is superimposed in this work with the dis-figure that deforms. The way in which invisibility also becomes a mise en abyme in Gilberte's signature, which is illegible because it is too detailed, is explained by the fact that this signature signifies too much at one time. It provides too many forms and thereby shields the sign from the desperate search for meaning. The exemplary dis-figure is the dis-figured figure of the impassioned loiterer. Visuality overdetermines the struggle with time, which weaves its cloth by means of the multiplicity of points of view that are juxtaposed in this work. This multiplicity constitutes the work's process of detailed spreading-out. The third term that takes charge of the detailing is the fragment, the hard, true "piece" that has been violently detached and that is the remainder of a past time that survives only as an image. The Proustian fragment cannot but lead to "flatness" in the second sense of the term, that is, in the sense of merciless banality, the best example of which is to be found in the last social gathering at the Guermantes' home.

In this work the search for pleasure makes common cause with the search for perception, which is the basis for knowledge. My purpose has been to suggest that, departing from conventional opinions on the matter, the most striking figurations of voluptuous pleasure in this work present a challenge to the traditionally available positions. Hence the explorations of fantasies that originate on the one hand in "maternal," swelling forms, even though they may have to be flattened if they are to be made one's own, and on the other, in culturally sanctioned dreams of virility.

I would like to insist that the analyses of the two imaginary systems figured around the "swelling hillsides" and the "fountain," which were anchored in "psycho-somatic" considerations, are not intended as psycho-criticism, nor do they purport to lead to a unified anamnesis or diagnosis of the writing subject. Once again, just as in the case of visual art where the aesthetics of the old masters served only as a springboard, the sexual fantasies are not used here to define a psyche, but to figure a poetics. The issue at stake was the need to flatten the swollen form in order to further a certain perception, the status of which is fundamentally indirect in three different, superimposed, and mutually reinforcing ways. Perception is delegated to an expert (Cottard, in the casino scene); it requires an optical instrument (the missing eyeglass); and it is off target in a temporal sense, since at the crucial moments the hero "forgets," is distracted, and has to rely on an interpretation suggested by his hearing. This deficiency in sight is highlighted by a total absence of diegetic motivation, which would have made it plausible.

The indirect status of perception defines what I have termed the "ethnographic" situation, a term that I chose to draw attention to the epistemological component of the voyeuristic and voluptuous enterprise. The issue at stake in ethnography is knowledge of the other. Now, the fact that Albertine, who functions as the embodiment of beauty, has to be asleep in order that this beauty be "offered up," shows that the visualization of the other is placed in opposition to the possibility of communicating with that other. This reduction of the other to a state of spectacle is another form of "flattening." The swelling hillsides seen from afar make the breasts untouchable, but the need to keep this beauty blind reconfirms that it remains just as untouchable in close-up perception.

Charlus's "big bum," which enchants Jupien, is the deliberately vulgar—flat—expression of the same problem. In the scene at the Guermantes' home the voyeuristic subject is defined by the split between seeing and being seen, which means that the subject must go into the closet at the very moment when Charlus, his model, "comes out." Ethnographically speaking, the partition that separates the other from the self, which is reduced here to the point of being almost insubstantial, remains nonetheless of radical importance, signifying that vision is a fundamentally problematic epistemological mode, perhaps even that it is

243

unsatisfactory in an absolute sense. The Proustian subject spreads himself out over the long pages of *La recherche* by "pressing" himself against all of the characters, who are nothing more than puppets, flat images that end up being flat images of himself. In this spreading-out the subject comes up against the partition that no ethnographic attempt at dialogical, communicative epistemology has managed to break down.[3]

I have used the notion of ethnography as a way of taking the "explorative" side of Proust's text seriously, regarding it as part of the whole and as fully integrated with the search for pleasure.[4] This search for knowledge of the other cannot be reduced to a sexual apprenticeship. But this does not mean to say that the sexual aspect is any less crucial. For it is in this area more than in any other that the "other" is seen, so to speak, up close, which is the reason for the constant interweaving of sensual desire and desire for knowledge.

The Proustian subject is undeniably male. The voyage of discovery, which the book recounts, brings about the commitment and the transformation of this subject, who has built himself up so enormously at the very center of the work. Traditional male identifications, while not particularly absent from this work, are shown to have many shortcomings. Among all the characters that appear in the novel, the male ones are either deprived of sexual symptoms and are, therefore, sexually "flattened," or are invested with such an excessive masculine identity that they are made ridiculous, revealed as fakes, and, to put it aptly, "inverted" by the narrator. Charlus is the character who makes the most of his virility, and this shows us immediately that his virility is far from being conventional. Saint-Loup is described as a virile character at the very moment when he becomes the object of male desire, that is, during the first meeting at Balbec, a meeting that is purely visual. He is too beautiful to be "true," and he cries with and for Marcel. He is also the military hero and, moreover, belongs to that group of men who take pleasure in being beaten, in being literally "flattened," until he falls in battle. His greatest feat of virile heroism is to fall.

The exploration of the self, that is, the figuration of different identifications in terms that signify masculinity, defines further the narrator's "ethnographic" quest and brings it closer to the epistemological and voluptuous ideal of "pressing against" the other in a way that renders the partition separating self from other obsolete. The fountain, an image that announces itself immediately as a hyperbolic figuration of conventional masculinity understood as ejaculation, picks up all the terms that were shown to form a network of meaning in the first part: from afar, it is deadened; up close, it is limp. The very thing sought after by this undeniably male apprentice is represented to us by the hand in the torrent of clear, cold water: a base for identification. This base would enable him to experience pleasure and knowledge. It would give him a knowledge through the lips that are able to go beyond the surface of the skin, but all the while stay on the surface in order to "explore" further.

Photography serves as a springboard, but also on occasion as a reference to a ground on which the ultimate fleeting being, light, can be fixed or "put down" in writing. Here the other can be known, time can be fixed, and space can be spread out. But this success can only be achieved on the condition that the photograph be a mental one. The mental photograph is "truer" than the material one, which is too docile as well as being too fixed. Here the link between the subject and the vision is broken in temporal terms by the discrepancy between the shot and what is seen at the time of the shot. But the link is as much broken in visual terms by the imperfection of the lens that is inserted as it is in ontological terms by the being-other of the subject that is represented.

But to suggest that the mental photograph represents the conclusion, the point of arrival of the voyage of discovery, is already to say too much. We are giving way to the desire to find a solution when Proust's text owes its truly marvelous nature to the very fact that it rejects conclusion. The zoom effect created by the movable lens figures the paradox of a centered vision that is empty at the center. It results from a lens that is operated by an omnipresent subject who nonetheless is absent to himself, who presses himself against others but is never filled with "shape and solidity." The contrast between clarity and indistinction, as it occurs in Chardin's work, is homologous to the contrast between the subject and the image. It is also slippery and unpredictable.

Knowledge according to vulgarized Cartesianism, according, that is, to the paradigm of physics or astronomy, is not and has never been without challengers. There are domains of knowledge in which the separation between subject and object sits awkwardly with the subjective status of the object, which, as a fully fledged subject, is always threatening to reverse the positions. If we can describe Cartesian epistemology in the way that Benveniste defines "history," that is, as a third-person discourse, then it can be seen in opposition to an epistemology structured around an object that is constituted by other people rather than things. This knowledge is, then, only accessible and approachable in the fundamentally unstable discourse elaborated through the reversible exchange between a first and a second person. The grammatical positions have once again to be taken literally. The exchange of positions that makes a first person into a second turns all the characters into Marcel, and Marcel into all the characters. Here we have indeed cause for casting a taboo on the first name of the "I," which would fix that which must remain fluid.

For at the end of Proust's visual experience we see that the image as site, springboard, and screen for the encounter between the "I" and the other, who is both respected and envied for his or her otherness, is ultimately that site of dreams which lies at the heart of Julia Kristeva's superb analysis of Proustian sensation. Kristeva restores to the Proustian image all its paradoxical depth when, at the end of her study of the language-based status of sensation, she writes: "The logic of an instant, of the simultaneity of opposites, out of time and beyond any plan: the chamber of sleep 'descends into the depths in which memory can no longer keep up with it, and on the brink of which the mind has been obliged to retrace its steps'" (*Les temps sensible*, 292, quoting *Sodome et Gomorrhe II*, SK 2.1013 / P 3.370). In these famous moments of sleep, either floating just under the surface of consciousness, or fully "gone," Marcel and the image, the other that comes to him, "dream each other." Kristeva looks to philosophical predecessors in order to link Proustian writing to a tradition, and finds one in Maurice Merleau-Ponty. In conclusion, I add a more diffuse, less historical, and more contemporary interdiscursive resonance that is capable of arousing philosophical interest in a way that is entirely oblique, but also striking.

246

Knowledge of the other: while ethnography, in the wake of the realization of the untenable nature of the imperialist, colonialist position, has elaborated endless reflections on the modalities of such knowledge, Proust, by declaring himself prisoner of his imprisoning jealousy, has already advanced across the enormous imaginary empire of his work in the direction in which these modalities could be sought. In this respect, this work of fiction can be associated with the type of philosophy of knowledge that is developed by, for example, the Canadian philosopher Lorraine Code. For Code knowledge of others is, indeed, the paradigm that offers an alternative to the Cartesian paradigm of physics. The model for this form of knowledge, or the figuration that models such a knowledge, is friendship. The reversible relation between first and second persons (grammatical persons in a "vital" grammar), which implies commitment without blinding passion, and which is constantly developing, is the form of discourse that constitutes such knowledge.

It is important to note here that it is friendship and not love that Code considers as her model. Again Proust enables us to understand why. Friendship as interpersonal communication is singularly lacking in *La recherche*. The friendship with Bloch serves only to represent a certain type of snobbery, and Saint-Loup as friend features only as a possible identification and an object of desire ("according to the other"). Proust's work is neither realist nor "humanist" in the psychologizing sense. Love, in contrast to friendship, may well be a constant theme in the novel, but it nonetheless only serves to figure the counterpart, the "Cartesian" knowledge that can only be envisaged in the context of complete subjection, and that is declared impossible. This is the meaning of jealousy, the driving force behind *La prisonnière*.

Code writes that normally we prefer—wrongly, according to her— clear and simple analyses of narratives that are in fact messy but infinitely richer than we suppose.[5] Faced with this dilemma the appeal of the Proustian text immediately takes on a philosophical aspect that has nothing to do with the author's argument or philosophy. The way to knowledge is embodied in this text, with its form and in particular with its figurations that inform (patches) and deform (dis-figures), thus reflecting its "messy" nature.

For Proust the pursuit of knowledge of the other cannot be figured **247** by the relation of friendship as it is advocated by Code. In a work of fiction this friendship would lead automatically to realist psychologism. However, using the means that are specific to it, *La recherche du temps perdu* offers a model that refuses to be straightforwardly positive. At the end of this exploration, my argument is that "flatness," in all the senses of the term and in all the ways that I have tried to reveal, offers a way out of the subjectifying epistemology and points, perhaps vaguely and into the distance, but nonetheless toward other possibilities. It is important for this exploration that the "I" be both below and beyond the partition that separates the self from the other. The "I" is both voyeur and participant in the "closet" of homosexuality. This is the crucial meaning of "pressing against" the other. The work itself is the kissing organ.

From the very beginning the photograph, a favored reference in the text, figures a representation—always of otherness—that transforms the ontological disjunction between the "I" as referent and the "I" as reference into a temporal disjunction, and then, in a second phase, into a spatial disjunction. This spatial disjunction is "flat" and visually accessible. It thereby gives the subjectivity a nonautonomous and nonrigid quality, which is centered but at the same time evacuated, leaving precisely a place for the other as object-subject.[6]

But the text, and this point must be emphasized, is literary, of a linguistic nature, written, and therefore deferred. It is not visual. This is also a necessity inherent to the exploratory project, and it goes beyond the author's gift and the choices he made. Knowledge by "pressing against" the other is an attempt to neutralize the gulf that separates subject from object. But there are more obviously linguistic means of doing just that. Thus Roland Barthes (in *Le bruissement de la langue*) reminds us that the middle voice in ancient Greek was capable of integrating the subject into the action of the verb, which created an intransitive writing. Barthes quotes Proust as an example. "Pressing against" would be, in this sense, a visual or visualizing form of this use of the middle voice.

Literary art, the material of which is language, articulates not only what the materially flat image shows, but also that which it hides; that which it allows and that which it forbids; what it is and what it is not. It is not as if we are dealing here with a veil that is lifted by visuality on the knowledge of a dazzling truth. Such a conception of the image would be simply and vulgarly Cartesian. The cut-up and stuck-down image, which is both banal and subjective, is neither an ideal nor a last resort. It is the map on which the explorer traces out his itinerary, if only he is able to "read" it as a sign, a wish. So, while neither the amateur of art nor the art historian will benefit from taking Proust at his word, the theory of art will find it most useful to do so for an understanding of the textual and coded character of the image, and *by this very fact*, of the image's epistemological productivity.

Within this framework the "we" that was symptomatic of the essayistic and generalizing discourse, and that we must not believe, is reintegrated with epistemological authority after all. For this *we* "without content is also described as a 'being' or a 'thing' that is traumatized by who knows what pleasure or pain: without a trace nor a memory, without any psychic unity; neither a me, nor a self, nor a subject. Nothing but 'blueness' or an 'unknown,' transformed, re-made, perhaps even invented by the narration of the dream" (Kristeva, *Les temps sensible*, 293). This *we* becomes the sign of a subject that "sticks," of a subject that accomplishes the miracle of perception without dehiscence. This subject is born from the encounter with an image that is flat and full. But I will stop before the temptation of a satisfying conclusion.

Allowing Proust to finish, I shall simply juxtapose two images. The seven fists of Robert de Saint-Loup administering a thrashing, on the one hand; and Gilberte / Albertine's exploded, illegible signature, on the other. They are both writing of time, done "by hand," the first "hieroglyphic," the second alphabetic. One allows us to see a desire that is denied, the other to read the subject as he changes positions with the other. Both are "downward slopes," mythical kissing organs, inscriptions of what is unstable, fleeting, unwritable. Visually writing the movement of time also implies dis-attributing the senses and therefore, provoking the abdication of full, sensual subjectivity. As a writing of "flatness," the Proustian text is that infinitely extensible thread which stretches out from the little room smelling of irises and traces its oscillations between space that flattens and time that spreads out.

Reference Matter

Notes

Introduction

1. This citation is representative of the passages of general discussion in *La recherche* that have been termed essayistic, philosophical, and aesthetic. This study will only deal rarely with such passages.

2. The French adjective *plat*, meaning "flat," is contained within the noun *platitude* (banality). The translation "flatness" has been chosen for the word *platitude*, and the reader must bear in mind the association of a figurative and a literal meaning in this word. —Trans.

3. In *Proust: Between Two Centuries*, Antoine Compagnon writes: "I would like to have shown that a work remains present and alive because of its flaws and its disparities, that these defects are what indicates that the work is rooted in time" (299).

4. See Georges Didi-Huberman, "Appendice," 279.

5. See *Expositions*, Philippe Hamon's fundamental work on the notion of exhibition as a sort of textual architecture. He writes notably: "The world of Michelet's 'brilliant trinkets,' of paper, signs, advertisement was also a place where objects were beginning to lose volume and depth. In such a world the great projects of historical and philosophical synthesis and of the collation of the document and the monument no longer seem capable of deploying their principle of all-embracing legibility. Before Marx and Benjamin, Baudelaire . . . equated this incapacity with the loss of memory's or culture's 'halo' or 'aura'" (125). In order to situate Proust "between two centuries," reference should, of course, also be made to Compagnon's *Proust entre deux siècles*.

Chapter 1

1. The question of detailed perception is elaborated in Part II. See Didi-Hu-
    berman, "Appendice," 273–81, and Gaston Bachelard, *Essai sur la connais-*
    sance approchée and *La formation de l'esprit scientifique*. A relevant discus-
    sion of Bachelard's discourse and its pictorial aspects can be found in Jon-
    athan Culler's influential *Framing the Sign*.

2. Proust and painting: the subject is too vast, and it would be useless to
    catalog all the references to painting, which are in any case easy to find
    with the help of the summaries at the end of each volume and the index
    of proper names at the end of the fourth volume of the Pléiade edition
    of the novel, as well as at the end of *Contre Sainte-Beuve*. The influential
    studies so far are Eméric Fiser's *L'esthétique de Marcel Proust* and *La théorie*
    du symbole littéraire chez Marcel Proust, and, more recently, Anne Henry's
    Marcel Proust and "Quand une peinture métaphysique"; John Theodore
    Johnson's *Painter and His Art*, "Proust and Giotto," and "Marcel Proust
    et Gustave Moreau"; and Barbara Bucknall's *Religion of Art in Proust*.
    None of these works emphasizes the fact that painting is above all else
    an image, and that these images are above all else flat; nor do they sug-
    gest that painting as such informs a properly literary poetics.

3. This is implied in Juliette Monnin-Hornung's remarks in *Proust et la pein-*
    ture, 17.

4. In this manner Rosine Georgin begins her diatribe against Proust (*Con-*
    tre Proust) by denouncing the insincerity of Marcel's friendship for Saint-
    Loup (9–20). She takes the whole of *La recherche* to be a serious declara-
    tion that intends to be both consistent and unified. She ends up by de-
    claring Marcel to be a monster (60).

5. "Le goût en peinture" (The taste for painting) is the title of an article by
    Jean-Pierre Guillerm. See also Jacques Derrida, *La vérité en peinture* (*Truth*
    in Painting): the ambiguities of this title are very relevant here.

6. See Taeko Uenishi, *Le style de Proust et la peinture*, 9, whose work has a
    certain relevance. However, despite the explicit intention to analyze the
    style of the work, too often, to my mind, Uenishi falls into paraphrasing
    what the narrator-essayist states openly, thus sometimes giving quite
    clearly erroneous interpretations. For example, when the narrator praises
    Elstir's creation of "a realm apart, with impenetrable frontiers, peerless
    in substance" (SK 2.126 / P 2.424; Uenishi, *Le style*, 21), he does not intend
    to subscribe to such a principle in his own work.

7. Anne Henry's disenchanted analysis (in *Marcel Proust* and "Quand une

peinture métaphysique"), for example, is definitely useful. She starts with Proust's amateur art-lover's taste, which can be quite surprising in its old-fashionedness and its heterogeneity. But she doesn't stop there. Elstir's studio has often been said to resemble a museum where "a good half-century of art" is stored. But what are we to do if the only painting by Elstir, the ekphrasis of which brings into play the most involved and in-dulgent means of visualization (SK 1.894 / P 2.192–94), fits with any num-ber of styles, subjects, and scales?

8. Sophie Bertho, "Asservir l'image," 28. I hesitate to adopt such a descrip-tion because it presupposes an aesthetic unity to the work, the existence of which I deny. Without a presupposition of aesthetic unity, the signi-fied of such a mise en abyme would not be a constant and relevant as-pect of the whole text.

9. Once again I would hesitate to unify the work by means of such a refer-ential visual aesthetics.

10. The other is that of the "rudder," whose firmness is opposed to the sug-gestions of fragility and furtive movement in the mottled screen.

11. Pierre-Louis Rey ends his analysis of the relations between the sketch and the final text of this ekphrastic piece in the following manner: "Con-firming Michel Butor's intuition that there are fortuitous similarities be-tween the description of the fictive painting *The Port at Carquethuit* and Seurat's *Afternoon at the Grand Jatte*, but no models, the sketch for the en-trance of the port proves that Elstir's painting was constituted from ele-ments invented by Proust to meet the needs of his novel" ("L'entrée," 16). The reference is to Butor's "Les oeuvres d'art imaginaires chez Proust."

12. The motivation for the description is a function of its realism. But it is obviously a realism that functions as a dated rhetorical device. See Philippe Hamon's *Introduction à l'analyse du descriptif*.

13. The term "dis-figure" is discussed in Chapter 6.

14. In terms of Lotman's semiotics, painting is understood here as a primary modeling system, and literature as a secondary modeling system. Be-tween the two, obviously, lies language. But according to this concep-tion, "primary" does not imply priority or primacy. See Yuriy Lotman, *The Structure of the Artistic Text.*

Chapter 2

1. In "Métonymie chez Proust," Gérard Genette discusses the mixture of metaphor with metonymy. Paul de Man writes about this passage : "*A la recherche du temps perdu* narrates the flight of meaning, but this does not prevent its own meaning from being, incessantly, in flight" (*Allegories of Reading*, 78).

2. See Harold Bloom's *Anxiety of Influence*, which makes this effect of emulation into the very principle of evolution in literature. Norman Bryson, in *Tradition and Desire*, applied this principle to French painting at the end of the eighteenth century and the beginning of the nineteenth.

3. See Mieke Bal, *Reading "Rembrandt,"* 361–98, for a discussion of this painting and its relation to "death in painting."

Chapter 3

1. See René Démoris's *Chardin*, to which this analysis is greatly indebted. I agree with most of Démoris's observations and with many of his interpretations, although I do necessarily depart from his analysis, since my interest is not historical. For his analysis of *The Skate*, see in particular *Chardin*, 28–38. For a general reading of Chardin, see the works of Pierre Rosenberg listed in the Bibliography; also see Philip Conisbee's *Chardin*. On *The Skate* in particular, see also Y.-A. Bois et al., "Le Raie," and François Lecercle, "Le regard dédoublé."

2. *Still Life with Skate and Basket of Onions*, 1731 (Raleigh, The North Carolina Museum of Art). Démoris claims that this painting could even date from 1728, that is, only one year after *The Skate* (*Chardin*, 51). This fish is, in any case, formally "ambiguous": seen from the front, it is very large, and from the side, it is very thin (cf. Claude Lévi-Strauss's notion of *zoème* in *The View from Afar*).

3. Lecercle interprets this knife as the embodiment of the problem of conflict between the near and the far ("Le regard dédoublé," 127). Démoris understands it rather as being linked to castration.

4. In a different context Lecercle writes of "a reduction in the depth of the field" ("Le regard dédoublé," 117).

5. This painting was, however, chosen by Yann le Pichon as representative of Proust's "Rembrandtism" (*Le musée retrouvé*, 125). According to the interpretation that I am developing here, this painting would be more "Chardinesque" than "Rembrandtesque."

6. Démoris is correct in attributing great importance to this hook. Lecercle offers an interpretation of it as a mise en abyme of the painting that would be hung from the same point.

7. In his remarkable study on still life, *Looking at the Overlooked*, Norman Bryson writes of "a studied informality of attention" and "a space where figuration is destined to appear" (91).

8. On the fundamentally disappointing aspect of perspective, see Hubert Damisch's *L'origine de la perspective*. The analysis that follows is greatly indebted to Bryson's *Looking at the Overlooked*, which has some very good pages on Chardin (see especially 90–95 and 165–70).

9. See in particular the detailed analysis by Michael Baxandall in *Patterns of Intention*, especially 74–104.

Chapter 4

1. The French term *nature morte* conveys more explicitly the idea of death than "still life" does. —Trans.

2. On this young man full of disgust, see also David Mendelson, *Le verre et l'objet de verre*, 54–55. Here the young man is cured by means of gracious transparency, which for the critic is a purely aesthetic category.

3. The French text plays here on the visual similarities between the words *le salé* meaning "saltiness" and *le sale*, meaning "filth" or "dirt."

4. Proust, *Cities of the Plain*, trans. C. K. Scott-Moncrieff and Terence Kilmartin (New York: Random House, 1982), 1074; cited in Eve Kosofsky Sedgwick's *Epistemology of the Closet*, 224.

5. This censorship in the translation has a long history, so much so that it is emblematic of a typical blindness in the face of cultural difference that is found even between cultures as close as French and American, or homosexual and heterosexual. A matrix example of this is to be found in Judges 19. In this, the most horrific story of the whole Bible, the husband of the said concubine—who is, in fact, a wife under a different matrimonial system—joins her after she has left him to return to her father's home. He "speaks to her heart," which means no more than that he "reasoned" with her, but critics have largely made a sentimental novel out of this ethnographic text by translating the expression as an appeal to emotion. For the questions this particular "mistake" seems to raise, see my *Death and Dissymmetry*.

6. This is an allusion to the Freudian "cover-memory." This is the transla-

tion of "screen-memory" on which Naomi Schor rightly insists in *Reading in Detail*.

7. For an in-depth analysis of Francis Bacon that takes a similar approach, see Ernst van Alphen's *Francis Bacon and the Loss of Self*.

8. I owe this reference to van Alphen's analysis in *Francis Bacon*, 21–59, particularly 25–27. The critic analyzes this painting as the embodiment of both Bacon's resistance to narrativity and the alternative—an affective performativeness—that the young Proust will make his own.

9. Pichon reproduces the fresco next to page 101 in *Le musée retrouvé*.

Chapter 5

1. I am referring here to the uses that Naomi Schor analyzes in her now classic study on the subject, *Reading in Detail*. My own analysis is greatly indebted to her work, which I consider indispensable to any study of text or image as a structured surface.

2. See my criticism of this particular form of "mastery" in my article "Avec son regard de maître." This sociocultural structure is always present in *La recherche*, which recounts a process of apprenticeship. However, given that it is the novice who does the recounting, its effects are most often neutralized.

3. See also "Details and Realism: The Curé de Tours" and "The Delusion of Interpretation: The Conquest of Plassans" in Schor's *Reading in Detail*.

4. In this study I use the term "semiotics" in Peirce's sense, as a logic of meaning production, and not in the Kristevian sense.

5. For the literary function of the discourse on etymology in the novel, see Compagnon, *Proust entre deux siècles*, 229–56.

6. "The fragment is to the detail as the ancient is to the modern, as depth is to surface, as scarcity is to surplus, and as reconstruction is to interpretation." Schor, *Reading in Detail*, 53. This distinction will evidently lose some of its sharpness in the analysis she later gives of the Freudian detail of the screen-memory. Incidentally, Proust develops a considerable poetics of the textual fragment—at the level, therefore, of the signifier, and not that of the signified, as is the case here. I cannot address this question in this context, although its relevance is unquestionable. See Luc Fraisse, *Le processus de la création chez Marcel Proust*.

7. Claude Simon has developed a complete rewriting of *La recherche*, taking his lead from these gaps, as Françoise van Rossum-Guyon has convinc-

ingly demonstrated in her analysis of Simon's 1969 novel *La Bataille de Pharsale*: "What, for Proust, was only a detail, becomes, for Simon, the essential element and *gradually invades the whole fiction*. A whole 'parasitical vegetation' has 'crept into the gaps opened up by the cracks' in the bits removed from the Proustian machine" ("De Claude Simon à Proust," 125; first emphasis Bal's, others van Rossum-Guyon's).

8. This visual coloring of the "spoken" detail is put fully to use by Nathalie Sarraute, who plays, according to Rachel Boué, on "the inextricable interweaving of meaning, sound, and vision" (Boué, "Lieux et figures," 61). Sarraute attributes to the sonority of the word as thing the same function that Proust occasionally attributes to the word when pronounced in accordance with its referent. As Boué says, citing Sarraute: the simple sonority of the word is able "to flow into all the hidden recesses, to seek out all the hidden corners, to suck in, to gather up in one whole block and to bring to light that which was there, but which was scattered, caresses, tenderness, pious contact, head buried in the lap, brusquely raised up, furious stares, hateful, all of that gathered together by just these words that rose up and pierced the gaze: he is jealous" (61; Sarraute, *Fools say, a novel*, 15). Sarraute is closer to our author than she seems to think when she reduces Proust to a problematic of memory (*L'ère du soupçon*, 65; Boué, "Lieux et figures," 65).

9. For this aspect of the Book of Esther and its relation to writing, see my article "Lots of Writing."

10. For this last symbolic function of Esther, see Sedgwick's *Epistemology of the Closet*. Sedgwick has elaborated brilliantly on the idea of the closet, beginning with the title of her work itself, "the epistemology of the closet," which she sums up in the phrase "it takes one to know one."

11. The reference here is to J. L. Austin's fundamental work *How To Do Things with Words*. Louis Marin makes use of Austin's theory in an analysis of images "in words" in his posthumous book *Les pouvoirs de l'image*.

12. On the glass jars as "glass objects" par excellence in *La recherche*, see Mendelson, *Le verre et l'objet de verre*, 184–85.

Chapter 6

1. On Mme de Villeparisis's magnifying glass, see also Mendelson, *Le verre et l'objet de verre*, 157. Mendelson establishes an interesting relation between this detail and the recurrent metaphor of the picture window at the hotel in Balbec.

2. Too young, that is, for the requirements of this passage. This does not
mean at all to say that there is a diegetic coherence to the age of the narrator in *A l'ombre des jeunes filles en fleurs*, from which the passage is taken,
or elsewhere. "Too young" is a semiotic verdict, "logically" derived from
the fact upon which this passage is based: Marcel's surprise is essential so
that the narrator can reflect upon the detail.

3. Tzvetan Todorov, *Théories du symbole*, 303: "The displacement is not a metonymy, is not a trope, for it is not a substitution of meaning, but rather
a linking-up of two equally present meanings." Cited in Schor, *Reading
in Detail*, 71.

4. It is generally agreed that this little patch of yellow wall is nowhere to be
seen in the painting at La Haye. According to Guillerm: "This delicious
detail, which puts into question Bergotte's literary practice, . . . is an
imaginary detail, and it would be a waste of a journey to La Haye to go
and attempt to see it on the real painting" ("Le goût en peinture," 139).
Philippe Boyer indeed made this journey, and he talks simply of the little patch in the painting, as if its presence were beyond doubt (*Le petit
pan*, 20). The patch that he sees is not part of the wall—it is part of an
awning—but this is of little importance to him. I have also encountered
occasional affirmations that the reference is to the little patch of light to
the far left of the painting. See Daniel Arasse, *Le détail*, 159. Whether it
is a wall or an awning, what we see in the painting-referent is not a patch.
There are two alternatives available here: either, it is a patch, in which
case it has no referential existence, or the narrator/Bergotte effectively
"sees" the wall at the extreme right of the painting, in which case, far
from being a "little wall," it is a quite robust-looking wall. The ambiguity on which Didi-Huberman bases his reasoning—is it the patch or the
wall that is yellow?—disappears.

5. The term "tearing-open" is the first in a series of violent metaphors that
the theorist uses to describe the meaning of his concept.

6. See, however, the opposition that Poulet establishes between superimposition and juxtaposition, in *Proustian Space*, 91–106.

7. The translation of Proust's text necessitates a variety of different solutions for the word *pan*, as in the following example in which *pan* is best
translated first as "patch" then as "panel." —Trans.

8. The French for firework is *feu d'artifice*, "artificial fire." —Trans.

9. Concerning Elstir and the visual aesthetics related to this character, see
Guillerm's "Le goût en peinture," Henry's *Marcel Proust* and "Quand une

peinture métaphysique," and the chapter "Dans l'atelier d'Elstir," in Vincent Descombes's *Proust: philosophie du roman*.

10. Doubrovsky has also insisted upon the aggression contained in the ideal of the closed body in reference to a passage situated close to the one I am examining (see *La place de la madeleine*, 134–37).

11. In *La peinture incarnée*, 37–39, Didi-Huberman develops a concept he calls *la subjectilité*, formed from the notions of subjectivity and projection.

12. The French text incorporates the notion of "trompe-l'oeil" as in trompe-l'oeil painting.

13. The reference is to "une faible mortelle" in Gustave Moreau's painting. —Trans.

14. With the exception of certain "details" about which I can say little here: the left hand that is too large, and the overly broad hips—perhaps a proleptic allusion to the future pregnancy and, in that case, another monstrosity that stems from the inscription of history painting as a genre.

15. For a more developed analysis of this painting, see my *Reading "Rembrandt,"* 216–46. On the Rembrandt corpus, which is essential for a reading of this image in Proust, see Gary Schwartz, *Rembrandt: His Life, His Paintings*. A further relevant study is Svetlana Alpers's *Rembrandt's Enterprise*.

16. See in particular Genette's analysis in "Métonymie chez Proust," which remains an essential work, the results of which I do not question.

17. W.T.J. Mitchell, *The Language of Images*, 8. This work, which develops complex analyses of image theories and how images differ from text, is of crucial importance for my purpose, so much so, in fact, that it would be impossible for me to do justice to it in notes and specific references. I cannot say as much for Mitchell's recent book, *Iconology*, which is disappointing. His *Language of Images* is vitally important for an understanding of the historical development of the tendency to turn the irreducible difference between text and visual objects into a reified opposition between semiotic nodes that are at play in both. Given the prevalent intellectual "fashion" at the moment for studying "text and image" it seems important to me, in the case of a study like this one, to encourage reflection on the interests that underpin both this "fashion" and the tendency to neglect the semiotic foundations of the different arts.

18. Mitchell, *Language of Images*, 9–31. He analyzes "the family of images" into the five domains I have here fleshed out with Proustian material. The image, conceived of as "likeness, resemblance, similitude," can be-

long to the graphic, the optical, the perceptual, the mental, or the verbal domain. The graphic consists in "pictures, statues, designs"; the optical in mirrors and projections; the perceptual in "sense data, 'species,' appearances"; the mental in dreams, memories, fantasies, and ideas; and the verbal in metaphors and descriptions.

19. Mirrors appear only rarely in *La recherche*. One occurrence of the motif is to be found in the scene of the "dance breast to breast" at the casino in Incarville, which I analyze in Chapter 7. The mirror reveals the direction of Albertine's gaze. Far from serving the narcissistic gaze, it takes this "fleeting being" elsewhere, ever further away.

20. See, among others, Georges Poulet's classic work, *L'Espace proustien*. On perception and optical instruments in the nineteenth century, see Jonathan Crary, *Techniques of the Observer*.

21. I would like to restrict the notion of voyeurism to this precise meaning in order to be able to show how Proust's text invests eroticism with an epistemological function. I disagree with Michel Erman, who expands the notion of voyeurism to encompass any form of visual perception.

22. Here as elsewhere, I am trying to avoid discussing questions and passages that have already been sufficiently analyzed by others, although the coherence of my work obviously requires occasional reworking of such questions. In the domain of the verbal image, for example, I do not reexamine the issue, which is of prime importance for my work, of the relation of metonymic motivation in many of Proust's metaphors simply because Genette has already sufficiently elucidated it. Likewise, I take Hamon's explanatory model for description as a basis, and, as a result, I examine only descriptions of visual objects.

23. For a brilliant analysis of world maps and other maps through history, see Christian Jacob, *L'empire des cartes*, from whom I have borrowed this characterization (152). Incidentally, Jacob works with the same passages from Alpers's work that Didi-Huberman criticizes. The fundamental flatness of geographical maps makes it tempting to associate them with Proust's enterprise.

24. Denis Diderot says almost exactly the same thing in reference to the "Chardin effect": "Come close and everything gets blurred, flattened and disappears; step back, everything is recreated and reproduced." See "Salon de 1763," 484.

Chapter 7

1. I am greatly indebted to Doubrovsky's *La place de la madeleine*, although I depart from it significantly. This departure occurs at the level of form, at the level of what I call the figuration: the written fantasies that, far from being derived from obsession, in fact produce these obsessions. I also depart from Doubrovsky when he insists too much, in my opinion, on the unity of the Proustian subject and text. In contrast, I see a rejection of unification as the fundamental characteristic of both of them.

2. The quotations from this text will be indicated by the letters *CSB* / G, thus clearly distinguishing the different editions of *Contre Sainte-Beuve*. This text appears only in the Gallimard edition.

3. The hill's "rump" refers to the French expression *la croupe*, which suggests both the human buttocks and the *croupe de la colline*, "the hilltop."
—Trans.

Chapter 8

1. For the relevant medical references—particularly those concerning Havelock Ellis, who claimed that dance and especially the waltz were erotic stimulants, and those concerning Krafft-Ebing, who held forth on the eroticism of breasts, see Antoine Compagnon's lecture "La danse contre-seins."

2. For an analysis of the problematics of ethnography and their bearing on this little scene, see Dan Sperber's relevant chapter, "Ethnographie interprétative et anthropologie théorique," in *Le Savoir des anthropologues*.

3. For the theory of these so-called homosocial relations, which consist in collaboration, rivalry, and imitation between men, and of which women are the derived objects, see Ernst van Alphen, "The Homosocial Gaze," who elaborates this theory from René Girard's *Mensonge romantique et vérité romanesque*, Lévi-Strauss's *Les structures élémentaires de la parenté*, Gayle Rubin, "The Traffic of Women," and Eve Kosofsky Sedgwick, *Between Men*.

4. In a forceful interpretation of the first sketches for this page, Compagnon suggests a "decadent" reading of this passage which links it to the combined characters of Medusa and Salomé by reference to a painting by Mantegna. See *Proust entre deux siècles*, 116–26.

5. Julia Kristeva associates the Baron's belly and his behind with his homo-

sexuality by means of an autoeroticism symbolized by the movement of these parts of the body. See Kristeva, *Le Temps sensible*, 114.

6. On the motivation of this scene, see Jean-Yves Tadié, *Proust et le roman*, 45.

7. J. E. Rivers, *Proust and the Art of Love*; Leo Bersani, *A Future for Astyanax*. I must add that these two studies are of quite different quality. Rivers tends himself toward the sentimental, which is not at all the case with Bersani's otherwise excellent book.

8. Sedgwick analyzes the diagnosis of sentimentalism with the help of the notion of the "closet" as spectacle, which is based on two principles. The first is that it takes one to know one. This is the slogan that she terms the "epistemology of the closet." The second principle is the specularity and speculativeness of the spectacle itself: the point of view on the closet—the one the narrator inhabits—necessarily also becomes the point of view from the closet, the one in which the narrator finds himself trapped after the theatrical comings and goings of his mobile voyeurism. See *Epistemology of the Closet*.

9. The French word referred to here is *vasistas*, the epistemological connotations of which will be discussed in detail shortly. —Trans.

10. See in particular Gilles Deleuze, *Proust et les signes*, 98–99.

11. The French here uses a play on words with *fleur* (flower) and *effleurer* (to touch lightly). —Trans.

12. The narrator defends himself from this danger precisely by stamping on, thus, flattening the Baron's hat. See SK 2.574–86 / P 2.842–53.

13. The French word is *soulèvements*, which recalls the expression discussed earlier of "soulever le coeur," translated here as "to turn the stomach."

14. I call this description a mise en abyme because I consider the elements that I have taken from it to be central, that is, important and constant, within the whole work. It is for this reason that this concept designates above all else a reading. See my analysis in "Reflections on Reflection," in *On Meaning-Making*, 45–58, of Lucien Dällenbach's *Mirror in the Text*.

15. Relatedly, one might think of the association that Naomi Schor makes in "Restricted Thematics" between milk and ink, which in Madame Bovary signifies the rejection of motherhood and the coming to writing.

16. The French text uses a play on words that combines "breast" (*sein*) with "sensuality" (*seinsualité*). —Trans.

17. See, for example, Sedgwick, who uses her ironic talent fully at the expense of Rivers's moralizing positivism (*Epistemology of the Closet*, 213–52). She also criticizes harshly Bersani's analysis in *Culture of Redemption*, which takes an opposing methodological point of view, and about which

I find Sedgwick to be much less fair. Both Rivers and Bersani treat *Sodome et Gomorrhe I* separately and consider it to be sentimental and reductive. They oppose it to *La prisonnière*, from which the above quotation is taken. Sedgwick is opposed to the way the violence, carried out first of all at a thematic level to "mastectomized" Albertine, is repeated at the level of the cutting-up of the text.

18. Homophobia, that felicitous parallel to xenophobia, complicates the hate of the homosexual by allying it with a fear of homosexuality within one-self and, thus, of a partial identification with the other, who is as a result made responsible for the elimination of everything that the subject feels as "other" within himself. In the "mastectomizing" interpretation of Albertine as "nude" the homophobia consists in the following two processes: first, the woman's body, the emblem of which is the breasts, is interpreted as "other," which explains the representation of the breasts as fruit; then, this otherness, made negative, is taken as a definition of disguised homosexuality, which is represented as a double negative. The repressed will not be long in "resurfacing," since the double negative produces a roundabout positive. [This "roundabout positive" evokes once more the idea of turning round, *détourné*. —Trans.]

19. On this subject, see Kaja Silverman, *Male Subjectivity at the Margin*, 378.

20. Thus, I find Kristeva's association, in *Le Temps sensible*, 100–101, between the dance "breast to breast," Albertine as nude, and the pleasure "a mother brings to a child" to be slightly gratuitous, even though it is formulated as a tentative hypothesis. The description of the "detachable" breasts, especially when related to the scene at the casino in which the breasts are seen as a reflection in the mirror, suggests above all else a fascination with radical otherness.

21. See Howard Hubbar's *Caravaggio* for a standard analysis of the painter's work and Andreas Sternweiler's study *Die Lust der Götter* for a discussion of his homosexual imagery.

22. For these passages, see also Compagnon, *Proust entre deux siècles*, 28. Proust often mentions Manet in this context of being between two centuries. See also SK 2.519 / P 2.790 and SK 2.840 / P 3.206.

23. Here is a case in which the redefinition of the concept of focalization takes on a specific importance. The point is that, far from indicating a simple distribution of information within the text, the focalization specifies the nature of the relation between the seeing subject and the object seen. Without a conception of focalization that is oriented according to this relation, literary criticism denies itself a term that is capable of giv-

ing nuance to specific visualities. See Bal, "Narration and Focalization," in *On Story-Telling*, 75–108, for the continuation of the discussion with Genette in which I reply to his original response in *Nouveau discours du récit*.

24. This vocabulary could lead to a misunderstanding: although the analysis seems to be slipping from a Lacanian discourse to a Derridean one, Silverman remains rigorously Lacanian in her method.

Chapter 9

1. The French *la langue* refers equally to the tongue and language. —Trans.
2. The last expression of this sentence is fundamentally ambiguous in French: "disant à Sarah qu'elle a à se départir du côté d'Isaac." The expression *se départir du côté de* suggests both to "tear herself away from" Isaac and "to turn away toward" Isaac. This very expression is the subject of discussion in the following pages and the French will be signaled in the text so that the reader is aware that the reference is to the same expression, despite slight necessary variations in the translation. —Trans.
3. The mechanisms of identification have been elaborated particularly within the framework of psychoanalytic studies of cinema. See in particular Kaja Silverman's works *The Acoustic Mirror, Male Subjectivity at the Margin*, and *Threshold of the Visible World*. Also, see the useful collection edited by Jacques Caïn (1978).
4. In Caïn (1978: 31).
5. Kristeva establishes a whole system of nuances of pink and red, which she links to sexuality and Judaism through Gilberte's red hair. See Kristeva, *Le Temps sensible*, 188.
6. There are other manifestations of orientalism in *La recherche*, in particular in the formal and intertextual aspects of the text that link it to *A Thousand and One Nights*. See Dominique Jullien's study *Proust et ses modèles*.
7. For an analysis of the expression "to turn away toward" as a formula for a sexual initiative and its ritual meanings, see my work *Murder and Difference*. In fact, the expression links two intertexts to this primal scene in Proust. In Genesis 16, Sarah, who is unable to conceive a child, had begun by encouraging her husband, still called Abram at that point, to conceive a child with Hagar. Then, she feels herself to be despised by Hagar and she banishes her. But Hagar comes back. In Genesis 21, after the birth of Isaac, Sarah no longer wants Hagar's son to share Abraham's heritage and she banishes Hagar and Ishmaël for good.

8. See Bal, Van Dijk, and Ginneken, *Und Sara lachte*, and for an anthropological explanation of this strange feature of the character, Carol Delaney, *The Legacy of Abraham*. For a theological interpretation, see Ann Marmesh, "Anti-Covenant."

9. For this very useful concept, see Brian Stock, *The Implications of Literacy*.

10. It is rather naive, therefore, of Guillerm to conclude from the "error" made here with regard to the biblical text that "obviously no fresco could illustrate a sequence of the text that does not exist" ("Le goût en peinture," 140). On the contrary, art history constructs its own traditions from confusions, the most famous example of which was the confusion between Judith and Salomé, which was highlighted by Erwin Panofsky, in his *Studies in Iconology*, 26–28.

11. Yann le Pichon was wise enough to leave this scene out of *Le musée retrouvé*.

12. I am using these two drawings, not as intertexts, but as samples of an interdiscourse; not as a semantic representation, but as a model of "syntactic" figuration.

Chapter 10

1. On primary narcissism, see Julia Kristeva, *Pouvoirs de l'horreur*; André Green, *Narcissisme*; Jean Laplanche, *Vie et mort en psychanalyse*; and Mikkel Borch-Jacobson, *The Freudian Subject*.

2. For an analytic model for descriptive discourse, see Hamon's now classic *Introduction*.

3. On Freud's book about "jokes" and their (anti-)feminist implications, see Sarah Kofman, *Pourquoi rit-on?*

4. This irony is difficult to classify because it is neither an irony of "words" nor of "situations," but rather of focalization. On irony in *La recherche*, see Pierre Schoentjes, *Recherche de l'ironie*.

5. Doubrovsky has already amply underlined the "place" of the madeleine in the orally based phantasmic schema of the novel. Silverman, who takes this orality as her starting point and as the linchpin of her "Leonardo" model, also considers the madeleine to be at the heart of the literary project of *La recherche* as a whole. See her *Male Subjectivity at the Margin*, 378.

6. The author uses the phrase "l'antre-deux" here to designate the threshold and to evoke the idea of *entre-deux*, or "between," as in the repeated notion of Proust lying "between" two centuries. —Trans.

7. See Françoise van Rossum-Guyon's elegant analysis of this intertextual relation, in "De Claude Simon à Proust," 121–26.

Chapter 11

1. Doubrovsky quotes the passage as one of the three matrices of the work, the other two being the madeleine and the solitary pleasure. He does not, however, develop extensively his analysis of the "public convenience." In *Le petit pan*, 213–53, Boyer analyzes the passage as one of the seven initiatory places, all of which he calls "public conveniences."
2. The French translation of Judges prepared by Dhorme and his team uses the verb *se détourner* here. —Trans.
3. Robert Alter, *The Art of Biblical Narrative*, interprets the penetration of the peg into Sisera's temple as an inverse figuration of rape. For more information on the story of the text, see James S. Ackerman, "Prophecy and Warfare in Early Israel." For a "military" interpretation, see A.D.H. Mayes, "The Historical Context of the Battles Against Sisera."
4. This passage presents a pastiche of orientalist discourse, which can be seen, for example, in the description of Moreau's painting *Salomé* in Huysmans's *A rebours*. This allusion does not fail to accentuate the danger immanent to this seduction: "An architectural cake, as urbane and familiar as it was imposing, seemed to be enthroned there on the off-chance as on any other day, in case the fancy seized Gilberte to discrown it of its chocolate battlements and to hew down the steep brown slopes of its ramparts, baked in the oven like the bastions of the palace of Darius. . . . [S]he extracted for me from the crumbling monument a whole glazed slab jewelled with scarlet fruits, in the oriental style" (SK 1.545 / P 1.497).
5. As was the case with the association between breasts and the mother, criticized earlier, I find the association between the sphincter and the drama of cleanliness a little mechanical. This is another case of the danger in psychoanalytic criticism to make everything uniformly banal. In the Proustian context, and in this specific context of a gathering of men in a public convenience, the more obvious association seems to me to be that of a certain homosexual practice. However, this association appears on a one-off basis and so is difficult to tie down. This is why I am not dwelling on the matter.
6. For the identification between Marcel and Phedre and a reading of Hip-

polyte as the love-object that Charlus gives up, see Compagnon, *Proust entre deux siècles*, 84.

7.   It is on this point that I differ from Silverman's analysis in *Male Subjectivity at the Margin*, 386, which describes the phantasmic organ as being, above all else, an organ of penetration, and which adds to the description an element that seems to me to be radically absent: an "imaginary appendage."

Chapter 12

1.   The notion of obscurity obviously refers here to the fact that the image is little known; however, in French the word *obscur* also echoes the opposition between light and shade. Moreover, the word "portrait" is used here in an archaic way to refer to a description of the town. This term is kept in the translation for its resonances with earlier uses of it. —Trans.

2.   Architectural archaeology, which is used here as a metaphoric springboard for the narrator's poetic reflections, appears also in Julia Kristeva's remarks on the objective of her book *Le Temps sensible*: "The aim is . . . to reveal the 'cornerstone' of Proustian aesthetics. . . . Venice is that cornerstone: it is the very characterization of embodied time" (151).

3.   Note that the quotation marks around "radiant sun" indicate a quotation from Baudelaire and, thus, locate this passage not only within the narrator's preoccupation with failed vision, but also within that of Proust's intermittent literary preferences. See Compagnon's genetic analysis of style in the novel, in *Proust entre deux siècles*, 187–228.

4.   As Didi-Huberman puts it so well: "It is according to a multiplicity of scales that painting is apprehended" (*Devant l'image*, 277).

5.   Hamon has asked the following question in relation to the prism: "If one lives for too long in a prism (if one is for too long a prism), does one not risk breaking down?" (*Expositions*, 91).

6.   The butterfly, like the skate, is a principal *zoème* in Lévi-Strauss's study, *The View from Afar*.

7.   In *Sodome et Gomorrhe II*, the narrator is himself compared to a butterfly by Celeste Albaret, one of the two sisters at Balbec, described as *courrières*, whose way of talking he records almost in free indirect speech: "It was impossible to tell when I slept, I fluttered about all night like a moth, and in the day-time I was as swift as the squirrels, 'you know, Marie,

269

which we used to see at home, so nimble that even with your eyes you can't follow them'" (SK 2.876 / P 3.241).

8. Given the close link between the fragmentary detail and jealousy, the following passage from Kristeva's *Le Temps sensible* seems most important to me: "The instability of Albertine is playfully betrayed . . . by the incessant migration of her beauty-spot: from the lip to the chin, from the chin to just under the eye. Through such a mist of details and confusion, we gather that the narrator cannot know his Albertine except "by subtraction" (96). Kristeva does not ponder the relation between migration/jealousy and fragmentation/violence, which seems, however, to be most striking.

9. Barthes, *La chambre claire*, 129. Obviously Barthes's denial here only bears on the platitude that reduces Proust to a problematic of memory. The lectures Barthes was giving when he died dealt precisely with photography in Proust. I intend to work with Barthes's book in order to explore an aspect of Proust's work that inverts the terms of this denial: if there is nothing Proustian in a photograph, there is much that is photographic in Proust.

Chapter 13

1. Of course, Barthes is well aware of this. On several occasions he reminds the reader of the similarity between his experience of the photograph of his mother at the Winter Garden and Marcel's involuntary recollection of his grandmother on the first night of his second stay at Balbec. But I would like to break partially the association between photography and memory in *La recherche* in order to grasp better the link between photography and "flatness." Photography in Proust is much more Barthesian than it is Proustian.

2. Peirce, in R. E. Innis, ed., *Semiotics*, 9–10.

3. The idea of having "a degree more of art," attributed ironically here to the grandmother, also participates in the poetics of reading associated with Marcel's mother. See in relation to this, Annick Bouillaguet, *Marcel Proust: Le jeu intertextuel*, 24: "It seems as if, by quoting [Mme de Sévigné], she quoted her own mother, adding thereby a further 'layer' of intertextuality since two different levels, one that is fictional (the grandmother's remark) and one that is not fictional (Mme de Sévigné's sentence) are superimposed. The fragment is taken from two sources: the Letters and the habits of speech of the narrator's grandmother. It

thereby acquires a supplementary signified, which results from its first transposition and which varies according to each of the different situations of the narrator's family."

4. This is an allusion to Kristeva's book *Etrangers à nous-mêmes*, which is very useful for this aspect of Proust's work.

5. See also Kristeva, *Le Temps sensible*, especially 224–25, for an analysis of this scene as generated by homosexual sadomasochism.

6. See Beckett's very beautiful passage on this matrix scene in *Proust*, 29–30.

7. For a study of deviation as a fundamental aspect of photography, see Rosalind Krauss's important book, *Le photographique*.

8. It goes without saying that this photographic reference should not be taken literally. Far be it from me to claim that Proust was a photographer, or that he saw how photography could help him in his literary work. On the contrary, there are good reasons for believing that he was not conscious of the importance of photography for his work.

Chapter 14

1. See Christine Buci-Glucksman, *La folie du voir*.

2. The word is borrowed from "Proust en de epiphanie" by Willem Brakman, the Dutch novelist, some of whose novels are self-conscious postmodern rewritings of *La recherche* based upon an exploitation of the work's visuality. See in particular Brakman's *De reis van de douanier naar Bentheim* and Ernst van Alphen's reading of it, "Reading Visually."

3. The more technical term "diaphragm" is interesting here for its anatomical reference to breath and, therefore, to asthma, the ailment that intermittently tortures Marcel all through his diegetic life. I thank Philippe Hamon for having pointed this out to me.

4. Part of an exhibition held at the Musée d'Orsay in Paris in 1995–96 was devoted to Proust's magic lantern.

5. See Jullien's chapter on the subject of projection as a poetic principle in *Proust et ses modèles*, 169–225.

Chapter 15

1. The author intends here to draw the reader's attention to the ambiguity in "sa place," which could refer to the photograph's place or that of the father. —Trans.

2. See Kristeva, *Le Temps sensible*, 105: "Through the intermediary of Al-

bertine the narrator gives himself the joy of picturing himself as a woman."

3. See van Alphen's analysis in *Francis Bacon*, 137–42. He quotes the following from Djuna Barnes's *Nightwood*, 112: "Love of woman for woman, what insane passion for unmitigated anguish and motherhood brought that into the mind?" to which he comments: "Motherhood in this view is in the first place splitting, cleaving, cloning" (139). The crucial matter for Barnes is a reconciliation between metaphor and metonymy in the reproduction of the same by means of contiguity.

4. Contra Uenishi, *Le style*, 83–167. This could perhaps be read as an example of cubism if it were not for the fact that the changes in perspective are so painstakingly spelled out. Compare the description of Yonville that begins the second part of *Madame Bovary*, where Flaubert ends up "dropping" his readers, leaving them without help, which quite wonderfully turns this description into a complete incongruity. See Jonathan Culler's excellent book *Flaubert: The Uses of Uncertainty*.

5. This genre can be defended as lying between realism and the fantastic: everything that happens can be explained in realistic terms but gradually these terms become less and less relevant.

6. The French plays on the two senses of the word *objectif*, which means here both "lens" and "objective." Therefore, the apparent aim of the narrator is also offset. —Trans.

7. In a seminal article ("Temporality"), Mary-Ann Doane emphasizes the resistance against the cinema in both Freud and Marey. Freud's reasons for resisting the cinema—he considered it redundant given the existence of the memory as a place where time is stored—relate only superficially to Proust's enterprise. In contrast, as the following analysis of the "promeneur passionné" will emphasize, Marey's wish to "de-familiarize, de-realize, and even de-iconize" (Doane 329) the photographic image is much more pertinent here. Marey, like Proust, was not interested in the recording of "what the eye can see" but in the eye as it is divested of subjectivity. Proust put this eye in tension with its opposite, a subjectivity that cannot see.

8. In reference to this passage, from which he isolates the "downward slope," Charles Bouazis writes: "The climax that is brought about only happens by virtue of a 'downward slope,' which makes it unreal even as it holds it out as a promise (not 'reaching' it)" (*Ce que Proust savait du symptôme*, 20).

9. The French plays on the homophony between *dégoutter* (to drip) and *dé-goûter* (to disgust). —Trans.

10. The French word play is more precise, since *figure* refers specifically to the man's face. —Trans.

11. See in particular *La chambre claire*, 49, 69, 74, 77, 81, 84, 88, 89, 148, 149.

12. The Tuché refers to Lacan's concept of the This, or the Encounter. —Trans.

13. The expression "tipped forward" is a translation of Barthes's phrase: "Ce quelque chose a fait tilt." In his translation of *La chambre claire* Richard Howard has chosen to render "a fait tilt" by "triggered me." This translation has been modified here to resonate with the concept of the downward slope. —Trans.

14. The text plays here on the homophony between the word for "touch" (*le toucher*) and the reference from Barthes's text to the Tuché. —Trans.

Conclusion

1. Descombes's study *Proust: philosophie du roman* offers a recent example of such an approach, as does that of Kristeva, *Le Temps sensible*, in particular 301–39. In *Freud, Proust, Lacan* Malcolm Bowie analyzes Proustian epistemology in a way that is, I believe, related to mine. He explores Proust's text, as well as that of Freud and Lacan, through their literary movements and images in order to delineate a specific epistemology located within the "novelistic" discourse.

2. "It is by this kind of general law that Proust hopes to give consistency to the novel over and above the dissipation of its individual instants. But do we have to believe in the law?" Compagnon, *Proust entre deux siècles*, 48. Compagnon puts this question in relation to the "theory of memory and knowledge" that for him is the conspicuous "detail" of the madeleine.

3. On this subject, see Johannes Fabian's *Power and Performance*, which describes an ethnographic experience in which the author/ethnographer pushes as far as possible the attempt to know the other "with" the other. In the domain of visual art Damisch's rhetorical experiments (in *L'orig-ine de la perspective*) have much in common with Fabian's work. Both of these works try to engage in a dialogue with their "object," the other. See my *Double Exposures*.

4. It is at this point that we should recall the relevance of Lévi-Strauss's title, *Le regard éloigné* (*The View from Afar*). While ethnography does at-

tempt to "see" a culture in its entirety from Olympian heights, as if from a bird's eye view, it also argues for an understanding from within the culture in question. This miracle of the ethnographic gaze is the aim that Proust pursues by literary means. I am thinking here of the kissing organ.

5. "Clean, uncluttered analyses are valued more highly than rich, multifaceted, but messy and ambiguous narratives." Lorraine Code, *What can she know?* 169.

6. It is in this respect that my interpretation of Proust's text accords with the linguistic hypotheses put forward by Ann Banfield in *Unspeakable Sentences*.

Bibliography

Ackerman, James S. "Prophecy and Warfare in Early Israel: A Study of the Deborah-Barak Story." *BASOR* 220 (1975): 5–15.

Agamben, Giorgio. *The Coming Community.* Trans. Michael Hardt. Minneapolis: University of Minnesota Press, 1993.

Alpers, Svetlana. *The Art of Describing: Dutch Art in the Seventeenth Century.* Chicago: University of Chicago Press, 1985.

———. *Rembrandt's Enterprise: The Studio and the Market.* Chicago: University of Chicago Press, 1988.

Alphen, Ernst van. *Francis Bacon and the Loss of Self.* Cambridge, Mass.: Harvard University Press; London: Reaktion Books, 1992.

———. "The Heterotopian Space of the Discussions on Postmodernism." *Poetics Today* 10 (1989): 819–38.

———. "The Homosocial Gaze, according to McEwan's *The Comfort of Strangers.*" In *Vision in Context: Historical and Contemporary Perspectives on Sight,* ed. Teresa Brennan and Martin Jay. New York: Routledge, 1996.

———. "Reading Visually." *Style* 22 (1988): 219–29.

Alter, Robert. *The Art of Biblical Narrative.* New York: Basic Books, 1981.

Arasse, Daniel. *Le détail: Pour une histoire rapprochée de la peinture.* Paris: Flammarion, 1992.

Austin, J. L. *How To Do Things with Words.* Cambridge, Mass.: Harvard University Press, 1975.

Bachelard, Gaston. *Essai sur la connaissance approchée.* Paris: Vrin, 1927.

———. *La formation de l'esprit scientifique.* Paris: Vrin, 1980.

Bal, Mieke. *Death and Dissymmetry: The Politics of Coherence in the Book of Judges.* Chicago: University of Chicago Press, 1988.

———. *Double Exposures: The Subject of Cultural Analysis.* New York: Routledge, 1996.

———. *Murder and Difference: Gender, Genre, and Scholarship on Sisera's Death.* Bloomington: Indiana University Press, 1988.

———. *On Meaning-Making: Essays in Semiotics*. Sonoma, Calif.: Polebridge Press, 1994.

———. *On Story-Telling: Essays in Narratology*. Sonoma, Calif.: Polebridge Press, 1991.

———. *Reading "Rembrandt": Beyond the Word-Image Opposition*. New York: Cambridge University Press, 1991.

Bal, Mieke, Fokkelien van Dijk, and Grietje van Ginneken. *Und Sara lachte . . . : Patriarchat und Widerstand in biblischen Geschichten*. Münster: Morgana Frauenverlag, 1988.

Banfield, Ann. "L'imparfait de l'objectif: The Imperfect of the Object Glass." *Camera Obscura* 24 (1990): 65–87.

———. *Unspeakable Sentences: Narration and Representation in the Language of Fiction*. Boston: Routledge & Kegan Paul, 1982.

Barnes, Djuna. *Nightwood*. With a preface by T. S. Eliot. 1936. Reprint. London: Faber & Faber, 1979.

Barthes, Roland. *Le bruissement de la langue*. Paris: Editions du Seuil, 1984. Trans. Richard Howard as *The Rustle of Language* (New York: Hill & Wang, 1986).

———. *La chambre claire: Note sur la photographie*. Paris: Editions de l'Etoile, Gallimard, Le Seuil, 1980. Trans. Richard Howard as *Camera Lucida: Reflections on Photography* (New York: Hill & Wang, 1981).

Baxandall, Michael. *Patterns of Intention: On the Historical Explanation of Pictures*. New Haven: Yale University Press, 1985.

Beckett, Samuel. *Proust*. 1931. Reprint. London: Chatto & Windus, 1965.

Belloï, Livio. *La scène proustienne: Proust, Goffman et le théâtre du monde*. Paris: Nathan, 1993.

Benjamin, Walter. "The Work of Art in the Age of Mechanical Reproduction." In *Illuminations*. New York: Schocken Books, 1969.

Benmussa, Simone. *Qui êtes-vous? Nathalie Sarraute*. Paris: La Manifacture, 1987.

Bersani, Leo. *The Culture of Redemption*. Cambridge, Mass.: Harvard University Press, 1990.

———. *A Future for Astyanax: Character and Desire in Language*. 2d ed. London: Marion Boyers, 1978.

Bertho, Sophie. "Asservir l'image, fonctions du tableau dans le récit." *CRIN* 23 (1990): 25–36.

Bloom, Harold. *The Anxiety of Influence: A Theory of Poetry*. Oxford: Oxford University Press, 1973.

Borch-Jacobsen, Mikkel. *The Freudian Subject*. Trans. Catherine Porter. Stanford: Stanford University Press, 1988.

Bouazis, Charles. *Ce que Proust savait du symptôme.* Paris: Méridiens Klincksieck, 1992.

Boué, Rachel. "Lieux et figures de la sensation dans l'oeuvre de Nathalie Sarraute." *Littérature* 89 (1993): 58–67.

Bougnoux, Daniel. "L'efficacité iconique." *Nouvelle Revue de Psychanalyse* 44 (Autumn 1991): 267–80.

Bouillaguet, Annick. *Marcel Proust: Le jeu intertextuel.* Paris: Editions du Titre, 1990.

Bowie, Malcolm. *Freud, Proust, Lacan: Theory as Knowledge.* Cambridge: Cambridge University Press, 1987.

Boyer, Philippe. *Le petit pan de mur jaune: Sur Proust.* Paris: Editions du Seuil, 1987.

Brakman, Willem. *De reis van de douanier naar Bentheim.* Amsterdam: Querido, 1983.

———. "Proust en de epifanie." Manuscript.

Bryson, Norman. *Looking at the Overlooked: Four Essays on Still-Life.* Cambridge, Mass.: Harvard University Press, 1989.

———. *Tradition and Desire.* Cambridge: Cambridge University Press, 1984.

Buci-Glucksmann, Christine. *La folie du voir: De l'esthétique baroque.* Paris: Galilée, 1986.

Bucknall, Barbara. *The Religion of Art in Proust.* Urbana: University of Illinois Press, 1969.

Butor, Michel. "Les oeuvres d'art imaginaires chez Proust." In *Répertoire II.* Paris: Editions de Minuit, 1964.

Caïn, Jacques. *L'identification.* Paris: Macula, 1978.

Chevrier, Jean-François. *Proust et la photographie.* With photographs by Pierr de Fenoyl and Holger Trülzsch. Paris: Editions de l'Etoile, 1982.

Clark, T. J. *The Painting of Modern Life: Paris in the Art of Manet and His Followers.* London: Thames & Hudson, 1985.

Code, Lorraine. *What can she know? Feminist Theory and the Construction of Knowledge.* Ithaca: Cornell University Press, 1991.

Collier, Peter. "La mise en abyme chez Proust." In *Ecrire la peinture*, ed. Philippe Delaveau. Paris: Editions Universitaires, 1991.

Compagnon, Antoine. "La danse contre-seins." Lecture delivered at the Université de Paris III, April 1993.

———. *Proust entre deux siècles.* Paris: Editions du Seuil, 1989. Trans. Richard E. Goodkin as *Proust: Between Two Centuries* (New York: Columbia University Press, 1992).

Conisbee, Philip. *Chardin.* Lewisburg: Bucknell University Press, 1986.

Crary, Jonathan. *Techniques of the Observer: On Vision and Modernity in the Nineteenth Century.* Cambridge, Mass.: MIT Press, 1990.

Culler, Jonathan. *Flaubert: The Uses of Uncertainty*. Ithaca: Cornell University Press, 1974.

———. *Framing the Sign: Criticism and Its Institutions*. Norman: University of Oklahoma Press, 1988.

Dagognet, François. *Etienne-Jules Marey: La passion de la trace*. Paris: Editions Hazan, 1987. Trans. Robert Galeta with Jeanine Herman as *Etienne-Jules Marey: A Passion for the Trace* (New York: Zone Books, 1992).

Dällenbach, Lucien. *Le récit spéculaire. Essai sur la mise en abyme*. Paris: Editions du Seuil, 1977. Trans. Jeremy Whitely with Emma Hughes as *The Mirror in the Text* (Cambridge: Polity Press, 1989).

Damisch, Hubert. *L'origine de la perspective*. Paris: Flammarion, 1987. Trans. John Goodman as *The Origin of Perspective* (Cambridge, Mass.: MIT Press, 1994).

Delaney, Carol. "The Legacy of Abraham." In *Anti-Covenant: Counter-Reading Women's Lives in the Hebrew Bible*, ed. M. Bal. Sheffield, U.K.: Sheffield Academic Press and the Almond Press, 1989.

Deleuze, Gilles. *Proust et les signes*. 3d ed. Paris: Presses Universitaires de France, 1964. Trans. Richard Howard as *Proust and Signs* (New York: George Braziller, 1972).

Démoris, René. *Chardin, la chair et l'object*. Paris: Adam Biro, 1991.

Derrida, Jacques. *De la grammatologie*. Paris: Editions de Minuit, 1967. Trans. and with an introduction by Gayatri Chakravorty Spivak as *Of Grammatology* (Baltimore: Johns Hopkins University Press, 1976).

———. *La dissémination*. Paris: Editions de Minuit, 1972. Trans. and with an introduction by Barbara Johnson as *Dissemination* (Chicago: University of Chicago Press, 1981).

———. *La vérité en peinture*. Paris: Editions du Seuil, 1978. Trans. Geoff Bennington and Ian McLeod as *Truth in Painting* (Chicago: University of Chicago Press, 1987).

Descombes, Vincent. *Proust: Philosophie du roman*. Paris: Editions de Minuit, 1987. Trans. Catherine Chance Macksey as *Proust: Philosophy of the Novel* (Stanford: Stanford University Press, 1992).

Dhorme, Edouard. *La Bible: Ancien Testament*. Vol. 1. Paris: Gallimard (Pléiade), 1956.

Diderot, Denis. "Salon de 1763." In *Oeuvres esthétiques*, ed. P. Verniere. Paris: Garnier, 1965.

Didi-Huberman, Georges. "Appendice: Question de détail, question de pan." In *Devant l'image: Question posée aux fins d'une histoire de l'art*. Paris: Editions de Minuit, 1990.

———. *Le Cube et le Visage: Autour d'une Sculpture d'Alberto Giacometti*. Paris: Macula, 1993.

———. *La peinture incarnée*. Paris: Editions de Minuit, 1985.

Doubrovsky, Serge. *La place de la madeleine: Ecriture et fantasme chez Proust*. Paris: Mercure de France, 1973. Trans. Carol Mastrangelo Bove with Paul A. Bove as *Writing and Fantasy in Proust: The Place of the Madeleine* (Lincoln: University of Nebraska Press, 1986).

Erman, Michel. *L'oeil de Proust: Ecriture et voyeurisme dans "A la recherche du temps perdu."* Paris: Nizet, 1988.

Fabian, Johannes. *Power and Performance: Ethnographic Explorations through Proverbial Wisdom and Theater in Shaba, Zaire*. Madison: University of Wisconsin Press, 1991.

Fiser, Eméric. *L'esthétique de Marcel Proust*. Paris: Rieder, 1933.

———. *La théorie du symbole littéraire chez Marcel Proust*. Paris: José Corti, 1941.

Fraisse, Luc. *Le processus de la création chez Marcel Proust: Le fragment expérimental*. Paris: José Corti, 1988.

Garrard, Mary D. "Artemesia and Susanna." In *Feminism and Art History. Questioning the Litany*. Ed. Norma Broude and Mary D. Garrard. New York: Harper & Row, 1982.

Genette, Gérard. "Flaubert par Proust." In *Palimpsestes: La littérature au second degré*. Paris: Editions du Seuil, 1982.

———. "Métonymie chez Proust." In *Figures III*. Paris: Editions du Seuil, 1972. Selections from this work were translated by Alan Sheridan as *Figures*, 3 vols. (New York: Columbia University Press, 1982).

———. *Nouveau discours du récit*. Paris: Editions du Seuil, 1983. Trans. Jane E. Lewin as *Narrative Discourse Revisited* (Ithaca: Cornell University Press, 1988).

———. "Proust et le langage indirect." In *Figures II*. Paris: Editions du Seuil, 1969.

———. "Proust palimpseste." In *Figures*. Paris: Editions du Seuil, 1966.

Georgin, Rosine. *Contre Proust*. Paris: Cistre / Essais, 1991.

Girard, René. *Mensonge romantique et vérité romanesque*. Paris: Grasset, 1961.

Green, André. *Narcissisme de vie, narcissisme de mort*. Paris: Editions de Minuit, 1983.

Groupe Mu. *Traité du signe visuel: Pour une rhétorique de l'image*. Paris: Editions du Seuil, 1992.

Guillerm, Jean-Pierre. "L'avènement du détail pictural: De Balzac à Proust." In *Ecrire la peinture*, ed. Philippe Delaveau. Paris: Editions Universitaires, 1991.

————. "Le goût en peinture: Les références à la peinture dans *A la recherche du temps perdu*." In *Des mots et des couleurs II*, ed. Jean-Pierre Guillerm. Lille: Presses Universitaires de Lille, 1987.

————. "La peinture comme ornement: Valérie, Maurice Denis, Gauguin." In *Les fins de la peinture*, ed. René Démoris. Paris: Desjonqueres, 1990.

Hamon, Philippe. *La description littéraire: Anthologie de textes théoriques et critiques*. Paris: Macula, 1991.

————. *Expositions: Littérature et architecture au XIXe siècle*. Paris: José Corti, 1989.

————. *Introduction à l'analyse du descriptif*. Paris: Hachette, 1981.

Henry, Anne. *Marcel Proust: Théories pour une esthétique*. Paris: Klincksieck, 1981.

————. "Quand une peinture métaphysique sert de propédeutique à l'écriture: Les métaphores d'Elstir dans *A la recherche du temps perdu*." In *La critique artistique: Un genre littéraire*, ed. Centre d'art, esthétique et littérature, Publications de l'université de Rouen. Paris: Presses Universitaires de France, 1983.

Hibbard, Howard. *Caravaggio*. New York: Harper & Row, 1983.

Innis, R. E., ed. *Semiotics: An Introductory Anthology*. Bloomington: Indiana University Press, 1984.

Jacob, Christian. *L'empire des cartes: Approche théorique de la cartographie à travers l'histoire*. Paris: Albin Michel, 1992.

Jay, Martin. "Of Plots, Witnesses, and Judgments." In *Probing the Limits of Representation: Nazism and the "Final Solution,"* ed. Saul Friedlander. Cambridge, Mass.: Harvard University Press, 1992.

Johnson, John Theodore. "Marcel Proust et Gustave Moreau." *BSAMP* 28 (1978): 614–39.

————. *The Painter and His Art in the Works of Marcel Proust*. London: Microfilms International, 1964.

————. "Proust and Giotto." In *Marcel Proust: A Critical Panorama*. Urbana: University of Illinois Press, 1974.

Jullien, Dominique. *Proust et ses modèles: Les "Milles et Une Nuits" et les "Mémoires" de Saint-Simon*. Paris: José Corti, 1989.

Kofman, Sarah. *Pourquoi rit-on?* Paris: Editions de Galilée, 1986.

Krauss, Rosalind. *Le photographique: Pour une théorie des écarts*. Paris: Macula, 1990.

Kristeva, Julia. *Etrangers à nous-mêmes*. Paris: Librairie Arthème Fayard, 1988. Trans. Leon Roudiez as *Strangers to Ourselves* (New York: Columbia University Press, 1991).

————. *Pouvoirs de l'horreur*. Paris: Editions du Seuil, 1980. Trans. Leon S.

Roudiez as *Powers of Horror: An Essay on Abjection* (New York: Columbia University Press, 1982).

———. *Le Temps sensible: Proust et l'expérience littéraire*. Paris: Gallimard, 1994.

Laplanche, Jean. *Vie et mort en psychanalyse*. Paris: Flammarion, 1970. Translated and introduced by Jeffrey Mehlman as *Life and Death in Psychoanalysis* (Baltimore: Johns Hopkins University Press, 1976).

Lecercle, François. "Le regard dédoublé." *Nouvelle Revue de Psychanalyse* 44 (1991): 101–28.

Lévi-Strauss, Claude. *Le regard éloigné*. Paris: Plon, 1983. Trans. Joachim Neugroschel and Phoebe Hoss as *The View from Afar* (New York: Basic Books, 1985).

———. *Les structures élémentaires de la parenté*. Paris: Plon, 1949. Trans. John Richard von Sturmer and Rodney Needham as *The Elementary Structures of Kinship* (Boston: Beacon Press, 1969).

Lichtenstein, Jacqueline. *La couleur éloquente*. Paris: Flammarion, 1989. Trans. Emily McVarish as *The Eloquence of Color: Rhetoric and Painting in the French Classical Age* (Berkeley and Los Angeles: University of California Press, 1993).

Lotman, Yuriy. *The Structure of the Artistic Text*. Trans. Gail Lenhoff and Ronald Vroon. Ann Arbor: University of Michigan Press, 1977.

Man, Paul de. *Allegories of Reading: Figural Language in Rousseau, Nietzsche, Rilke, and Proust*. New Haven: Yale University Press, 1979.

Mannoni, O. "Je sais bien, mais quand-même. . . ." In *Clefs pour l'Imaginaire ou l'Autre Scène*. Paris: Editions du Seuil, 1969.

Marey, Etienne-Jules. *Le mouvement*. Paris: Masson, 1894.

———. *Le vol des oiseaux*. Paris: Masson, 1890.

Marin, Louis. *Les pouvoirs de l'image: Gloses*. Paris: Editions du Seuil, 1993.

Marmesh, Ann. "Anti-Covenant." In *Anti-Covenant: Counter-Reading Women's Lives in the Hebrew Bible*, ed. M. Bal. Sheffield, U.K.: Sheffield Academic Press and the Almond Press, 1989.

Mayes, A.D.H. "The Historical Context of the Battles Against Sisera." *Vetus Testamentum* 19 (1969): 353–60.

McEwan, Ian. *The Comfort of Strangers*. London: Jonathan Cape, 1981.

McHale, Brian. *Postmodernist Fiction*. London and New York: Methuen, 1987.

Mendelson, David. *Le verre et l'objet de verre dans l'univers imaginaire de Marcel Proust*. Paris: Librairie José Corti, 1968.

Mitchell, W.T.J. *Iconology: Image, Text, Ideology*. Chicago: University of Chicago Press, 1984.

———. *The Language of Images*. Chicago: University of Chicago Press, 1985.

———. *Picture Theory*. Chicago: University of Chicago Press, 1994.

Monnin-Hornung, Juliette. *Proust et la peinture*. Genève: Droz, 1951.

Muybridge, Eadweard. *Muybridge's Complete Human and Animal Locomotion: All 781 Plates from the 1887 "Animal Locomotion."* New York: Dover Publications, 1979.

Navarro, Annie. *Qui a tué le participe passé? Comédie policière et grammaticale*. Paris: Collège Saint Germain de Charonne, 1993.

Panofsky, Erwin. *Studies in Iconology: Humanistic Themes in the Art of the Renaissance*. New York: Harper & Row, 1962.

Pichon, Yann le. *Le musée retrouvé de Marcel Proust*. Paris: Stock, 1990.

Poulet, Georges. *L'Espace proustien*. Paris: Gallimard, 1988 [1960]. Trans. Eliott Coleman as *Proustian Space* (Baltimore: Johns Hopkins University Press, 1977).

Proust, Marcel. *A la recherche du temps perdu*. 4 vols. Ed. under the direction of Jean-Yves Tadié. Paris: Gallimard, Bibliothèque de la Pléiade, 1987–89. Trans. C. K. Scott-Moncrieff and Terence Kilmartin as *Remembrance of Things Past* (London: Penguin Books, 1981).

———. *Contre Saint-Beuve* (including *Pastiches et mélanges* and *Essais et articles*). Edition established by Pierre Clarac with the collaboration of Yves Sandre. Paris: Gallimard, Bibliothèque de la Pléiade, 1971.

Revel, Jean-François. *Sur Proust: Remarques sur "A la recherche du temps perdu."* Paris: Grasset, 1987 [1970]. Trans. Martin Turnell as *On Proust* (New York: Library Press, 1972).

Rey, Pierre-Louis. "L'entrée du port peinte par Elstir." In *Marcel Proust I: A la recherche du temps perdu, des personnages aux structures*, ed. Pierre-Edmond Robert. Paris: Lettres Modernes, 1992.

Rivers, J. E. *Proust and the Art of Love: The Aesthetics of Sexuality in the Life, Times and Art of Marcel Proust*. New York: Columbia University Press, 1980.

Rosenberg, Pierre. *Chardin*. Paris: Skira, 1963. Trans. Helga Harrison (New York: Rizzoli, 1991).

———. *Chardin*. Catalogue de l'exposition au Grand Palais, 1979. Trans. Emilie P. Kadish and Ursula Korneitchouk (Cleveland: Cleveland Museum of Art, 1979).

———. *Toute l'oeuvre peinte de Chardin*. Paris: Flammarion, 1983.

Rossum-Guyon, Françoise van. "De Claude Simon à Proust: Un exemple d'intertextualité." *Les Lettres Nouvelles* (Sept. 1972): 107–36.

Rubin, Gayle. "The Traffic of Women: Notes on the 'Political Economy' of

Sex." In *Towards an Anthropology of Women*, ed. Rayna R. Reiter. New York and London: Monthly Review Press, 1975.

Sarraute, Nathalie. *Disent les imbéciles*. Paris: Gallimard (Folio), 1976. Trans. Maria Jolas as *"Fools say": A novel* (New York: George Braziller, 1977).

———. *L'ère du soupçon*. Paris: Gallimard (Folio/Essais), 1956. Trans. Maria Jolas as *The Age of Suspicion: Essays on the Novel* (New York: George Braziller, 1990).

Schoentjes, Pierre. *Recherche de l'ironie et ironie de la Recherche*. Gent: Rijksuniversiteit Gent, 1993.

Schor, Naomi. "Le détail chez Freud." *Littérature* 37 (1980): 3–14.

———. *Reading in Detail: Esthetics and the Feminine*. New York and London: Methuen, 1987.

———. "Restricted Thematics." In *Breaking the Chain: Women, Theory, and French Realist Fiction*. New York: Columbia University Press, 1985.

Schwartz, Gary. *Rembrandt: His Life, His Paintings*. Harmondsworth: Penguin, 1985.

Sedgwick, Eve Kosofsky. *Between Men: English Literature and Male Homosocial Desire*. New York: Columbia University Press, 1985.

———. *Epistemology of the Closet*. New York: Harvester/Wheatsheaf, 1990.

Silverman, Kaja. *The Acoustic Mirror*. Bloomington: Indiana University Press, 1988.

———. *Male Subjectivity at the Margin*. New York: Routledge, 1992.

———. *Threshold of the Visible World*. New York: Routledge, 1995.

Sperber, Dan. "Ethnographie interprétative et anthropologie théorique." In *Le Savoir des anthropologues*. Paris: Hermann, 1982.

Steinberg, Leo. *The Sexuality of Christ in Renaissance Art and Modern Oblivion*. New York: Pantheon Books, 1983.

Sternweiler, Andreas. *Die Lust der Götter. Homosexualität in der italienischen Kunst von Donatello zu Caravaggio*. Berlin: Rosa Winkel, 1993.

Stock, Brian. *The Implications of Literacy: Written Language and Models of Interpretation in the Eleventh and Twelfth Centuries*. Princeton: Princeton University Press, 1983.

Tadié, Jean-Yves. *Proust et le roman*. Paris: Gallimard, 1971.

Todorov, Tzvetan. *Théories du symbole*. Paris: Editions du Seuil, 1977. Trans. Catherine Porter as *Theories of the Symbol* (Ithaca: Cornell University Press, 1982).

Uenishi, Taeko. *Le style de Proust et la peinture*. Paris: SEDES, 1988.

White, Hayden. "The Forms of Wildness: Archeology of an Idea." In *Tropics of Discourse*. Baltimore: Johns Hopkins University Press, 1978.

————. "Historical Emplotment and the Problem of Truth." In *Probing the Limits of Representation: Nazism and the "Final Solution,"* ed. Saul Friedlander. Cambridge, Mass.: Harvard University Press, 1992.

————. "Interpretation in History." In *Tropics of Discourse*. Baltimore: Johns Hopkins University Press, 1978.

————. *Metahistory: The Historical Imagination in Nineteenth-Century Europe*. Baltimore: Johns Hopkins University Press, 1973.

Žižek, Slavoj. *The Sublime Object of Ideology*. London: Verso, 1989.

Library of Congress Cataloging-in-Publication Data

Bal, Mieke.
[Images Proustiennes, ou, Comment lire visuellement. English]
The mottled screen : reading Proust visually / Mieke Bal.
    p.   cm.
Includes bibliographical references.
ISBN 0-8047-2807-0 (cl.)
ISBN 0-8047-2808-9 (pbk.)
1. Proust, Marcel, 1871-1922—Technique. 2. Visual communica-
tion. 3. Optical instruments in literature. I. Title.
PQ2631.R63Z52513 1997
843'.912—dc21   96-49839
CIP

♾ This book is printed on acid-free, recycled paper.

Original printing 1997
Last figure below indicates year of this printing:
06 05 04 03 02 01 00 99 98 97